LeeWards
Complete
Library of
Needlecraft

FULLER & DEES
TIMES MIRROR

New York • Los Angeles • Montgomery

Contributors

Fuller and Dees

PRESIDENT
James Lueck

ART DIRECTOR
George Alexandres

PRODUCTION DIRECTOR
William Holmes
George Jenks

EXECUTIVE EDITOR
Carter Houck

PROJECT EDITOR
Nell McInnish

EDITORIAL STAFF
Phyllis Fenn
Carl Richardson
Pat Warner

LAY-OUT DIRECTOR
Nancy Crippen
Mary Veitch

PHOTOGRAPHER
Myron Miller

ILLUSTRATORS
Jacqueline Butler
Marilyn Heard Eubanks
Janice Culbertson
Debbie Benedict
Patrick Gibson
Eleanor Palmer

CONTRIBUTING AUTHORS
Carter Houck
Sewing

Jinny Avery
Embroidery, Patchwork, Appliqué
Teacher, Lecturer, Designer

CONTRIBUTING EDITOR
John Bade (Hook Arts)

CREATIVE STAFF
Courtney Bede
Kathy Crowe
Martha Ann Crowe
Grace Harding
Joe Ann Helms
Marion Moffat
Sandy Singer

ACKNOWLEDGEMENTS
Brunswick Yarn Company
Lily Yarn Company
C.J. Bates & Son

© Fuller & Dees MCMLXXV
3734 Atlanta Highway, Montgomery, Alabama 36109
Library of Congress Cataloging in Publication Data
Main entry under title:

A Complete Library of Needlecraft
Includes index.
1. Needlework   2. Fancy work.   3. Textile crafts.
TT705.C75   746   74-32451

Complete Set ISBN 0-87197-085-6
Volume 3 ISBN 0-87197-088-0

Contents

Volume 3

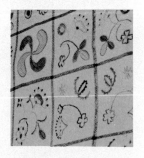

Sewing has grown from the early use of bone needles to the elaborate machinery used in today's bustling garment industry. And sewing, however, has been recently rediscovered as an art with the spectrum of creative activities broadening day by day.

An individual and functional craft, patchwork today includes pieced work, patching with paper liners, and Crazy Patch, as well as variations of both traditional and modern appliqué. It is popular on clothing and personal accessories, wall hangings, pillows, and other home accents.

The art of appliqué, cutting a design from one fabric and sewing it on to another fabric, is centuries old. Today this creative art has few limits or rules, and provides adventure and self-expression with fabrics.

Introduction

Sewing is often considered a necessity in saving money on clothing and home decorations. However, when this technique is coupled with patchwork and appliqué, it becomes a very creative art form. Although mending clothing seems more necessary than pleasurable, the planning and designing of original fashion is indeed a rewarding pastime. Once the reader attempts original designs, she will want to work more and more from her own ideas and patterns rather than from those produced commercially.

The idea that any woman can sew without training may have originated in an era when all young girls were taught to sew and embroider. This practice ended during the Industrial Revolution when ready-to-wear clothing became more practical than handmade work. It is now recognized, however, that a long period of training and practice is necessary to learn the finer points of this craft. Thus, many seamstresses continue to attend classes, seminars, and lectures designed to enhance their basic sewing knowledge.

A sense of color and proportion, some simple arithmetic and patience are assets in learning to sew. The basic technical information on Sewing, Patchwork and Appliqué is included in this volume. It is suggested that the beginner start by practicing the simple stitches. It is necessary to become proficient in these rudiments before attempting the projects or traditional art designs contained in these three chapters.

There are many project patterns from which to choose. Start with some of the simpler ones and progress to the more difficult only after the basic techniques have been established.

The alphabetical arrangement of the sewing terms and the full explanation of each will be useful to a seamstress at any level of development. This volume will make it easy for the beginner to teach herself, and will be a handy reference and guide for future projects of all types.

As these arts are closely related, the projects in this volume may be combined to suit individual taste. For instance, most of the appliqué and patchwork terminology can be found in the dictionary of sewing terms. Many of the patchwork designs may be enlarged for blouses, skirts or dresses. The proportions of the Genesis Wall-Hanging in Appliqué may be reduced and placed on a large skirt pocket or a patchwork coverlet. Thus, an understanding of the basic needlework techniques is essential in creating individual designs and unique uses for them.

Sewing

Shortly after man began to drape himself in the skins of other animals, sewing was invented. At first, needles were carved from bone and threaded with strips of leather so that skins could be sewn together into more practical shapes. The invention of spinning and weaving techniques made sewing an even greater necessity. At first, garment shapes were simple and so was the sewing. However, by the Middle Ages in Europe and somewhat earlier in the Far East, clothing was elaborate in both style and decoration. Every stitch and each bit of embroidery was done by hand. The hours of labor on each garment became long and arduous.

When the Industrial Revolution began and faster ways of spinning and weaving by machine became practical, inventors saw a need for a machine which could sew garments together. The first known sewing machine patent was issued in England in 1790 to Thomas Saint. Nothing came of this first machine except perhaps that it spurred the imagination of other inventors.

Until the beginning of the 19th century every piece of cloth for dresses, suits, curtains and quilts was woven on looms like this. The working original shown here is in Richmondtown Restoration, Staten Island, New York.

◁ **THE WAY IT WAS: Shown with 19th century equipment in Richmondtown Restoration, Staten Island, New York. Ann Anderson is the expert at the loom.**

In 1830, a patent was issued in France to Barthelemy Thimonnier for a sewing machine made entirely of wood. He created eighty of these machines which worked well enough to be used for the manufacture of uniforms for the French Army. Hand craftsmen were alarmed about their futures and in a typical gesture of the times, a group of tailors destroyed the machines. Thimonnier worked undaunted to make an improved model and succeeded in getting an American patent for a metal sewing machine in 1850. He met with no further success and died in poverty in 1857.

In the interim, Elias Howe had patented his machine in 1846. He had no success with it in America and so attempted to collaborate with an Englishman named William Thomas to manufacture the machine in that country. The two men did not work well together and Howe returned to the United States.

By this time there were many other names (now familiar to the users of sewing machines) competing in the field. Wheeler and Wilson and Singer were among the manufacturers of sewing machines in the decade before the Civil War. In 1854, Howe won a number of law suits against these men for infringing on his patents, thus, his years of hard work were rewarded.

Women continued to sew by hand, but tailors and manufacturers of clothing soon saw the sewing machine as a way to more rapid manufacture and so, more money. After the Civil War, the home sewing machine became a standard piece of equipment in many homes. Of course, electricity made the machine even more desirable; the invention of buttonhole and embroidery stitches have recently made it more fun.

Inventors through the ages realized that people needed and wanted all types of sewing aids and accessories. Cabinet makers, silver smiths, artists and artisans of all kinds, to say nothing of seamstresses themselves, invented and embellished a variety of attractive, useful sewing tools. Needles were of primary importance and were valued possessions prior to the time when they could be mass produced. Thimbles have not only been considered useful in most cultures, but in some cases, they have reached a stage of ornamentation much like that of jewelry. There are now people who collect thimbles and many companies design and produce them especially to please collectors.

At one time, during the 18th and 19th century, hemming clamps were popular and became extremely decorative. They were used to hold one end of a hem while the seamstress held the fabric and worked rapidly along the taut edge. Scissors, shears and clippers have been made and decorated — from tiniest embroidery scissors in the shape of a bird to the large steel shears used by tailors.

Once ladies began to acquire this variety of equipment, they needed storage areas. The variety of boxes, needle cases, needle books, pin cushions and reticules that have been created through the ages are charming works of art. Many of them have found their way into private collections and museums. These have been made of wood, metal, ivory and fine fabrics and decorated with jewels, mother-of-pearl, scrimshaw and embroidery. They have been painted and padded and lined, made with secret compartments and fine locks. In the Middle Ages, ladies wore their sewing equipment on chatelaines suspended from the waist to prevent theft. In the 18th century, chatelaines again became popular and extremely elaborate — sometimes made of silver and gold, engraved and set with stones.

HOW TO USE THIS SECTION

Because sewing covers such a variety of things and these are not necessarily learned in any exact order, it seemed wise to put the "nuts and bolts" of sewing in dictionary form so that the reader can find buttonholes or zippers with a flip of the pages. There is some cross-referencing so that the problem of varied terminology should be covered. The diagrams have been planned so that it is almost possible to find the answer to how to make a French seam, for instance, without reading the words. However, all the fine points and the warnings about possible pitfalls will be found in the copy accompanying the diagrams.

Not only are the techniques of sewing covered, but information is given on equipment, sewing machines and pattern alteration. For beginners, especially, the material should act as a useful expansion of the limited information which can be printed in the guide sheet accompanying a commercial pattern.

The sewing projects which follow the dictionary make ample use of the techniques so that the combination of the two work together as a self-teaching program. There are many simple designs given which do not even require patterns, but are made by measuring the proper pieces of fabric to fit the situation. These include such designs as curtains, bedspreads and tablecloths. Many of the smaller designs, such as hats and bags, are given with full-size patterns which can be traced from the pages of the book and used as described. These have certain notations which are consistent throughout. There is a notation for patterns, indicating which pieces should be cut double on a folded paper when they are traced. There is another notation for patterns which can be traced as is and, then laid on a fold of fabric like a commercial pattern so that the doubling is done on the fabric, not the paper. There are some pattern pieces which are so large that it is necessary to put them on two pages and give a special line for joining so that this can be done in the tracing process. Almost all the patterns require that seams be added and dimensions are given as finished, not as cut. This allows some choice on seams. On fine, small items, such as scarves, where the seams might have to be trimmed, it will be necessary to add only ¼-inch seams. On materials which ravel easily, add ¾ or 1-inch seams.

The few actual garments provided in this section are primarily planned on geometric shapes, circles and rectangles, and fitting is not a great problem. Darts and other lines which would be hard for a beginner to draft have been avoided. A measurement chart of the figure for which the garment is being made and some simple arithmetic is all that is needed to draft these patterns. It is suggested that the patterns be drawn out in their entirety on large sheets of brown paper or tissue or even newspaper. Add the seams, make the fold line notations, etc. and then, cut them out of old sheets for a trial run if there is any uncertainty of pattern making. If the garment does not work out, go back and read the instructions over; nothing is lost except a little time and an old sheet. Each attempt will be beneficial.

The words which are printed in bold-face type in each of the instructions for the projects are ones which can be looked up in the sewing dictionary for complete step-by-step descriptions. In this way, the instructions can be kept shorter and less confusing. The advanced seamstress will not even need to look up these words, but the beginner may find that the information will come in handy.

The sewing projects will not only be useful personally, but are especially good for making gifts. There are things which everyone can use, such as the big canvas tote bag and the scarves and ties. These take only an evening or less to make and have no size problem. The designs for several of the sewing projects combine well with the embroidery patterns in other sections.

ALTERATIONS (Clothing)

Alteration is a necessary part of maintaining a family wardrobe. The largest amount of time allocated to this job is in shortening and lengthening garments. Most of the information on Hems (pg. 631) applies equally to new and old garments. However, there are a few tricks involved in working with the altered hem which will be explained here.

Hems: If the hemline of a garment is even, it can be changed by measurement. But, if it looks uneven at all, take out the old hem and have someone remark it. Before it is remarked or any other work is done on it, brush out the inside of the old hemline where dirt has collected, then steam it. If an obvious line remains on the outside, it is wise to wash or dry-clean the garment while the hem is out.

If a hem is being let down, it may be necessary to face the edge with another fabric to give enough length. A skimpy hem, in most cases anything under 1½ inches, looks a bit sad. Bias hem facing can be bought in packs or by the yard. A better quality can be obtained by cutting your own from lining fabrics. Be sure that the fabric chosen responds to washing or dry-cleaning in the same manner as the garment fabric! By directions (pg. 588), cut and piece bias 2½ to 3 inches wide. Seam it, right sides together, with the edge of the garment, turn it up, baste and hem it as you would any other hem (Hems, pg. 631). Use as narrow a seam as possible so that a little of the garment fabric will turn up, preventing the facing from showing at the edge. **Fig. 1 and 2.**

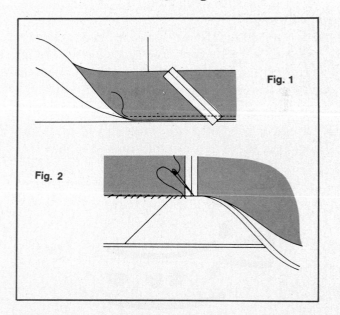

Fig. 1

Fig. 2

Other more elaborate camouflages can be used for lengthening children's clothes, sport clothes, coats, etc.

Turn up ½ to ¾ inch and machine triple stitch the edge. Use straight or zigzag stitching and matching or contrasting thread.

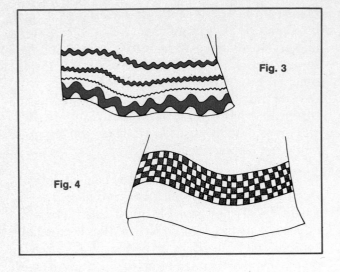

Fig. 3

Fig. 4

Fig. 7

Make a decorative band using one or more rows of rickrack. This will enable you to cover the hemline that shows. **Fig. 3.**

Set in a band of contrasting fabric, then add contrasting collars, cuffs, belts or buttons to tie in the effect. **Fig. 4.**

On jeans, add a wide band of embroidered cotton braid at the lower edge. **Fig. 5.**

On boys' cuffed trousers make a 1³/₄-inch hem by machine stitching very close to the top edge of the hem. On the outside of the garment, pick up the fabric 1¹/₄ inches from the lower edge and fold it up as far as it will go, forming a tuck to resemble the upper edge of a cuff. Press this in place and tack it at the sides onto the seams. **Fig. 6.**

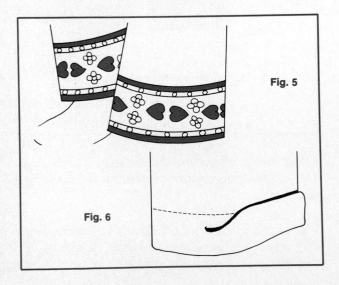

Fig. 5

Fig. 6

If a coat is let down and faced, several rows of heavy rayon braid will freshen the appearance of the lower edge and can be applied to collar or cuffs to match.

A coat can be let down even farther by adding a piece of fabric to the lower edge and covering the whole area with a band of real or fake fur. Fake fur, cut to the shape of the lower part of the coat, may be as wide as 8 or 10 inches.

Waists: Lengthening a waistline is nearly impossible — one of the main reasons for long-waisted people to learn to make their own clothes. It is possible in some few bodices to insert a band of trim or of contrasting fabric and to repeat this in the skirt. **Fig. 7.**

Shortening a waist properly requires partially removing the zipper from the skirt part of the dress and remaking the waist length. **Fig. 8.** Sometimes the skirt can be made to hang better at the same time by dipping the waistline seam down into the skirt a bit in the back. **Fig. 9.** (Also see Waistbands, pg. 683.)

The balance or hang of a bought skirt can often be improved by lowering the band across the back. Occasionally this should be done in the front instead. For a complete description of hanging a skirt properly, see Waistbands, page

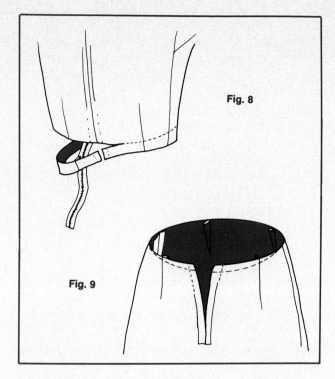

Fig. 8

Fig. 9

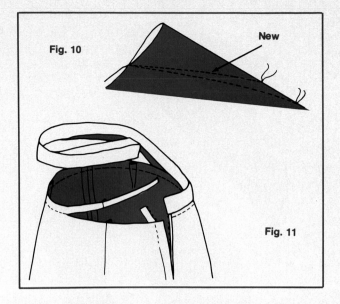

Fig. 10

New

Fig. 11

of the hip, though not down in the seat area. **Fig. 10.** (Also see Darts, pg. 607.)

683. If the hip of a skirt or pants fits, but the waist is too large, or too small, the alteration should be made in the darts. If a waist is made larger, an addition may have to be made on the under end of the band, matching the fabric as closely as possible. On pants, the center back seam can be increased or decreased for a slight waist alteration. In that case only the end of the band between the back seam and a side zipper needs to be removed. In men's pants and some others, there is a seam in the band itself in the center back. Removing a few inches of the band at the center back seam will simultaneously alter both pants and band.

Hips: It is an unfortunate fact, that on many people, clothes which fit perfectly everywhere else are tight in the hips. One way out of this dilemma, besides constant dieting, is to buy two-piece outfits in different sizes. For one-piece dresses, a seam line alteration is the easiest way to enlarge hips. So, inspect what you buy to make sure that there is a generous side seam. This goes for skirts and pants also. Pants very often have a good seam in the center back which can be used to allow a bit more room at the top of the hip and into the waist.

The darts in skirts and pants can often be tapered to allow a bit more room on that high round part

If a skirt, either on a band or on a waistline dress, is a bit too long as well as too tight, it can be raised from the top. This will shorten and widen it at the same time. If it has darts, they may need to be reshaped when this is done. **Fig. 11.**

Neck and Shoulder Lines: A woman who is very small boned but full busted will find that most clothes are too large in the shoulder and neck and often on into the armhole. This problem requires nothing short of a radical operation on dresses and blouses, to say nothing of coats and jackets! Remove facings around neck and armholes, and/or collars and sleeves. Pull the shoulder seams up until the neck fits properly. Reseam the facing to match the neckline. **Fig. 12.**

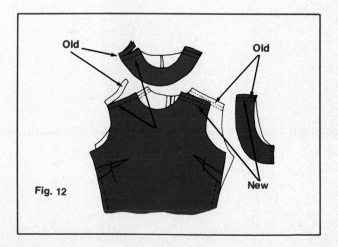

Old

Old

Fig. 12

New

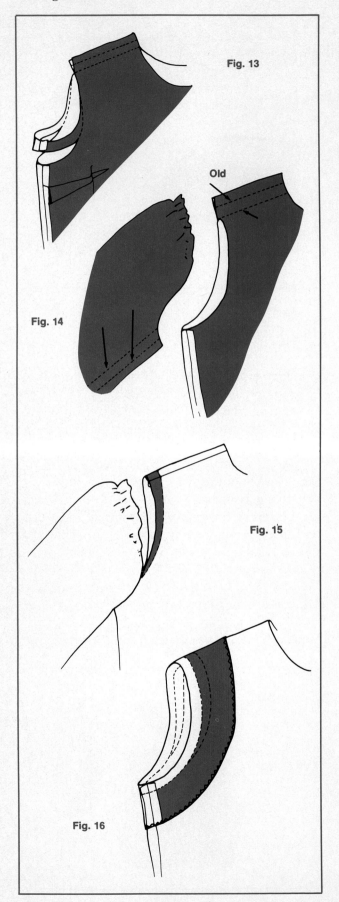

Fig. 13

Old

Fig. 14

Fig. 15

Fig. 16

Reduce the collar in size by shortening from the end. Reassemble the neck in the order in which it was originally done. If the armhole was all right before the shoulder was lifted, cut it back down at the bottom to accommodate the sleeve or facing. **Fig. 13.** If it was necessary to make the armhole smaller, reduce the sleeve to fit by taking in the underarm seam. **Fig. 14.** In the case of a facing, it is better to alter it at the shoulder, creating a seam there if necessary, to correspond to the shoulder alteration on the garment.

If the shoulder is too wide, remove the sleeve around the upper three-fourths of the armhole and set it in farther. **Fig. 15.** Retrim and clip the seam as before. If it is a faced armhole, stitch in more deeply at shoulder, trim, clip, and reunderstitch. **Fig. 16.** (Also see Facings, pg. 617.)

Armholes: In either sleeved or sleeveless dresses, a tight armhole can be enlarged by simply stitching a deeper seam in the lower curve. The excess seam will then be trimmed away. **Fig. 17.**

Sleeves: Lengthening sleeves is a bit like lengthening waists. But, in the case of shirt sleeves, it is possible to add a wider cuff in a contrast fabric, possibly doing a new collar to match.

Shortening straight sleeves is easy, as they are usually hemmed or faced. Shirt-type sleeves are generally best shortened from the bottom by removing the cuff and placket, cutting the proper amount from the sleeves and reassembling everything. If the cuff seems too complicated to touch,

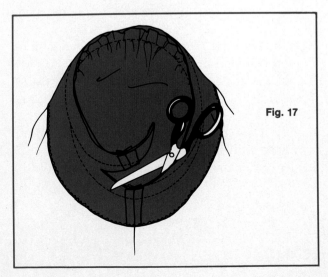

Fig. 17

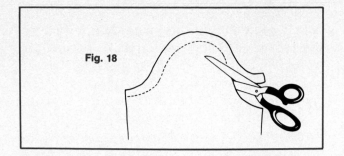

Fig. 18

and there is no elaborate flat-felled seam at the armhole, it may be easier to remove the sleeve from the armhole and recut the top. Press out the sleeve, draw a pattern around the cap and armhole section and recut by it, as much lower down as is necessary. **Fig. 18.** Reset the sleeve as described on page 671.

It is wise to shorten a child's shirt sleeve so that it can be let down again. Make a tuck, with large machine stitching, on the inside of the sleeve above the elbow.

Enlarging a sleeve is very difficult as there is usually no appreciable extra seam. However, for a person with a very heavy upper arm, a V-shaped gusset can be set in. **Fig. 19.** The armhole will then have to be enlarged on the garment. (See **Fig. 17.**) In the case of a woman who is also heavy busted, a gusset will also be set into the bodice in the same manner as the sleeve. The armhole is automatically enlarged on both pieces.

Long sleeves often need taking in along the lower arm and wrist, for which they will not even need to be removed from the armhole. In the case of a shirt type sleeve the cuff button can be moved over as much as $^3/_4$ inch but beyond that it is best to unstitch at least a few inches of the cuff at the button end and pleat or gather the sleeve in. Reduce the length of the cuff at that end and reapply it to the sleeve.

Bust Lines: Darts and side seams control the appearance of the bust lines. Some fullness can be taken out or added in seams. For a very full bust, a V-shaped gusset can be added to the side seam. **Fig. 20.** The armhole on the sleeve will have to be cut larger to correspond, unless a gusset is also being added to the sleeve. When a side seam is taken in, the armhole will have to be adjusted also, either by trimming it back to its original size or by reducing the sleeve or facing to the new size.

For a low bust, the darts should all be moved down or shortened to come to the correct point.

Unfortunately, many commercial garments have a punch mark just inside the end of most darts, making it impossible to lower them. Check for this in buying! If there are no punch marks, rip out stitching of darts and lower the entire side dart parallel to the original lines. Shorten the

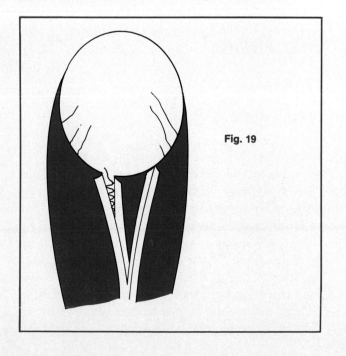

Fig. 19

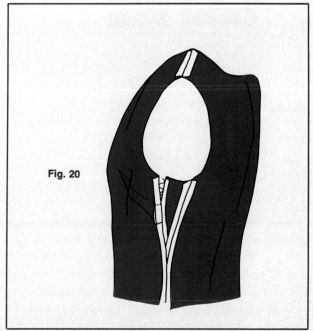

Fig. 20

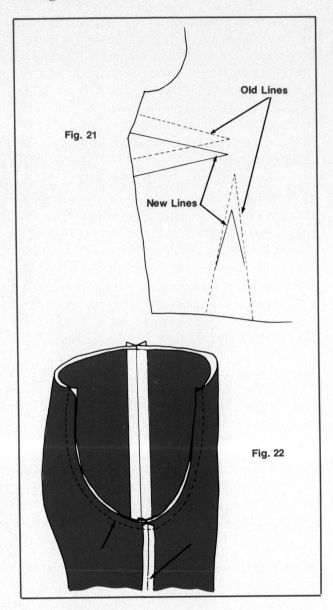

Fig. 21

Old Lines

New Lines

Fig. 22

dart that comes up from the waist. **Fig. 21.** This change will give slightly more room and a far better appearance. In the case of a high bust line, the darts should be transferred upward to give a trim look.

Pants: Waist and hip alterations in pants are identical to those in any other garment. There are strange problems in the fit of the seat that require serious analysis. If the seat is short, the crotch seam can be stitched lower, as in the armhole (pg. 584) then retrimmed to allow greater depth. If the seat is short *and* the upper thigh tight, you can kill two birds by putting in a long narrow V-shaped gusset in the inseam of each leg (**Fig. 19** and **20**). The opposite treatment works for taking

in the thigh and for shortening the seat. Undo the crotch where it intersects the inseam, take in the inseam on each leg and carefully restitch the crotch. **Fig. 22.**

APPLIQUÉ

Applying a cut out design of one fabric to another fabric for decorative purposes is called appliqué. It can be done with a close wide zigzag machine stitch. Draw the design on the right side of decorative fabric. Do not trim away the excess fabric around the design. Pin or baste it in place on the surface to which it is to be attached. Follow the outline of the design with the stitching, then trim the edges neatly with fine scissors close to the stitching. **Fig. 23.**

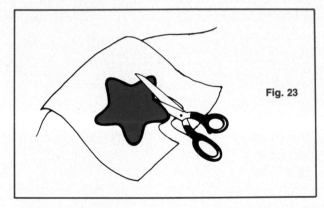

Fig. 23

There are many hand embroidery techniques also used for appliqué.

BALL FRINGE

(See Braid, page 591.)

BASTING

Basting is simply a temporary stitching using long, loose stitches which can easily be pulled out when no longer needed. It is used to hold portions of a garment in place during fittings or for final stitching. Basting can be done either by hand (see Stitches, pg. 674) or on the sewing machine. Some newer machines have a true basting stitch, but the older ones recommend using a long stitch — about six stitches per inch. Machine basting many fabrics is a dangerous practice as the stitching may leave marks or you may snag the fabric while trying to remove stitches of this small size.

Basting is especially useful when a garment needs to be carefully fitted. (See Fitting, page 621.)

(Also see Pin Basting, page 656.)

BEADING

In embroidery, beading refers to covering a surface with fine glass beads, often called bugle beads. They are sewn on by hand with a beading needle to form patterns.

Beading is also a narrow lace or eyelet trim through which ribbon can be run. **Fig. 24.** It is used to trim lingerie, children's clothes, blouses and bed linens. It can be applied to the surface of

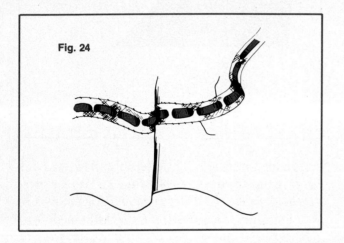

Fig. 24

the fabric, frequently after the garment is assembled. Using matching thread, machine stitch along each edge of the beading which has been pinned or basted in place. It may be much easier to apply very fine lace beading by hand. Run ribbon through with a bodkin and tack it if necessary to keep it from slipping. In some cases the ribbon is purely decorative and in some it is used to draw up a waistline, neckline or the edge of a sleeve.

BELTS

Belts in any width can be made to match your garments without a pattern. There are several types of stiffening for belts available; you may also find grosgrain ribbon is particularly satisfactory in some cases or it may be a good idea to cut it from interfacing fabric. No matter which type of stiffening is used, make sure that it is compatible with the fabric used regarding washability and shrinkage.

Cut both fabric and belting 6 to 8 inches longer than your waist measurement. Cut fabric twice as wide as belting plus allowance for two 1/2-inch seams. Cut end of stiffening in a point if desired.

Lay 1/2 inch of fabric wrong side down onto belting as shown. Machine stitch in place. **Fig. 25.** Fold fabric around point, press and clip out excess wedges. Bring the rest of the fabric all the way around the stiffening, turn under the other 1/2 inch and slip stitch the folded edge over the machine stitching. **Fig. 26.** Finish the belt with a row of machine top stitching on each edge or leave it plain. **Fig. 27.**

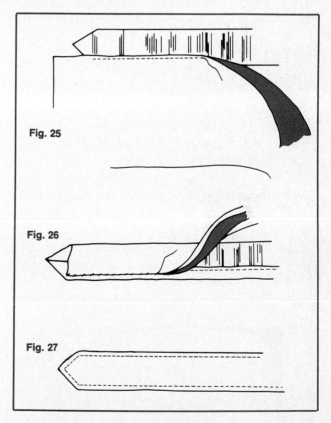

Fig. 25

Fig. 26

Fig. 27

The belt may be fastened with a buckle and eyelets, either metal or hand worked. Velcro, grippers or buttons and buttonholes may be used in place of a buckle. **Fig. 28.**

When choosing a link buckle with two pieces, one of which locks into the other, you can eliminate the extra length over and above your waist measurement. There is also no necessity for finishing either end. **Fig. 29.**

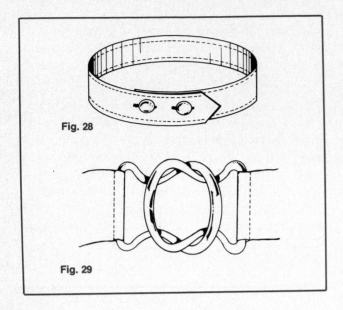

Fig. 28

Fig. 29

BIAS

If the *length grain* (selvage) of a piece of fabric is laid on the *cross grain* (end cut from the bolt) the fold will be on the *bias* or at a 45-degree angle to either straight grain. **Fig. 30.** Many directions require that a strip of bias fabric be cut for binding or facing or trimming. This can be done by folding the fabric as described to find the bias and then marking along the fold with a yard stick and chalk or pencil. Measure and mark along parallel lines and cut as many pieces as are needed to make up the required length. The pieces should have the ends

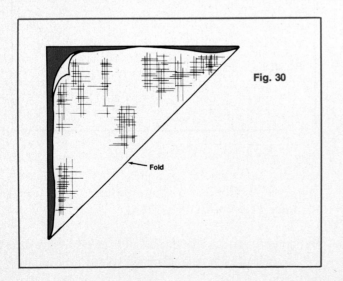

Fig. 30

Fold

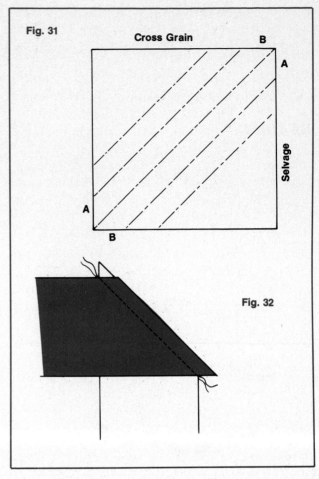

Fig. 31

Cross Grain

B

A

Selvage

A

B

Fig. 32

cut on the straight grain (preferably all length or all cross) to make joining easier. **Fig. 31.** Lay the strips right sides together to form an angle, as shown, so that the edges meet to form a V $\frac{1}{2}$ inch back from each straight end. Stitch a $\frac{1}{4}$-inch seam, starting and stopping directly at the V. **Fig. 32.** Press the seams open flat and clip off the small triangles that extend over the sides.

BIAS BINDING

Bias binding can be made in any width desired by the directions in the previous paragraph or it can be purchased ready-cut in several widths. There are a number of ways to use bias binding as edging or trimming or a clean finish for seams.

For simple bias binding over a raw edge or as a seam finish, you may use any of these methods, depending on the fabric you are using and the finished effect that you want. For all three methods cut the bias four times wider than the desired finished width.

Method No. 1: Lay *right* side of binding to *right* side of fabric and seam them together, taking up slightly less than one-fourth the width of the binding. Turn the binding over the edge and press, then turn under the raw edge and slip stitch to the stitching line that shows on the wrong side of the fabric. **Fig. 33.** This method is useful for medium-weight fabrics and in cases where the wrong side does not show.

Method No. 2: Lay *right* side of binding to *wrong* side of fabric and seam them together, taking up slightly less than one-fourth the width of the binding. Turn the binding over the edge and press, then turn under the raw edge, being sure not to make the binding too narrow to conceal completely the original stitching line. At this point it is a good idea to baste it in place, covering the stitching line by a very small amount. Stitch on the machine very close to the folded edge, using a medium stitch and keeping it very even. **Fig. 34.** If this is done properly so that the stitching shows right along the edge of the binding on both sides, it is especially good for areas in which both sides are visible.

Method No. 3: Start as in Method No. 1. After the binding is folded over the edge of the fabric, *do not turn under the raw edge* of the binding! On the right side of the fabric, machine stitch close to, but not on the binding, catching the underneath edge of the binding to the fabric. **Fig. 35.** Trim the raw edge of the binding, leaving about 1/8 inch beyond the stitching line. **Fig. 36.** As bias cannot ravel away, there is no problem about the unfinished edge, except that it can only be used in places where that side never shows. This is an especially good finish for heavy materials such as linen and wool because it is less bulky than a turned edge. It is also a very good seam or hem finish.

French double-bias binding: In very thin fabrics and where a very delicate bound edge is desired, try French double bias. Cut the strips six times wider than desired finished width. Fold the binding, wrong sides together, along the center so that the two raw edges are even, press. Seam the raw edges of the binding to the right side of the fabric, taking up slightly less than one-third of the width of the binding on both. Press the bind-

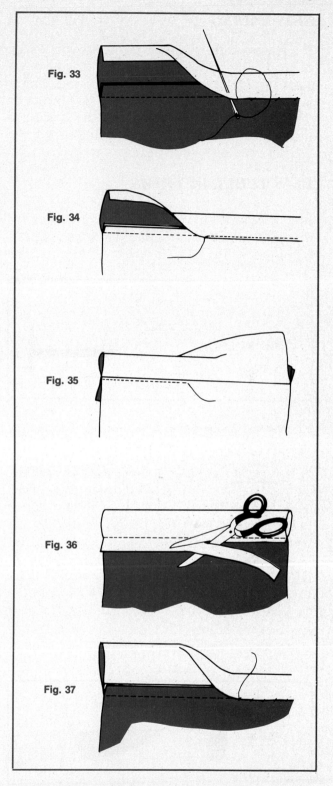

Fig. 33

Fig. 34

Fig. 35

Fig. 36

Fig. 37

ing over the edge and slip stitch the folded edge to the stitching line on the wrong side of the fabric. **Fig. 37.** If an even narrower seam is used when you stitch the binding to the edge, the folded edge can then be brought over the stitching line far enough to finish, as in Method No. 3.

BIAS FACING

If a pattern calls for a bias facing around a neck or armhole, or if one is needed for lengthening a skirt (pg. 581), cut it by the directions under bias. For a skirt hem, it should be 2½ inches or more, for a neckline or armhole, cut it about 1 inch so that it will be about ½ inch finished. See section on Facings for details.

BIAS TUBULAR TRIMS

Bias self-fabric ties, bows or loops are called for in many patterns. For some purposes a folded and top stitched piece is adequate. **Fig. 38.** For

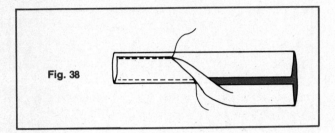

Fig. 38

others, such as very fine button loops, try spaghetti strips, as follows:

For small ties and button loops use fine cording, ⅛ inch diameter or less; cut the bias strips 1 inch wide; if possible, work with a length of no more than 12 inches. For larger things like tie belts, use a ⅜-inch diameter cording and cut the bias about 2 inches wide and as long as necessary. In all cases cut the cording two and one-half times longer than the bias.

Lay the bias wrong side down with one end in the exact center of the cord. Stitch back and forth to

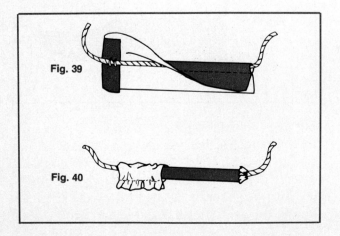

Fig. 39

Fig. 40

secure fabric to cord about ¼ inch from end of bias. Lay bias back over the other half of the cord and fold it around the cord, right sides together. With a *cording or zipper foot* on the machine, seam the bias, not too close to the cording, and be careful not to catch the ¼ inch turned back at the end. **Fig. 39.** Trim the seam to ⅛ inch and start gently pulling the tube of fabric along until it covers the other end of the cord. **Fig. 40.** Cut off remaining cord.

BONING

Patterns for low-necked gowns, cummerbunds and some accessories suggest whaleboning to hold the shape. This is a stiff but flexible material, similar to a very thin bone and is encased in fabric. It can be sewn in place by hand or on the machine with a zipper foot, working in the flange of fabric which extends beyond the bone. Whaleboning may be purchased by the yard at most notions counters. **Fig. 41.**

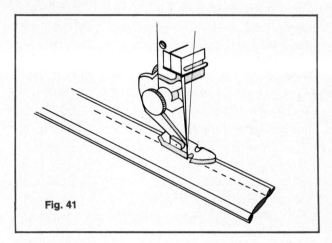

Fig. 41

BRAS (Built in)

If bathing suits and certain types of evening gowns are being made, a built-in bra may be necessary. It is possible to purchase these in a variety of sizes. Some are made especially for bathing suits of materials which will withstand constant exposure to sun and water. When making the bra from scratch — either by a pattern provided with the garment pattern or by an old bra which has been discarded — use washable, preshrunk, quick drying fabrics and a non-woven, washable interfacing to give shape. Nylon elastic is the best for use in bathing suit bras.

BRAID

The term braid is used to cover a wide variety of items. The most practical way to divide the categories of braids and tapes is to say that tapes are utilitarian and braids are decorative. The most common braids are rickrack and ball fringe. However, there are other varieties of beautiful decorative braids sold by the yard at trimming counters. They range from cotton and rayon through all the washable synthetics to wool. Occasionally a silk braid may be found. Following are some tips on choosing and applying these various decorative braids.

If the fabric is washable, choose a braid which is guaranteed washable and colorfast. If in doubt, get a sample, wash it and lay it on a white towel to see whether the color bleeds. *Preshrink all* cotton and washable braids before applying them to fabric. This will save a great deal of trouble in pressing the garment later. In the case of very long lengths of braid, such as would be used on draperies and other household items, it is possible to "full" the braid onto the edge. To do this, allow about one-fourth again as much braid as the length of the edge to be trimmed. Work in the extra length of braid and pin in place before stitching. This way makes it unnecessary to preshrink the braid.

Braids can be stitched along the edges with either straight or zigzag machine stitching, **Fig. 42,** or sewn on by hand. The hand method is especially good when applying wool or silk types of braids to clothing. If the trim needs to curve around a neckline, choose a braid which will bend easily into a curve, not a stiff one such as grosgrain ribbon. **Fig. 43.** Turn the ends under and carefully catch down by hand.

Rickrack can be applied in two ways — flat on the surface or as an edging (Edgings, pg. 608). In either case, one row of straight machine stitching along the center is all that is necessary. **Fig. 44.**

Ball fringe can be applied on the surface in the same manner as rickrack, using straight or zigzag machine stitching. **Fig. 45.** It may also be used as a finishing for a raw edge. Lay the fringe on the edge of the fabric, wrong side to wrong side, overlapping the raw edge about ³/₈ inch. Be sure that the balls are lying toward the fabric and not hanging off the edge as you will want them to be when finished. **Fig. 46.** Pin or baste in place and stitch the edge of the braid nearest the balls to the fabric. Turn the braid up onto the right side of the fabric, press in place and stitch the other edge in place. **Fig. 47.**

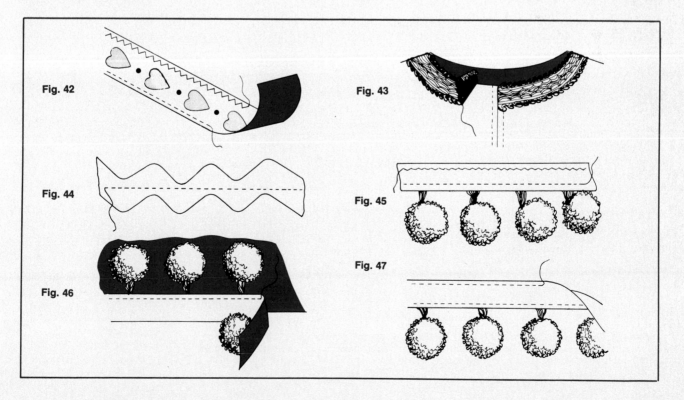

Fig. 42

Fig. 43

Fig. 44

Fig. 45

Fig. 46

Fig. 47

Braids for Many Uses: From top to bottom, cotton peasant, rayon and metallic woven, machine embroidered novelty tennis, flat wool cable, flat rayon cable, miniature rayon novelty, miniature wool cable, woven fold, blazer, cotton fringe, ball fringe.

BUTTONHOLES

Buttonholes fall into two categories — bound (with fabric) and worked (with thread). Modern sewing machines (almost any that zigzag) can be used to work very nice buttonholes on cottons and any other light to medium-weight fabrics, without the aid of a special attachment. Use your sewing machine manual for exact instructions. Hand-worked buttonholes are appropriate for fine fabrics such as silks and light to medium-weight woolens. Bound buttonholes are appropriate for suits, coats and other tailored garments made of medium to heavy-weight fabrics.

There are several methods for making bound buttonholes. The most foolproof one, the patch method, is described here. An alternate method is described in the section on Bound Buttonhole Pockets (pg. 596). These are interchangeable, though for most people the one given here works best in the necessarily small area allotted for buttonholes.

GENERAL INSTRUCTIONS FOR BUTTONHOLES

Mark buttonholes accurately by the pattern. If you have altered the length of the pattern in the buttonhole area, redistribute the marks between the top one and the bottom one so that the buttons are again equally spaced. In a single-breasted garment, be sure that the buttonhole begins $1/8$ inch from the center front line (toward the edge of the garment). The length of the buttonhole can be altered at the other end to conform to the size of the button. **Fig. 48.** The buttonhole should be $1/8$ inch longer than a flat button and $1/4$ inch longer than a raised or rough one. On a double-breasted garment, treat both rows of buttonholes alike: the ends nearest the front edge of the garment remain as they were marked on the pattern. Any adjustment of the length occurs at the other ends. **Fig. 49.** On almost all garments, the buttonholes should run perpendicular to the center front line and exactly on the cross grain.

Remember that buttonholes in women's and girls' clothes are placed on the right side of the garment; in men's and boys' wear, on the left side.

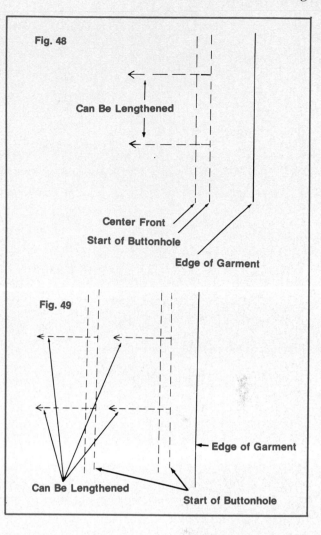

Fig. 48
Can Be Lengthened
Center Front
Start of Buttonhole
Edge of Garment

Fig. 49
Edge of Garment
Can Be Lengthened
Start of Buttonhole

Important Note: Bound buttonholes are stitched and cut through the body and interfacing of the garment in an early stage of construction before the facing is joined to the garment. Worked buttonholes are made when the garment is completed.

BOUND BUTTONHOLES

Every bound buttonhole turns out in an individual manner, depending upon the fabric, the size of the buttonhole and whether you cut the patch (which is the binding) on the straight or the bias. For this reason it is wise to build up a sample piece, including interfacing, and try one or two buttonholes for size and effect. The practice will also boost your confidence.

Once the interfacing is basted in place on the wrong side of the garment piece, mark the exact

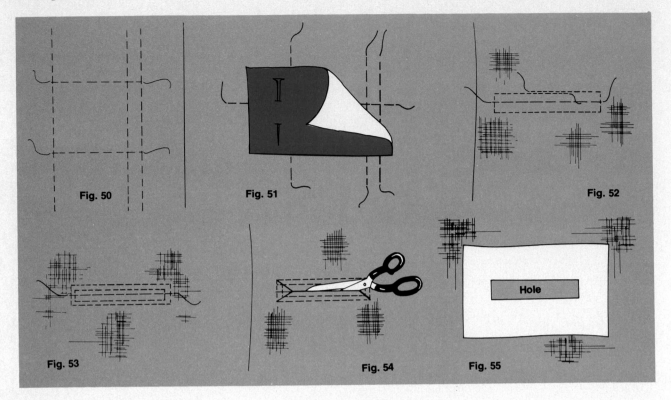

Fig. 50   Fig. 51   Fig. 52

Fig. 53   Fig. 54   Fig. 55

Hole

length of the buttonhole through the layers using a hand-basting stitch. **Fig. 50.**

Using the true straight grain of the fabric or the true bias, cut a patch approximately 3 x 4 inches. Bias is more flexible, easier to handle and ravels less; it also has a more pleasing effect in plaids and checks. Straight grain is preferable for rib weaves and some twill weaves.

Lay the patch on the garment with right sides together. Center the patch directly over the basted line and pin it in place. **Fig. 51.** Turn the garment over so that you are working on the wrong side (or the interfacing). Set the sewing machine for twelve stitches to the inch and stitch a neat rectangle around the basted line. The stitching should start in the center of one long side of the buttonhole and finish by overlapping the initial stitches by at least three stitches. The width of the buttonhole can be anything from four stitches wide for fine fabrics, to seven for very heavy suitings. **Fig. 52.** Check the corners to make sure that the stitch is tight at that point. If the tension of the machine is loose, the corners will not be neat and square.

When the stitching is completed around all the buttonholes in the garment, check them for ac-curacy and spacing, you may further reinforce them by stitching around again on exactly the same line. Then stitch smaller rectangles inside the first one to prevent ravelling after the buttonhole is cut. **Fig. 53.**

With very sharp-pointed scissors, cut through all layers, using a "buttonhole cut" as shown. Be sure to cut all the way to the corner stitch. You will be cutting through those reinforcing smaller rectangles which were stitched. **Fig. 54.** Pull up the patch at each corner to make sure that you did not clip through the corners on the outermost row of stitching. If this should happen, *restitch it immediately* before you start turning the patch.

Pull the patch through to wrong side of garment so there is a rectangular opening. **Fig. 55.**

Press only the ends with the point of a steam iron. On the patch, mark the center of each end with fine chalk or a light pencil. **Fig. 56.**

Fold one side of the patch over the opening, leaving the small side seam turned away from the opening. Press lightly. **Fig. 57.** Fold that side back on itself so that it covers half of the opening and just touches the marks. **Fig. 58.** Press it gently in place and repeat with the other side. At

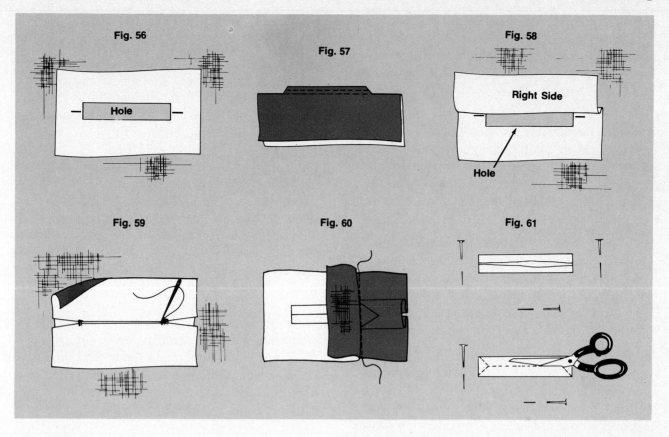

Fig. 56   Hole

Fig. 57

Fig. 58   Right Side   Hole

Fig. 59

Fig. 60

Fig. 61

each end, tack the two pleats or lips together by hand. **Fig. 59.**

Place the garment, patch down and right side of garment up, on the sewing machine. Fold the garment back to expose the triangular ends of the buttonhole. Stitch across the triangular ends and the pleats, starting and ending at the edges of the patch. **Fig. 60.** This will make the end of the buttonhole very straight and firm looking. Tack the pleats by hand along the sides to keep them even, though this will not be necessary if the fabric takes a hard press.

When the garment is nearer completion and the facing has been sewn on, trim seam and finish the buttonholes through the facing. On a flat surface, fold the facing back over the buttonholes. Hold it firmly in place and pin it to the garment around each buttonhole. With sharp scissors, clip the facing through the center of the opening of the buttonhole. **Fig. 61.** Once a cut of approximately 1/4 inch has been made, work from the facing side. There are two types of cuts which may be used a long straight one for thin fabrics and a "buttonhole cut" for heavy ones. Either cut should be the exact length of the opening.

Start in the center of one side, tuck under the edge of the cut and blind stitch it with very small stitches. Reinforce the corners or ends with several very close overcast stitches. **Fig. 62.**

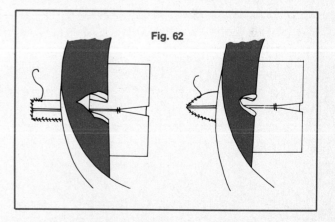

Fig. 62

HANDWORKED BUTTONHOLES

Because worked buttonholes are made after the garment is assembled, the cut is made through several layers of fabric at once — body, interfacing and facing. It is wise to remember to keep all the layers together by stitching a rectangle the length of the buttonhole and about 1/8 inch wide around the small buttonhole area. **Fig. 63.** Use a straight machine stitch of about twelve stitches to the inch, a tiny running stitch or backstitch by hand. With very sharp scissors, cut between the rows of stitches to the desired length.

The thread must be chosen according to the weight of the fabric. Cotton or polyester thread is best for light-to medium-weight washable fabrics, silk thread for light-to medium-weight silks and woolens; silk buttonhole twist for heavy woolens. The thread may be used single or double depending on the effect desired.

Start at the end of the buttonhole which will be under the button — the end nearest the garment edge. Use a buttonhole stitch as shown, being careful to pull the stitch tight each time so that the loop or ridge forms evenly along the cut edge of the fabric. **Fig. 64.**

In lightweight fabrics, both ends may be finished with a fan of stitches. In heavier fabrics, it is customary to make a bar at the end away from the button. Lay down two stitches across the end of the buttonhole and work over them as shown. **Fig. 65.** In very tailored buttonholes of this type, a small hole can be cut at the button end. This necessitates stitching a circular area in the reinforcement stitching. These are called "keyhole" buttonholes. **Fig. 66.**

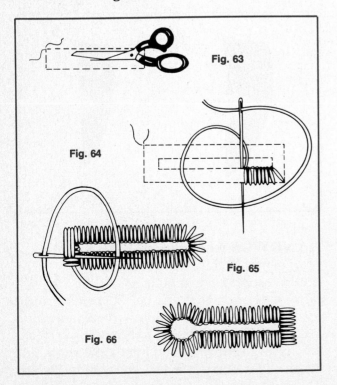

Fig. 63

Fig. 64

Fig. 65

Fig. 66

BUTTONHOLE POCKETS

Another version of the bound buttonhole is especially suitable for use as a bound buttonhole pocket. It is generally known as the five-line method. (See General Instructions on Buttonholes for comparison of patch method and five-line method, pg. 593.)

Cut a strip of fabric 3 inches long and two seam allowances wider than the finished width of the pocket. The strip is usually straight grain, though it may be bias for purposes of design — as with a plaid or check. If the body of the garment is underlined, it is wise to underline the strip also, cutting the underlining on the same grain as the strip.

Mark the pocket line with basting which can be seen clearly on the reverse side of the garment. Using chalk or pencil, mark the width of the strip on the wrong side — once along the center and once $5/8$ inch on either side of this line. Mark across the ends of these lines at the desired width of the pocket opening. **Fig. 67.**

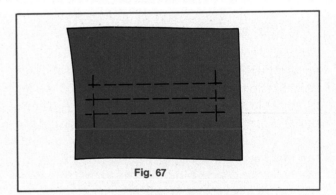

Fig. 67

Lay the strip on the garment with right sides together, placing the center line exactly over the basted marking on the garment. **Fig. 68.** Pin across the center line in several places to secure it. Turn the garment over and baste by machine on the original basted marking. Then, machine baste along the lines marked on the wrong side of the strip. **Fig. 69.** Fold one side of the strip toward the center and press. **Fig. 70.** It is helpful to chalk the end lines on the wrong side of the garment, using the ends of the three basted lines as your guide. Working from the wrong side of the garment, with the machine set at 12 stitches per inch, stitch through all layers of fabric exactly

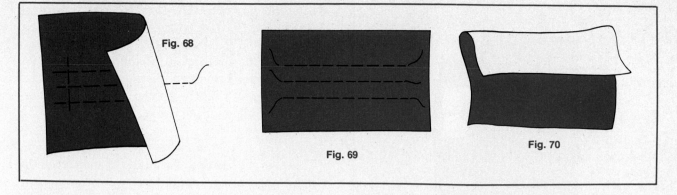

Fig. 68

Fig. 69

Fig. 70

between the center line and the basted line. The stitching should begin at one marked end line and stop at the other end line. Secure the stitching at each end by backstitching about three stitches. Lift the free edge of the stitched, folded side and repeat the folding, pressing and stitching for the other side. You now have five lines of stitching showing on the wrong side of the garment. **Fig. 71.**

Pull out the three basting lines. Split the strip down the center. Working from the wrong side of

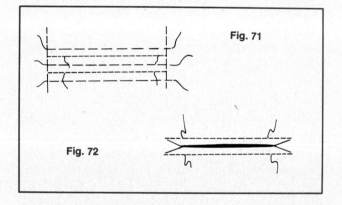

Fig. 71

Fig. 72

the garment, make a buttonhole cut in the garment fabric only. Do not cut into the strip. **Fig. 72.** Turn the strip through the opening. Straighten the lips of the opening and diagonally baste them together. Be sure that the lips of the buttonhole meet, but do not overlap. Lay the garment wrong side down on the machine and fold it back to expose the small triangles at the ends of the buttonhole pocket. Stitch across the strip as closely as possible to the corners of the buttonhole, crossing the triangle. **Fig. 73.**

There are usually two pattern pieces provided to complete this type pocket, or an original pattern may be cut if the buttonhole pocket is being cre-

ated from scratch. Both pieces will be as wide as the buttonhole strip. Cut one of the pieces from lining fabric — the length and width being equal. Cut the other piece from garment fabric — $5/8$ inch longer. Sewing directly on the original stitching lines (on the wrong side of garment), seam the longer piece (garment fabric) right sides together with the upper edge of the strip. Be careful not to catch the right side of the finished opening in the stitching. Seam the shorter piece (lining fabric) right sides together with the lower edge of the strip. **Fig. 74.**

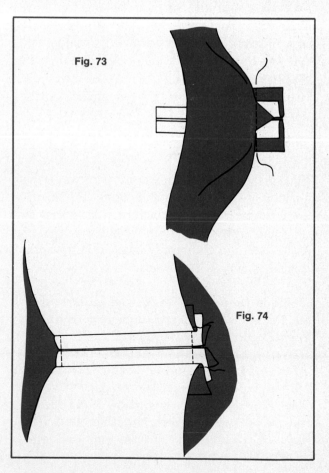

Fig. 73

Fig. 74

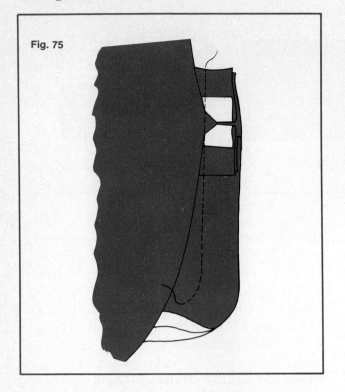

Fig. 75

Lay the garment wrong side down on the machine and fold it back to expose the edges of the pocket; pin and stitch from one top corner around the pocket to the other top corner. Be sure to stitch across the exposed triangles, thus squaring the corners of the pocket opening. **Fig. 75.** (The lower corners may be curved if desired.) Remove basting from pocket opening and press.

BUTTONLOOPS

Buttonloops can be made in two ways: with fabric or worked by hand using thread. The fabric loops are a fine touch for silks, dressy cottons, and light-to medium-weight woolens. The thread ones are commonly used on baby clothes, lingerie and delicate fabrics.

Fabric Buttonloops: Using strips of fabric cut on the bias and very fine cotton cable cord or heavy crochet cotton, make spaghetti strips by directions on page 590, Bias Tubular Trims. Lay out the plan for buttonloop placement with pencil and ruler on typewriter-weight paper. With the paper representing the right side of the garment, draw a line to represent the seam line. Then, mark the spacings on the seam line for loops to correspond with the buttons.

Draw line A on the left side and parallel to the seam line at the desired depth of the buttonloops. **Fig. 76a.** A little experimentation is necessary to decide on the spacing and depth of the loops. A general rule is that the circumference of the loop should appear slightly smaller than the circumference of the button.

Draw line B on the right side of seam line and parallel to it. This line should be $^5/_8$ inch from the seam line, representing the seam allowance of the garment.

Cut the spaghetti strip into lengths that will fit the length of the curve from line B to line A and back to line B. Lay the strips in place with each seamed side exposed and machine stitch along the $^5/_8$-inch seam line so that each loop is held in place on the paper. **Fig. 76b.** Lay the paper on the right side of the garment, seam lines matching, and stitch together. Tear away the paper. Lay the facing on the garment with right sides together, covering the loops. **Fig. 77.** Pin it in place and on the wrong side of the garment, stitch exactly on top of the line of stitching which shows there. The buttonloops will be evenly spaced on the right side of the garment when the facing is turned and pressed. **Fig. 78.**

Thread Buttonloops: You may use ordinary sewing thread for buttonloops, silk thread for fine fabrics, or buttonhole twist for heavy fabrics. Thread the needle double, knot the end and start between the garment and facing. Bring the needle through to the right side and make a loose loop along the edge of the garment. Check to see that the button goes through easily, then, double back on the loop so that it is four threads in all. **Fig. 79.** Work a buttonhole stitch over this loop, keeping stitches tight and even. (If the needle is backed through, it usually will not catch in the fabric.) **Fig. 80.** Fasten the thread inside the facing at the end.

BUTTONS

Buttons are decorative as well as useful, so select them as carefully as you select your pattern and fabric. Most fashion buttons are of the two-hole sew-through type or are shanked. Four-hole sew-through buttons are used mainly on sports wear,

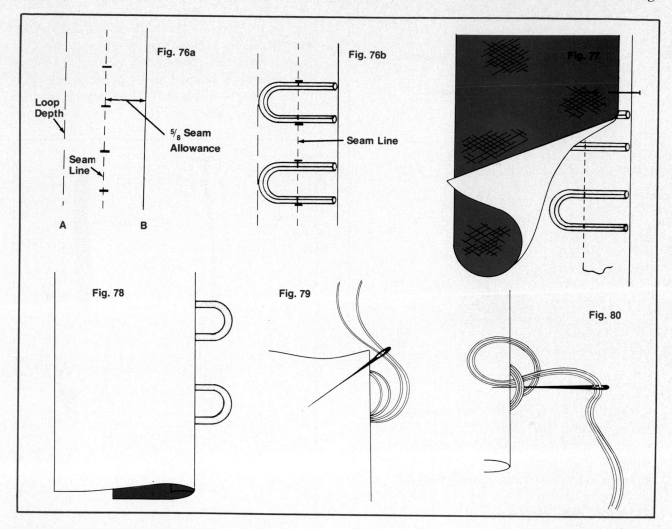

Fig. 76a

Loop Depth

Seam Line

⁵/₈ Seam Allowance

A

B

Fig. 76b

Seam Line

Fig. 77

Fig. 78

Fig. 79

Fig. 80

men's wear and children's clothes. **Fig. 81.** Besides choosing buttons for looks and size, make sure that they are as washable or as dry-cleanable as the fabric on which they will be sewn. No jeweled button should be washed or dry-cleaned. However, these are usually shanked and can be put on with a special safety pin made just for attaching buttons. **Fig. 82.**

Ordinary sewing thread is adequate for sewing on most buttons. If it is waxed, it is stronger and easier to use, so keep beeswax handy. Silk thread is nice for silks and fine woolens. Very heavy button thread can be purchased for use on overcoats and work clothes.

Shanked buttons and most sew-through buttons used on lightweight fabrics can be sewn tightly to the fabric with a double thread. Start with the knot on the right side of the fabric so that it will be concealed under the button; finish the stitch-

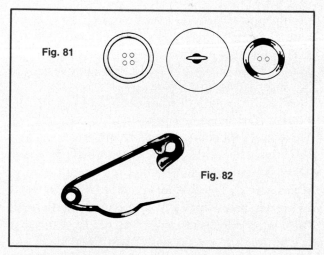

Fig. 81

Fig. 82

ing tightly on the back of the fabric by going through the stitches several times.

Sew-through buttons on heavier fabrics should be shanked up from the fabric during sewing. To do this, place a toothpick or match between the but-

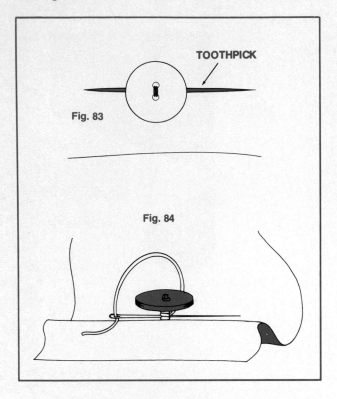

Fig. 83

TOOTHPICK

Fig. 84

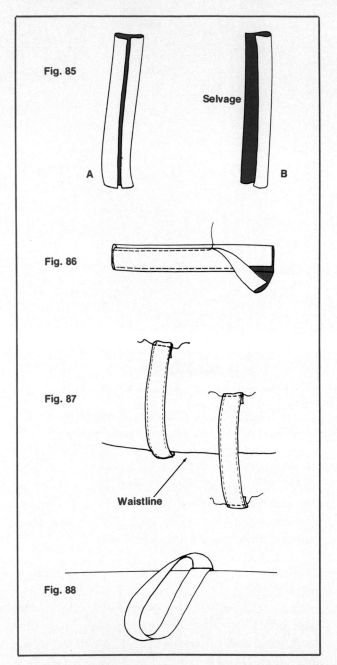

Fig. 85

Selvage

A   B

Fig. 86

Fig. 87

Waistline

Fig. 88

ton and the fabric. **Fig. 83.** Sew back and forth as usual, remove the stick and wrap the thread several times around the shank of loose stitches. Fasten off by running the needle back and forth through the shank several times. **Fig. 84.**

CARRIERS (Belt Loops)

Carriers are used on pants, skirts, dresses and some jackets to keep belts in place and to add a decorative touch. The most attractive varieties are made of fabric, but strictly utilitarian carriers can be made by hand with thread.

Fabric Carriers: For fabric carriers, such as those used on pants, cut a straight strip of fabric four times wider than the desired finished width. (If cutting along the selvage, cut the strip three times wider.) Fold under one fourth of the width along the raw edges and press. (Fold under one third when selvage is used.) **Fig. 85.** Fold the strip down the center so that finished edges meet and top stitch about $1/16$ inch from edge. **Fig. 86.**

Fabric carriers can be attached to a garment in several ways. **Fig. 87.** One method is to incorporate one end of a carrier into the waistband seam, turn under the other end, pin or baste in desired position, and top stitch. Another method

is to pin or baste the carrier in place on top of the garment, turn under and top stitch both ends. For narrow belts, the carrier may be folded in half and both ends seamed into the waistline of a dress, so that they are loose except at the waistline. **Fig. 88.**

Thread Carriers: Thread a large needle with two threads — cotton, silk or buttonhole twist, depending on the fabric. Double the thread and knot it so that you have four threads. Bring the needle through from the wrong side of the garment and anchor it tightly with one stitch. Start

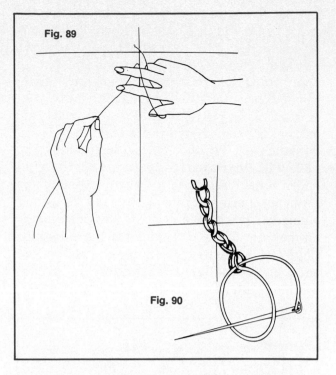

Fig. 89

Fig. 90

CASINGS

A casing is simply a tunnel of fabric through which elastic or cording is run. Casings may be required on an edge of a garment or used directly behind the fabric for shirring. **Fig. 91.** Usually, a casing along an edge is simply a hem slightly wider than the elastic. An opening must be left through which the elastic or cording can be run. Hem by machine as close as possible to the edge of the hem, leaving an opening of about $1/2$ inch between the points of starting and stopping. Backstitch at each end for security. **Fig. 92.**

If a ribbon is to be run as a decorative touch, the opening should be made by means of working two buttonholes (machine ones are fine) through the single layer of fabric before the hem is made. Place the buttonholes about $1/2$ inch apart at the point where the ribbon ends should appear. The length of the buttonholes should be slightly less than the width of the casing. **Fig. 93.**

another stitch, but do not pull it up; leave a loop about 3 inches long. Use the fingers much like a crochet hook, pulling another loop through the first one; pull the first loop tight, repeat the process through the second loop and continue until you have a crocheted chain of the desired length. **Fig. 89.** Pass the needle through the last loop to anchor it and fasten the end into the fabric with several stitches, ending on wrong side. **Fig. 90.**

Use bias strips of lining fabric, compatible with the garment fabric. Cut them $1/2$ inch wider than the elastic plus $1/2$ inch to turn under. Cut a piece of thin cardboard the finished width of the casing strip. Lay the cardboard on the wrong side of the strip and press the edges back over it so that they will be uniform. **Fig. 94.** Pin or baste the strip in

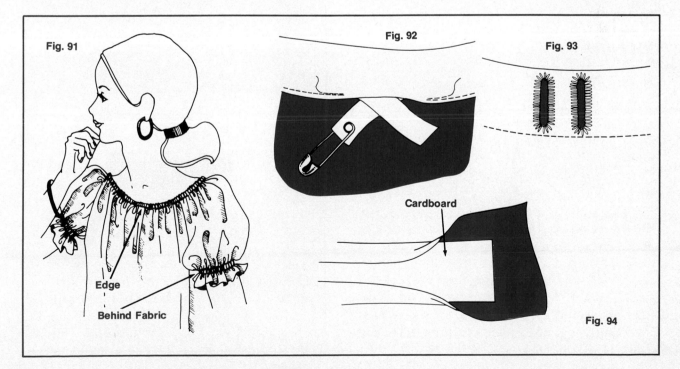

Fig. 91

Fig. 92

Fig. 93

Edge

Behind Fabric

Cardboard

Fig. 94

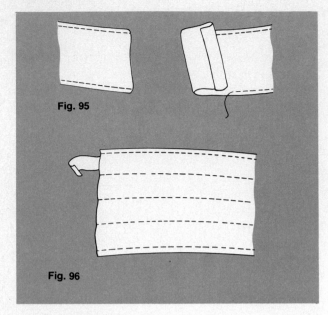

Fig. 95

Fig. 96

Lay the interfacing on the wrong side of the under collar, pin in place and stitch. Pin the upper and under collar right sides together, making sure that the under collar is very taut and that the upper collar has been eased in slightly. Stitch; trim the seam; notch the curves or clip the corners as is necessary. **Fig. 97.** Turn the collar right side out and understitch by hand around the edge to hold the seam in place. (See Understitching, pg. 682.) **Fig. 98.** Press lightly. Lay the collar with under collar side down, on the neckline of the garment, matching center fronts and backs and all marked points. Pin in place, working directly on the seam line and shaping the curve over the fingers while pinning. Check to see that the front ends of the collar are identical in length. Machine baste along the pinned seam. **Fig. 99.**

place against the wrong side of the garment, turning each end under $1/2$ inch so that there will be an opening between. Stitch as close as possible to the edges. **Fig. 95.**

Many clothes show a multiple shirring which can be made with elastic thread. However, this is extremely hard to handle on many machines so an alternative is suggested. Use a wide bias casing, stitch it through in even rows and run a narrow elastic band in each of the tunnels formed. This method is easier to do and will outlast the elastic thread. **Fig. 96.**

COLLARS

Several types of collars can be found on clothing for everyday wear and most of them can be applied in one of two ways. This section deals with the application of dress collars, i.e. collars used on light to medium-weight fabrics. For collars on heavyweight fabrics or suits and coats, see the section on Tailoring, page 672.

Patterns usually call for interfacing on collars; be careful not to get it too heavy. In some cases it is wise to leave it out and use a crisp lining fabric, such as an underlining, through the entire collar instead. In knits it is usually not necessary to use either underlining or interfacing. (See section on Underlining, pg. 682; Interfacing, pg. 636; and Knits, pg. 637.)

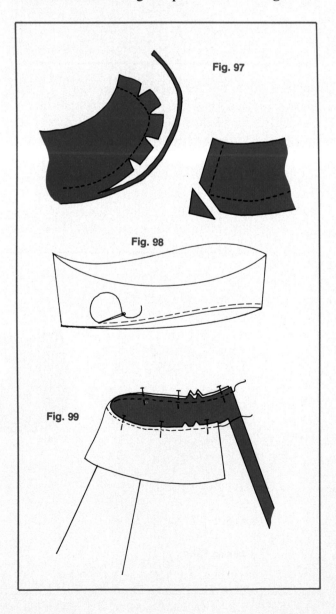

Fig. 97

Fig. 98

Fig. 99

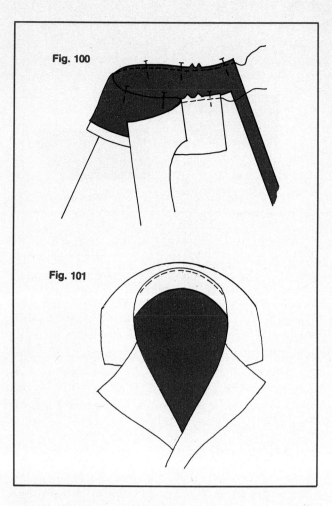

Fig. 100

Fig. 101

Pointed collars with very sharp corners can be turned more easily if the interfacing is omitted in the corners at a point just above the seam line. **Fig. 102.** After turning the collar right side out, be careful when pushing the corner into shape. The best equipment for this purpose is a small crochet hook or a wooden pointer made specifically for this purpose. Never use scissors or other sharp implements.

Mandarin collars should stand up around the neck. This effect is best achieved by using a stiff interfacing, preferably a nonwoven one. The best patterns for true mandarin collars are those which have a slight curve, making them fit around the neck without puckering. **Fig. 103.**

Bias Collars

There are several collar styles which can be made from a strip of bias. The most common one is the rolled down or turtleneck collar and its popular modification, the mock turtleneck. Bias collars are used on low necks also and are sometimes referred to as cowl collars. **Fig. 104.**

Pin the facing right sides together over the collar. Stitch from the wrong side of the garment, following the first line of stitching. **Fig. 100.** Working around a curve with several layers requires skill in handling the machine, so always check to see that a pleat has not formed in the bottom layer of fabric. If this happens, rip out about an inch of stitching at that point, smooth out the pleat and restitch. Trim the collar seam to about ¼ inch and the other seams to ½ inch. Clip almost to the stitching at ½-inch intervals all around the neckline. (See Curved Seams, pg. 665.) Turn right side out. If the neckline is to be worn open, understitch only across the back so that the stitching doesn't show. **Fig. 101.**

Tips on Specific Types of Collars

Rounded or Peter Pan collars can be marked with chalk or a light pencil on the seam line, using a French curve or curved dressmaker's ruler. This will make the ends identical when stitched.

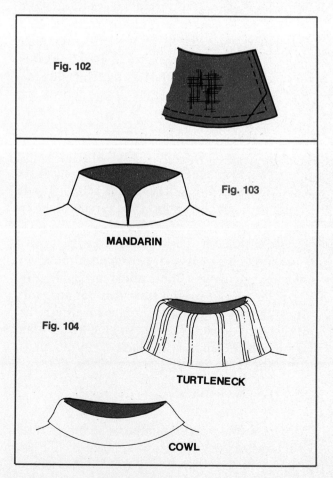

Fig. 102

Fig. 103

MANDARIN

Fig. 104

TURTLENECK

COWL

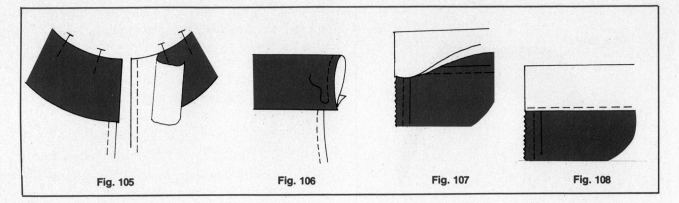

Fig. 105   Fig. 106   Fig. 107   Fig. 108

These collars may be applied to the neckline with a facing exactly like the ones just described. An easier application is made by treating them as bands.

Lay one long edge of the bias strip, right sides together with the neckline. Pin into place, matching centers, shoulders and other markings. If the garment has a back zipper, it should already be completed so there will be a seam allowance on each end of the collar extending beyond the zipper edge. **Fig. 105.** Stitch the collar band in place. Grade the seam as follows: the collar fabric, trimmed to $1/4$ inch and the garment fabric trimmed to $3/8$ inch. Clip the neckline seam almost to the stitching line at $1/2$-inch intervals. Smooth the collar out flat (away from the garment) so that the right sides of the fabrics are showing.

Turn under the raw edge and fold over the ends of the band, sides together, matching edges. Pin and stitch a seam across each end, stopping at the end of the neckline stitching and securing with several back stitches. **Fig. 106.** Grade seam by trimming one layer to $1/4$ inch and one to $3/8$ inch. Turn right side out. Turn under raw edge around the collar and pin in place over neckline seam, matching markings. Blind stitch by hand. **Fig. 107.** If the fabric is very heavy, it is not necessary to turn the raw edge under, as bias ravels very little. Lay it flat inside the neck, matching the seam lines and slip stitch it in place. Trim about $1/4$ inch from raw edge. **Fig. 108.**

CORD

The cord most commonly used in sewing is cable cord, a twisted cotton cord which is used to make Corded Piping and spaghetti cord (Bias Tubular

Trims, pg. 590). It ranges in size from about $1/8$ inch in diameter to $1/2$ inch. Stores carrying drapery fabrics usually have the best selection.

There are decorative twisted rayon cords used for drapery ties and for trimming cushions and household items. This type of cord can also be used effectively for belts on dresses. If the appearance of cord around the edge of a garment is needed, use the type which has a flat braid lip on one edge, called blazed braid. (See illustration of Types of Braids, pg. 592.)

CORDED PIPING

One of the most effective trims is corded piping, made from cable cord and fabric cut on the bias. It can either match or contrast; be made of an entirely different fabric, such as velveteen or wool; show off a check or plaid on the bias; and lift an otherwise plain dress out of the doldrums. Use it in necklines for a smooth finish and at waistlines in place of a belt.

Cut and piece bias strips, about $1 1/2$ inches wide. Fold the piece, wrong sides together, over cable cord — usually sizes $1/8$ inch to $1/4$ inch for clothing. Machine stitch close to cord with cording or zipper foot. **Fig. 109.** Use a fairly long stitch and hold the fabric so that you are not stretching either layer. (For applying the piping to garments see Edgings, pg. 608.)

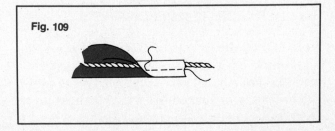

Fig. 109

CUFFS

Cuffs are somewhat like collars; they are either applied to sleeves with facings or they go on like bands. Pants cuffs and some sleeve cuffs are no more than wide hems turned back. French cuffs are very wide band cuffs turned back. **Fig. 110.**

Like collars, cuffs may be interfaced. If they are to have buttons and buttonholes, interfacing is a necessity. Avoid using an interfacing which is too heavy, especially if you are putting on a cuff with a facing. The seam can get very thick and distort the shape of the sleeve. If the cuff is a band type, the interfacing should not run throughout the entire cuff. Cut it off ¹/₂ inch beyond the fold line and catch stitch it into place. **Fig. 111.** Some bias cuffs really require no interfacing. If a cuff is made of two shaped pieces, interface, stitch and trim them as you would a collar. *Understitch* the edge by hand if you wish. (See pg. 682.)

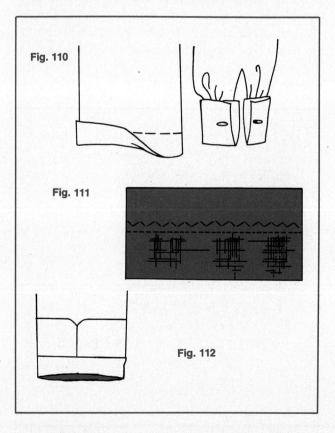

Fig. 110

Fig. 111

Fig. 112

If a sleeve facing is necessary, it can be cut from a lighter material to avoid bulk. Pin and stitch the cuff, wrong side down, to the right side of the sleeve, using a long machine stitch. Lay the facing right side down over the cuff, pin and stitch it in place. **Fig. 112.** Trim the cuff seam to ¹/₄ inch and the other seams to approximately ¹/₂ inch. Turn facing and understitch the facing seam. (See Facings, pg. 618.)

Bias Band Cuffs

Bias band cuffs are sometimes used on short sleeves. Seam the sides of the cuff together. Lay right side of the cuff on the wrong side of the seamed sleeve. Pin the two together, matching all markings, and stitch. Turn the raw edge under and blind stitch it on the outside of the sleeve, covering the machine stitching. **Fig. 113.** It is not usually necessary to trim or grade this seam but you may if you wish.

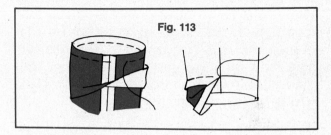

Fig. 113

Shirt Sleeve Cuffs

The cuff on a shirt sleeve is a band cuff, made with one piece folded or two pieces seamed together. In either case, they can be put onto the sleeve in much the same way. Interface one side. (See above suggestion for interfacing only one-half of a folded cuff.) Adjust the gathers or pleats at the lower edge of the sleeve after the opening has been bound or finished (see pg. 657). Unless it is a French cuff, the cuff will have an underlap extension of ¹/₂ inch to 1 inch at the end nearest the underarm seam of the sleeve. Pin the sleeve and the interfaced piece of cuff right sides together. Start at the seam line at the overlap end and pin to the point where the underlap starts. Stitch this seam, trim off about ¹/₄ inch. **Fig. 114.**

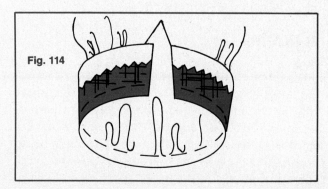

Fig. 114

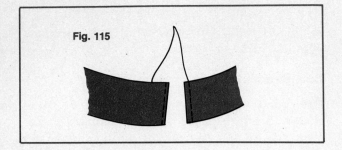

Fig. 115

If the cuff is made in one piece, stitch it to the sleeve with right sides together. Fold the cuff back, right sides together, pin the ends, stitch and turn cuff. **Fig. 115.** If the cuff is in two pieces, pin the other half, right sides together, with the piece joined to the sleeve, keeping the new piece very tight so that it will lie smoothly inside the cuff when finished. Stitch around the seam and trim or grade the seam (see pg. 665). Turn the cuff right side out, turn under the raw edge and blind stitch to the seam inside the cuff. This type of cuff is often top stitched.

Make machine or handworked buttonholes on the overlap end of the cuffs. If the cuff is a French cuff, remember to fold the cuff back into its correct position and then, mark the spacings for buttonholes. This will ensure that the garment is not ruined by working buttonholes from the wrong side of the cuff.

CUFF LINKS

A finishing touch for French cuffs is to make cuff links to match the shirt buttons. Two shanked buttons can be held together with double thread which has been run through the shanks several times and knotted securely. They may also be held together with a strong jewelry link. Sew-through buttons can be held together by a thread chain ½ inch long, (see method, Buttonloops, pg. 598; or Carriers, pg. 600.)

DARNING

The oldest form of mending is darning. Though few people still bother to darn stockings, there may be times when mending a favorite pair of wool ski socks or a good tweed skirt will be a necessity. For either, the basic principle is to weave over the hole, as smoothly as possible, with thread or yarn similar to the garment.

Darning Knitted Apparel

For socks and sweaters, there are small packs or spools of darning thread available at notions counters. Wool, nylon or cotton threads usually work best. Use single or double thread in the needle, depending upon the weight of the fabric. Trim away the ragged edges of the hole. Without knotting the thread, make a row of running stitches just outside the edges of the hole, leaving a 1-inch end of thread. **Fig. 116.** Catch this in under subsequent stitches. Run another row, parallel to the first. Continue to do this, allowing the threads to lie across the hole. When two rows of stitching are completed on the other side of the hole, start working in the same manner in the other direction, perpendicular to the first rows. Across the center of the hole, weave the stitches into the first threads-over and under alternately on each row. **Fig. 117.** Finish off the thread by running under several stitches. A small hole is easily darned by holding it taut over the fingers of your other hand. However, a large hole should be held over an old-fashioned darning egg or a light bulb. These help prevent puckering the fabric and making it knotty.

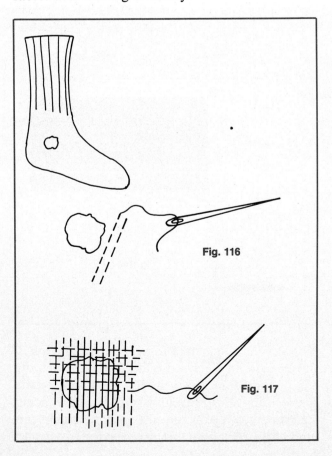

Fig. 116

Fig. 117

Darning Woven Apparel

When darning a woven fabric, find a seam or other raw edge which is wide enough to allow a few long threads to be pulled out. These should be long enough to thread a fairly large darning needle. Weave the two rows along the first edge and all subsequent edges. Try to weave into the original weave. Work from the wrong side of the fabric and steam press the mended area.

DARTS

Darts are used to give garments shape. There are slight differences in them, depending on which section of a garment they will contour. Some darts are stitched in perfectly straight lines. These are usually the short ones found at the back neck, at the bust or at the elbow of a sleeve. Hip darts are shaped to conform to the curve of the body: convex to give more room just below the waist; concave to take up slight excess of fabric. Sometimes in very fitted garments, under bust darts are given a concave curve to make the bodice hug the rib cage under the bust. **Fig. 118.**

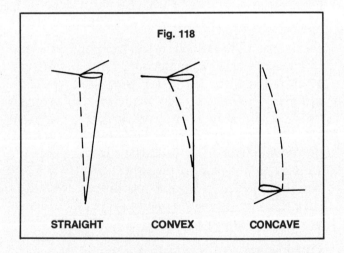

Fig. 118

STRAIGHT   CONVEX   CONCAVE

Single-ended darts are used most often. However, in princess line garments, double-ended darts are used. These are much like two darts put together in the middle. When stitching a single-ended dart, begin at the widest end of the dart and follow the markings to the fine point. The last few stitches should be very near the folded edge of the fabric. Backstitch about three stitches along the fold to secure the end. **Fig. 119.**

It is easier to stitch a double-ended dart if you treat it as two single-ended ones. Start at the

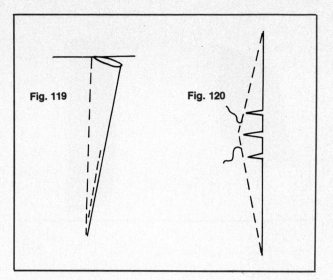

Fig. 119   Fig. 120

center or wide part each time and let about four stitches overlap at this point for security. Treat the lower dart as a hip dart and the upper one as a bodice dart. Clip the dart about three times at the widest part before pressing. **Fig. 120.** (For further instructions on pressing darts, see pg. 660.)

EASE

There are two definitions of "ease" in sewing terminology. It may refer to the amount of extra room in a garment in excess of the body measurements. Most patterns allow at least 3 to 4 inches ease in the bust and 2 inches in the hips. This is sometimes referred to as ease allowance.

The other kind is similar gathering. This kind of ease means that a longer piece of fabric is worked in by hand to fit a shorter piece. The main difference between this and gathering is the amount of cloth to be worked in; with ease, there should not be enough extra fabric to create puckers. In certain places on the seam line of a pattern, the word "ease" and two notches or tailor tack marks may appear. To ease a section, run a single line of large machine stitches along this seam line. With the fabric pieces right sides together, match these markings to the corresponding markings. **Fig. 121.** Gently pull the bobbin thread and distribute the fullness between the marks smoothly and evenly so that the pieces can be stitched together without a pleat forming. Pin in place along the seam line and stitch with the full side up so that you can see and control the ease. **Fig. 122.**

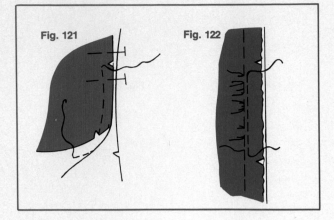

Fig. 121   Fig. 122

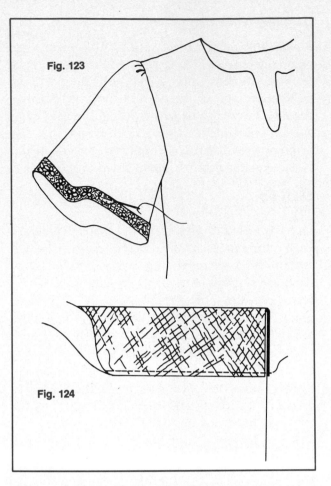

Fig. 123

Fig. 124

Soft fabrics, especially knits, can be eased more successfully than hard finish fabrics such as chintz. Most fabrics can be eased on the bias better than on the straight grain and on the cross grain slightly better than on the length grain. For this reason, "ease" is not usually marked on the length grain of patterns, except those patterns made exclusively for knits. Thus, it is unwise to use "for knits only" patterns for any other fabrics.

Easing is sometimes used to mean "fulling." "Fulling" is generally used in cases where an ease thread will not be used.

EDGE STITCHING

Top stitching is done to enhance the tailored appearance of shirts, jackets, and other sport clothes. When it is done along the finished edge of a garment, it is sometimes referred to as edge stitching. (See directions for Top Stitching, found on pg. 681.)

EDGINGS

Many types of braids, bindings and pipings are used along the edges of garments for decoration and are then called edgings. Some are applied flat on the top of the fabric when the edge has already been finished with a facing or hem. This is generally done by hand with a blind stitch or backstitch so that the stitches do not show through on the facing. The flat braids can be used as an edge finish as described for Ball Fringe in Braids, page 591. **Fig. 123.**

Bound Edges

Bias bindings can also be used to finish an edge. Several methods are described in the section on them, pg. 588. Folded braid, so popular with knits, can be applied in much the same manner as Method No. 1 or No. 2 for Bias Binding. The difference is that the edge of the folded braid is finished so that it can be laid flat on the fabric, stitched and then the other half brought over to the other side and finished. The edges are woven so there is no need to turn them under as bias binding. Folded braid can be slipped over the edge and stitched in one operation but the results are never as good. **Fig. 124.**

Piped Edges

Corded piping, rickrack and ruffling can be set into the seam between the fabric and the facing, making a very smooth edge finish. Lay the seam line of the piping or ruffling (or the center line of the rickrack) on the seam line of the garment, right sides together. Pin in place and stitch. Lay the facing over the trim, right sides together with the garment, matching all notches and markings and pin in place. Working from the wrong side of the garment, stitch facing in place, following the first line of stitching. Trim and clip the seam and

Two Easy Edgings for Finishing Sleeves and Neckline (especially good on knits): On the left is a sport blouse in cotton knit, finished with fold braid which is stitched on the machine with zigzag. On the right is the same blouse in a dressier version in polyester bouclé finished with corded piping acting as its own bias facing.

turn the garment right side out. Understitch if necessary. (See Facings, pg. 617.) **Fig. 125.**

The same method should be used to set in any piping or trim in a seam, as with slipcovers. Never try to pin or baste all three layers together to stitch in one operation. Always stitch the trim to one layer and then, following the first stitching, stitch the other layer in place.

Special Piping Finish

Another useful way of finishing an edge with corded piping is to use the piping bias itself as a facing. This eliminates the extra bulk of another layer and is especially good as a finish for knits. It also prevents the problem of a facing rolling out from a low neck.

When making the piping, cut the bias 2 inches wide for $1/8$-inch cording. Stitch it onto the neck or armhole as in the first step in the method just described. Trim the layer of bias nearest the garment fabric; trim and clip the garment seam. Turn under the raw edge of the remaining long bias edge and pin in place. Stitch it to the garment by hand, using a lock stitch, with about $1/2$ inch between the stitches. (See Stitches, pg. 674.) Take very small stitches and be careful not to pull them tight enough to show on the right side.

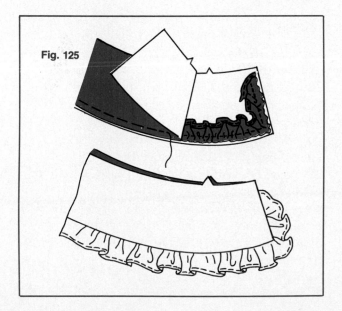

Fig. 125

ELASTIC

When buying elastic, pay special attention to the fiber content. It is also desirable to be able to feel the softness or hardness of the elastic. Hard elastic can be most uncomfortable in puffed sleeves and panty legs. If the elastic is marked "lingerie," it is usually soft. Nylon elastic is a necessity for bathing suits, as it retains its holding properties when wet.

Most elastics are run in Casings. (See pg. 601.) There is an elastic thread available which can be used in the bobbin of the sewing machine. This thread is difficult to handle and not all machines will react well to it. Use regular sewing thread on the top of the machine and a long stitch when experimenting with this. Further directions may be found on the pack of elastic.

Lingerie elastic around the waistline of panties and half slips can be put on with a straight machine stitch. However, zigzag stitching is ideal. Measure the elastic 2 to 4 inches shorter than the waist; stitch the ends together and mark it off in quarters. Divide the garment into quarters. Pin the elastic on the right side of the garment, matching the markings and overlapping the raw edge of the fabric about ³/₈ inch. Stretch the elastic so that the elastic lies flat on the fabric in one quarter section. Stitch along the edge. Proceed in the same manner with the remaining three sections. Repeat the process, stitching closer to the raw edge of the fabric. **Fig. 126.**

Fig. 126

ELASTIC

A similar stretch-and-stitch process can be used to put wide webbing elastic in bathing trunks and pajama pants. Measure and join the elastic, marking the quarters as before. Turn under the seam allowance on the upper edge of the pants and press. Pin that folded edge over the edge of the

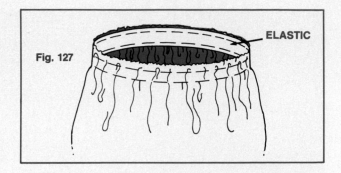

Fig. 127

ELASTIC

elastic, matching markings. It may be necessary to divide and pin in each quarter to prevent the edge of the elastic from curving. Using a straight machine stitch, about eight or ten per inch, stitch ¹/₈ inch from the folded edge, catching the edge of the elastic. Pin the lower edge, stretch and stitch it. **Fig. 127.**

EQUIPMENT

In planning space for sewing and equipment, maximum efficiency with minimum clutter is the primary objective. A few well-chosen tools are better than all the gadgets in the world! Below is a list of essentials:

Sewing machine: Clean and in perfect running order.

Steam iron: Preferably a small one made especially for sewing.

Ironing board: A small apartment-size ironing board is perfect.

Sleeve board: Use in shaping and pressing sleeves.

Press mitt: Desirable for pressing curves and small areas.

Shears: Bent-handled with blades up to 6 inches long and always sharp.

Clipping scissors: Small, sharp; the best of which are those known as "buttonhole scissors."

Box of fine pins: Called "silk pins."

Hand sewing needles: Selection in various sizes.

First quality thread: Selection in various colors, poly-wrap, poly-core or mercerized cotton.

Emery bag: For cleaning needles.

Beeswax: For rubbing thread to keep it from tangling.

Firm, 60-inch measuring tape: Preferably with centimeter conversions on reverse side.

Small 6-inch ruler: One which has a slide for setting hem depths.

Tailor's chalk or chalk pencil

Wooden pointer and curver

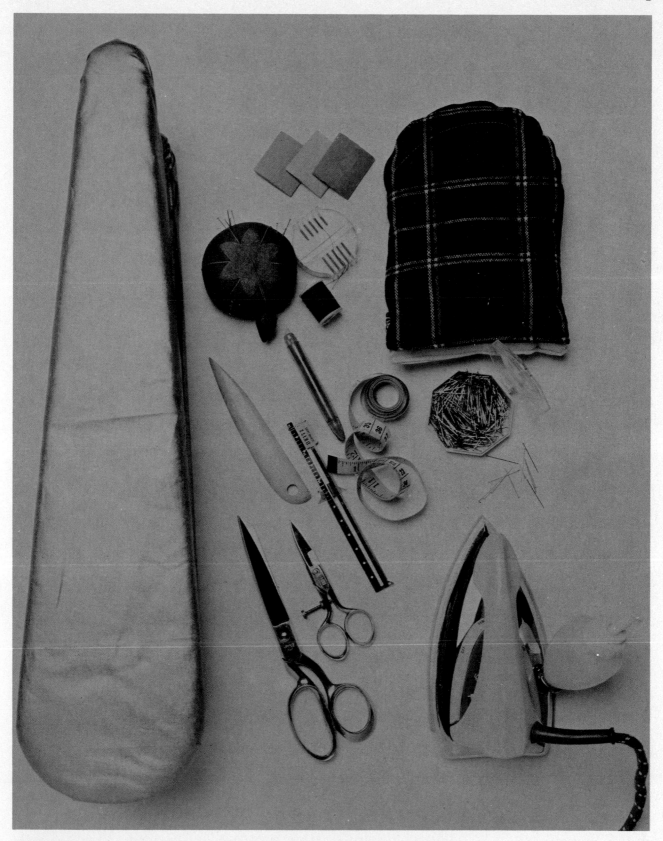

Well-Equipped Sewing Space (Clockwise from left): sleeve board, pin cushion with emery bag, thread, beeswax in holder, three-color chalk, press mitt, silk pins, sewing iron, buttonhole scissors, cutting shears, wooden pointer and curver, measuring gauge, chalk pencil, measuring tape with inches and centimeters.

Optional items are: Other sizes of scissors and pinking shears; variety of pressing hams, corner boards, etc; tracing wheel and carbon; measured cutting board; weights for holding fabric and pattern; and, dress forms.

Weights can be made with two 4-inch circles of heavy felt or vinyl, stitched together and loaded with shot, pebbles or coarse sand.

Dress forms may be of some help in checking pattern sizes and fitting. The best are the ones made to fit the individual figure. Dress forms are particularly helpful in shaping and handling the heavy fabrics used for coats and jackets.

FABRICS (Types of Cloth)

Batik: Originally, a way of printing fabric by hand, using a lost wax process. Now refers to painting designs on cloth with waxes and immersing the cloth into dyes. This process may be done either by hand or machine.

Batiste: Fine soft lingerie or blouse fabric, usually made of cotton or cotton blend.

Blend: Any combination of fibers such as wool blend, meaning wool and synthetic or wool and silk; or a cotton blend such as polyester and cotton or dacron and cotton.

Broadcloth: Silk or cotton shirting with a high luster; also a wool suiting.

Brocade: Jacquarded fabric with a woven design, usually raised and often tone-on-tone.

Burlap: Rough loosely woven fabric of jute or hemp or a more refined variation of these.

Calico: Plain, woven cotton cloth usually printed with a distinctive type of design, often referred to as Early American.

Canvas: Very heavy, sturdy fabric, usually a woven cotton.

Challis: Fine dress fabric made of wool or other fibers and usually delicately printed.

Chambray: Yarn-dyed cotton or silk fabric with an iridescent effect due to the use of two tones of yarn.

Chiffon: Fine, floating fabric of silk or synthetic.

China silk: Thin, smooth plain-woven silk.

Chintz: Plain, woven cotton, usually glazed, often printed.

Ciré: Originally a finish applied to give a shiny effect but now used as a name for any one of several fabrics thus finished.

Cloqué: A type of Matelassé, usually cotton, with a raised or blistered design, often called cloqué piqué.

Corduroy: Napped fabric with wales or stripes of cut pile. Now also available uncut which is more like velveteen.

Covert: Twill weave, worsted fabric for suits and coats.

Crepe: Slightly textured fabric of silk, synthetic, cotton or wool, frequently solid colored.

Crepe de Chine: Fine delicate silk crepe.

Crinoline: Stiffener or interfacing used in hats and petticoats of a certain era.

Damask: Flat Jacquarded fabric with a tone-on-tone design. Most often made of linen for table use.

Denim: Twill weave, heavy sport fabric, most often seen in blue jeans.

Dimity: Cotton or cotton blend, sheer with a woven stripe or check.

Doeskin: Wool fabric somewhat like wool broadcloth.

Dotted Swiss: Cotton sheer with woven or flocked dots.

Double Knit: Fabric knit on two sets of needles so that it is double-layered and looks the same on both sides.

Duck: Canvas-like fabric of cotton or cotton blend.

Eyelet: Openwork embroidered fabric, usually cotton or cotton blend.

Faille: Medium-weight, dress fabric, usually of silk or synthetic, with a fine cross rib woven in. A heavier type is called Bengaline or Bengaline Faille.

Felt: Nonwoven, matted fabric of wool or wool blend.

Flannel: Smooth wool or synthetic fabric, sometimes having a twill weave. Also *Outing Flannel,* a soft cotton fabric with a brushed nap.

Flannelette: Same as Outing Flannel, see above.

Fleece: Heavy-napped coating, usually wool. Also, fake fur fabrics used mostly for lining coats and jackets.

#1 Top Group, l. to r.: Velveteen, Metallic Matelassé, Sheer Lamé, Satin, Velour.
Center Group, l. to r.: Hound's Tooth Flannel, Challis with Paisley Design, Corduroy, Moiré, Faille, Printed Velvet.
Bottom Group, l. to r.: Wool Double Knit, Herringbone Tweed, Wool Gabardine, Donegal Tweed, Tartan Wool Flannel.

Flocked Cotton: Fabric decorated with a raised design of powdered fibers adhered to the cloth.

Gabardine: Strong twill weave, often wool but can be silk, cotton or synthetic.

Georgette: Sheer fabric, slightly heavier than chiffon, lighter than crepe de chine, but with some of the qualities of both. Silk or synthetic.

Gingham: Yarn-dyed cotton with woven geometric designs such as checks.

Herringbone: Striped design with chevron motifs woven in, usually a wool tweed, but can be cotton or silk.

Hopsacking: Thick cotton fabric with a fairly loose basket weave.

Houndstooth: Checkered design woven in, usually wool but can be cotton or silk.

Jacquard: Weaving process which has also given its name to the fabric thus woven. The design is woven in; all damasks, brocades and Matelassés are Jacquard.

Jersey: Lightweight single-knit fabric of any fiber.

Knit: A variety of fabrics made on knitting machines.

Lace: Openwork fabric, usually of cotton or linen and with a repeating pattern.

Lamé: Shimmery metallic cloth, usually a crepe weave.

Lawn: Thin, plain-weave cotton, similar to voile, sometimes used for lightweight interfacing.

Leno: Open-weave cotton used for summer wear and curtains.

Linen: Rough textured fabric made from flax.

Loden: Rough water-resistant wool used for coats. Originally from Austria, usually in a distinctive dull green or beige.

Madras: Cotton from India, originally hand-woven with geometric designs usually plaids woven in. Can be colorfast or bleeding. Also a fine white cotton shirting with small tone-on-tone designs similar to damask.

Marquisette: Sheer open-weave fabric, usually of synthetic fiber and used mostly for curtains.

Matelassé: Jacquard fabric with a raised or padded design. Imitation Matelassé is embossed, not Jacquard.

Melton: Heavy coating with a soft nap. Though it is a twill weave, it has the appearance of felt.

Moiré: Watered silk or synthetic, (i.e., a smooth fabric with a watery design created with heat and pressure).

Monk's Cloth: Heavy, basket-weave cotton, similar to hopsacking. Used mainly for draperies.

Muslin: Basic, plain-weave cotton bleached, may be unbleached or printed.

Napped Fabric: Velvets, velveteens, corduroys and many wools which have a pile that can be stroked in one direction. (See Layouts, pg. 640.)

Organdy: Sheer, crisp cotton with a permanent finish.

Organza: Sheer silk fabric similar to organdy but softer and more transparent. Now also made of synthetics.

Ottoman: Heavy, ribbed fabric of silk, wool or synthetic, much used for women's coats.

Oxford Cloth: Modified basket-weave, cotton shirting.

Paisley: A distinctive type of print design, which often gives its name to any fabric on which it is used.

Peau de Soie: "Skin of Silk," a heavy, smooth silk or synthetic formal fabric.

Percale: Smooth cotton, solid or printed.

Piqué: Firm cotton fabric with woven, raised designs in stripes or novelties. The heavier ones are sometimes known as cloqué piqué.

Plisse: Puckered fabric with a less definite stripe than seersucker.

Polished Cotton: Any of a number of shiny, plain-weave or satin-weave cottons resembling chintz.

Pongee: Originally a natural colored, lightweight raw silk from China, now several imitations.

Poplin: Smooth, medium-weight cotton with a very slight rib.

Sailcloth: Plain-weave cotton, heavier than poplin, but lighter than canvas.

Sateen: Highly mercerized cotton with a satin weave.

Satin: A type of very smooth, shiny weave and any of a number of fabrics thus woven, usually silk or synthetic.

Seersucker: Cotton fabric with a firm texture and alternating plain and puckered stripes.

Serge: Twill weave, woolen fabric with a very hard finish.

Top Group, L. to R.: Striped Seersucker, Cotton and Rayon Brocade, Linen, Silk Chiffon with Novelty Stripe, Flocked Batiste.
Center Group, L. to R.: Eyelet Batiste, Checked Gingham, Bird's Eye Pique, Printed Percale, Polyester Crepe, Chambray.
Bottom Group, L. to R.: Batik, Silk Shantung, Polyester Damask, Novelty Leno.

Shantung: Fabric woven of thick-and-thin yarns to give a slubbed effect. Originally of silk from the Shantung Province in China; now silk, cotton or synthetic.

Sharkskin: Firm, wool suiting or a hard finish synthetic.

Taffeta: Crisp plain-weave silk, cotton or synthetic, used for formal wear and linings.

Tartans: Plaids, usually wool, associated with the clans of Scotland.

Terry: Woven or knitted cotton fabric with a looped surface for absorbency.

Ticking: Strong cotton fabric, usually striped, used for mattresses and pillows.

Tricot: Warp knit, synthetic fabric used for lingerie.

Tulle: Fine silk or synthetic net used for wedding veils.

Tweed: Rough wool fabric of several types and designs, including donegal, herringbone and plaid. Also copied in silk, cotton and blends.

Twill: Basic weave with diagonal rib or any one of several fabrics thus woven.

Velour: Any of several soft, pile fabrics. Generally used in reference to a thick fabric with a knitted backing used for sport wear.

Velvet: Luxurious pile fabric of silk, cotton or synthetic.

Velveteen: Practical pile fabric of cotton, often washable.

Voile: Crisp plain-weave cotton or cotton blend, often printed.

TERMS

Basket Weave: Plain-weave with two or more yarns laid in at once.

Bird's-eye Weave: A small woven-in diamond pattern.

Bull's-eye Weave: A larger version of the bird's-eye weave.

Bleaching: Removing all natural color from fibers.

Bleeding: Running or blending of dye, desirable in such fabrics as Madras.

Block Print: Type of printing done on fabric by hand.

Bolt: Length of cloth cut and rolled for sale.

Bonding: Process of backing a fabric with another fabric, using glue to hold them together.

Carding: A process of cleaning of fibers, preparatory to spinning.

Count: Number of threads per inch in either warp or filling of fabric.

Dyeing: Applying color to fabric or fiber.

Embossing: Process of pressing designs into fabrics with rollers and heat.

Filling: Cross yarn in woven fabric.

Greige (Gray) Goods: Unfinished fabrics direct from the loom.

Honeycomb Weave: Textured woven in square design.

Mercerize: To finish cotton using a special process giving it a higher luster and making it stronger.

Piece-Dye: Process of coloring after the fabric has been woven or knitted.

Pile: The nap, cut or uncut, on the surface of such fabrics as velour, velvet and terry.

Plain Knit: Simplest type of knit, with a distinct right and wrong side.

Plain Weave: Simplest type of weave, with one thread over and one under alternately, in each direction.

Preshrink: To process fabric to avoid further shrinkage.

Rib: Variation of plain weave, having a raised line or rib either vertically or horizontally.

Roller Print: Process of printing fabric using high speed machines.

Satin Weave: Specific weaving pattern that produces a smooth, shiny surface.

Screen Print: Process of printing fabric by a very slow painstaking hand method; used for rather exclusive designs.

Seconds: Fabrics with flaws, generally sold at greatly reduced prices.

Selvage (Selvedge): Finished lengthwise edges of fabric.

Square Weave: Plain woven fabric with the same thread count in both directions.

Thread Count: Same as Count.

Tie-Dye: A process of dyeing in which areas of the cloth are tied with twine to resist the dye.

Twill Weave: Fabric in which the weave creates a diagonal line across the face.

Vat Dye: Superior form of dyeing for either yarn dyeing or printing.

Warp: Yarns laid lengthwise on the loom.

Warp Knit: Type of flat knitting done on very intricate machines; best known is tricot.

Warp Print: Design printed on the warp threads only to give an elusive effect.

Weft: Also woof or filling, threads woven crosswise.

Yarn Dye: Process, in which the yarn has been dyed before weaving, used in most checks, stripes, plaids and iridescents.

FABRIC CARE

The care of all fabrics is most important. If fabrics are not to be used immediately after purchase, store them in a dark place, preferably on a roller or over a hanger. Label them for easy identification and cleaning instructions. Mothproof all woolens.

Washable cotton prints and most plain colors will remain brighter much longer if washed by hand or on the delicate cycle in the washing machine. Then, machine dry them for no more than five minutes. This removes the washer wrinkles and, if hung immediately, little or no pressing is required. Many fine washables are cleaned most successfully in cool water with a liquid soap designed for this purpose.

Storing clothes makes a big difference in their durability and appearance. Wire hangers are the least desirable of all hangers. Use smooth plastic or wooden hangers, or padded hangers for these items; and velvet bar hangers for knits and large stoles. For between season storage, knit clothes and garments with bias skirts will store better if they are laid on a flat surface. Be sure everything is clean and use moth spray.

FABRIC PREPARATION

Preshrinking: When buying fabric, read labels and ask questions; then if required, prepare the fabric before cutting out a garment. If there is any doubt about preshrinking, it is wise to preshrink to be sure. Any washable fabric can be dipped in warm water and hung correctly to drip dry. All linings and trims which are used with the garment should be treated in the same manner. When trims have been dipped, test them for colorfastness: lay the wet trim on a white towel to dry to see that there is no color bleed.

Nonwashable woolens can be preshrunk by a reputable dry cleaner. This is especially wise if fabrics were bought abroad or are hand-loomed. Nonwashable silks and synthetics of good quality do not need to be preshrunk.

Also remember the dryer is the villain in the gradual shrinkage of synthetic knits and even preshrinking won't prevent this.

Straightening: When fabric is cut from the bolt it is not always true to the grain along the cut ends. If a thread can be pulled easily, cut along the pulled thread line to be sure that the grain is straight. In some fabrics, the grain line is so strong that it is quite plain. In others, it may be necessary to ravel the end, one thread at a time, until a thread pulls all the way across. With knits, it is impossible to be sure of a straight or cross grain; before cutting, lay the fabric on a flat surface as carefully as possible without pulling it out of shape. (For further instructions see Layouts, page 640.)

FACINGS

A facing is an extra piece of fabric used frequently in finishing certain garment edges that are too curved to be hemmed; or edges that are shaped to be finished without a hem. The facing for this area is cut to conform with the garment edge. It is then sewn to the garment, turned back and stitched into place in the same manner as a hem. Facings can also be used in alterations where additional length is necessary.

Neckline and Armhole Facings: Necklines, both with and without collars, are usually finished with shaped facings. These can be made of the same material as the garment or of a lighter, firmer or smoother fabric. People who are sensitive to wool will find that a silk or synthetic facing around a neck or armhole can make a garment more comfortable to wear. Knit fabrics hold their shape better if a thin, firmly woven fabric is used for facings. Heavy fabrics will lie flatter and smoother around a neckline if a thinner fabric is used for facings. Try to keep the colors compatible, if not an exact match. Be sure that the dry cleaning or washing properties of both fabrics are the same.

Facings are cut in exactly the same shape as the neckline or armhole to which they are to be attached, the grain lines usually being the same.

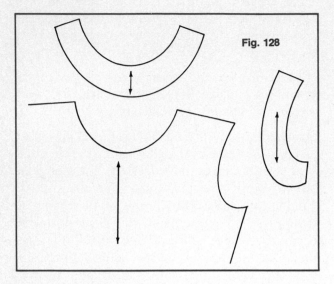

Fig. 128

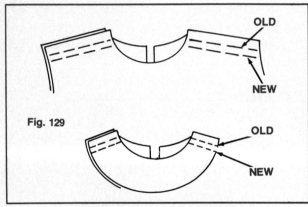

Fig. 129

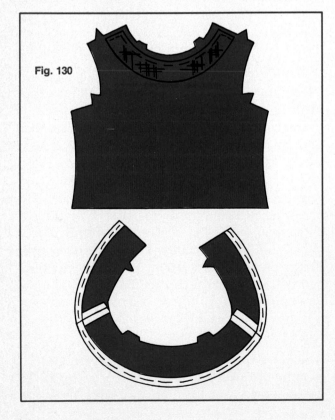

Fig. 130

Fig. 128. Do not change grain lines to save fabric. Be careful that all seams are kept the same width so that the size of the piece is not altered. For instance, if you take a deeper shoulder seam at the neck of a dress for fitting purposes, take a deeper seam in the facing at that same point. **Fig. 129.**

If an interfacing is to be used, it is generally basted onto the wrong side of the garment. The facing is completed and finished around the edge with any of the Finishes on page 620. **Fig. 130.**

Pin the facing, right sides together with the garment neckline or armhole, matching all seams and markings. If the garment has a back neck zipper, there will be a seam allowance left over at each end of the facing where it lies over the zipper. Turn this back toward itself and pin into place. **Fig. 131.** Stitch around the neckline or armhole. Trim or grade the seams (see Seams, pg. 665). Clip, almost to the stitching line, every $1/2$ inch all around, so that the seams will lay flat. Turn the facing to the wrong side and understitch by hand or on the machine before pressing. Hand tack the edges in place. **Fig. 132.**

Understitching: After sewing the facing to the garment (and trimming and clipping), fold the facing back over the seam so that the right sides of both garment and facing are exposed. Holding the facing away from the garment, with the right side up, machine stitch on the facing $1/8$ inch from the seam line. All layers of the facing and seam should be stitched but not garment. Pull gently from left to right as you do this to keep the facing and the seam underneath lying flat and smooth. The same process can be done by hand with a small backstitch about every $1/4$ inch. Nothing holds a facing in place as well as understitching.

Bias Neckline and Armhole Facings: Sometimes a bias facing is called for around a neck or armhole instead of a fitted facing. By the rules for Bias, page 588, cut and piece strips $1^1/2$ inches wide and long enough to go around the areas to be finished, allowing enough to overlap. Use $3/8$ inch as a seam allowance for the bias facing. Pin this $3/8$-inch seam line, right sides together, on the $5/8$-inch seam line of the garment, easing in the bias around the curves. **Fig. 133.** (When using commercial bias binding, use a $1/4$-inch seam

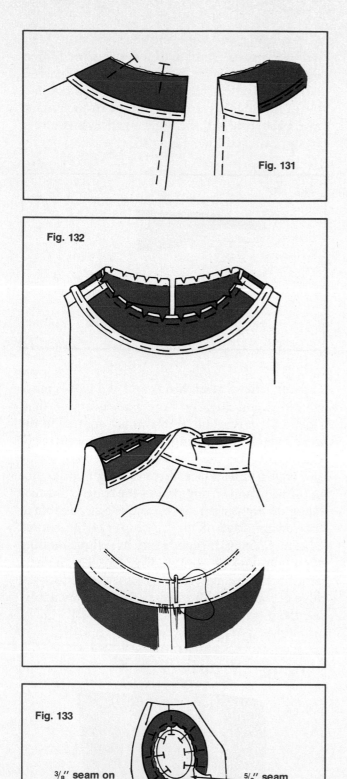

Fig. 131

Fig. 132

Fig. 133

3/8" seam on bias facing

5/8" seam on garment

allowance instead of 3/8 inch.) The outer edge should lie almost flat on the garment so that when it is turned to the inside, it can be hemmed

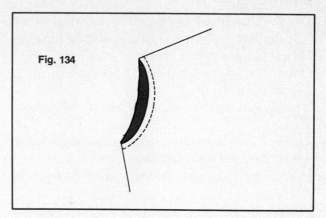

Fig. 134

without pulling and puckering the fabric. For this reason, it is necessary that the fabric for bias be soft and pliable.

Trim the seam, clip every 1/2 inch, and turn the bias to the wrong side. It is not necessary to understitch, but it will add strength to the edge. Turn under the seam allowance for the hem on the opposite edge of the bias and pin into place. Hem with a lock stitch (see Stitches, pg. 674) or baste into place and top stitch. **Fig. 134.**

FIBERS

Synthetic fibers appear and disappear so quickly that it is impossible to give a complete view of them. The following are the generic names of the ones now in common use: Acetate, Acrylic, Nylon, Polyester, Rayon. Many synthetics are produced by a large number of companies and therefore have many trade names.

Natural fibers are simpler to define and to recognize. Most of the ones in common use are as follows:

Alpaca: Fine, long, wooly hair from a small mountain animal in South America.

Angora: Hair from the Angora goat or may refer to Angora rabbit fur.

Camel: Fine silky hair from animal of the same name.

Cashmere: Hair of the Kashmir goat.

Cotton: From the seed boll of the cotton plant; Sea Island and Pima are especially fine varieties.

Flax: Fiber from the stalk of the flax plant; used for making linen.

Hemp: Coarse fiber from an Asiatic herb (of the mulberry family); used for making rope.

Jute: Coarse, glossy fiber from either of two East Indian plants (of the linden family).

Kapok: Silky fibers surrounding the seeds of the Ceiba (silk-cotton) tree; used as filling for mattresses, life preservers, sleeping bags, etc.
Linen: The fabric from flax; also used in referring to the fiber itself.
Mohair: Another name for the hair of the Angora goat.
Ramie: Fiber from the stalk of a plant grown in Japan; used for straw-cloth.
Sisal: Fiber from the Yucatan agave plant; very coarse.
Vicuna: Hair from a South American llama; the most expensive natural fiber in use.
Wool: Hair from a variety of sheep; also Lamb's Wool from very young sheep.

FINISHES

Hems, seams and facings can all be finished in a variety of ways. The type selected depends upon the weight of the fabric, the delicacy of the garment and the amount of time which can be spent in making the inside of the garment as finished as the outside. Many seams require no finishing as the fabrics ravel very little. Knit fabrics are really better without any seam finish. Hems and facings are usually finished or trimmed in one of the following manners.

Stay stitch and pink: Any fabric which is tightly woven and ravels very little may be finished in this way to avoid unnecessary bulk. Set the machine for ten stitches per inch and run a row of stitching ¼ inch from the fabric edge. Pink off a scant ⅛ inch of the raw edge. **Fig. 135.**

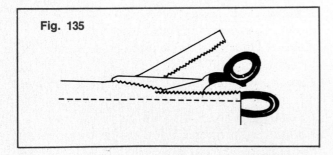

Fig. 135

Turn and stitch: This is the edge usually described in patterns for finishing facings. It should be used only for medium to lightweight fabrics. This method can be used on long straight seams and on the hems of moderately straight skirts or pants where little easing is required. Turn under

¼ inch of the raw edge and machine stitch it to itself as close as possible to the turned or folded edge. When using this method on a very curved area such as a neck facing, it is helpful to put in a row of machine stay stitching at the ¼-inch mark first. The fabric will then turn more evenly along the stay-stitched line. **Fig. 136.**

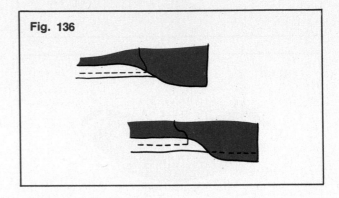

Fig. 136

Lace or ribbon seam binding: Hem lace is more attractive and slightly more maneuverable than ribbon seam binding, but both are applied in the same manner. Working with both pieces right side up, overlap the binding about ⅜ inch on the raw edge. (In hem lace, there is a slight difference in the right and wrong side — the rougher surface being the right side). Stitch as close as possible to the selvage edge of the binding. On the curved edge of a facing, it is necessary to full the binding slightly to make it lie flat. **Fig. 137.** On the hem of a flared garment, it is necessary to reduce the edge of the hem with an ease thread before applying the binding. (See Hems, page 631.)

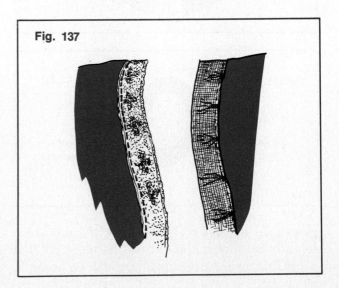

Fig. 137

Bias or Hong Kong binding: Unlined jackets require an especially finished look for seams, hems, and facings, since the inside is sometimes seen. Cut a bias strip of lining fabric about 1¼ inches wide and apply as in Method #3, Bias Binding, page 588. This is also a good binding for fabrics that ravel badly, such as glitter brocades, and for hems of an underlined garment. **Fig. 138.**

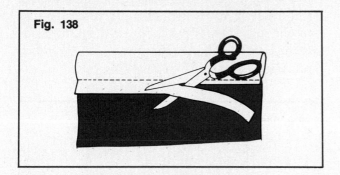

Fig. 138

Zigzag or lock stitch edging: If you intend to finish a fabric which ravels easily with a wide zigzag stitch, it is wise to cut an extra ⅛ inch all around. As soon as you take the pattern off, run a wide zigzag stitch all around, ⅛ inch from the raw edge. Trim off the excess close to the stitching. **Fig. 139.** Some machines have special overlock stitches for finishing knit edges. Check the machine manual for use of these.

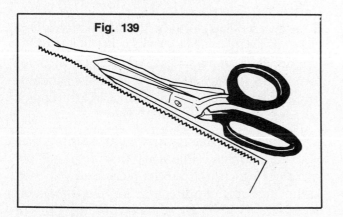

Fig. 139

FITTING

An entire book can be written on the subject of fitting, so only the essentials will appear here. (See Patterns, pg. 651, for details of prefitting patterns before cutting fabric.) Once a garment is cut, small darts and some nonfitting seams can be stitched immediately. **Fig. 140.** Yokes and other such nonfitting seams are called "style

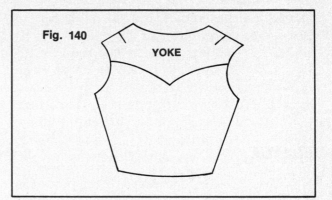

Fig. 140

YOKE

lines" and are usually not altered for fit. When fitting, baste seams such as side and shoulder seams so that the garment can be tried on. **Fig. 141.** Hand basting is preferable unless the machine has a true basting stitch — not just six stitches to the inch — because machine basting is as slow to pick out as hand basting is to put in. Machine basting stitches are very tight and the fabric may be damaged when they are pulled out. *Do not press seams in a basted garment.*

Separately, baste together the skirt seams, the bodice seams and one sleeve. Try on each part, right side out, and pin where adjustments are necessary. Stitch, remove basting and press.

Fig. 141

BASTING

BASTING

Then, baste the bodice and skirt together; try them on to make sure that the waist is correct. Sleeves may be pinned and basted before stitching or, if there are no fitting problems at the shoulders, the sleeves may be pinned and stitched, omitting the basting step. (See Alterations, pg. 581 to 586, for suggestions on fitting.)

FLANGE

A flange is a wide, decorative, overlapped seam with top stitching. On a straight line, the edge is folded back and allowance is made for this extra width in the pattern. On a curved line, a facing is stitched on the edge and turned before the finished edge is top stitched to the adjoining garment piece. **Fig. 142.**

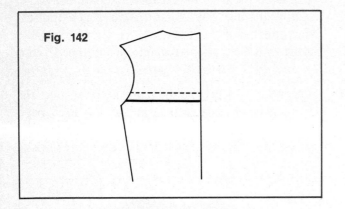

Fig. 142

FLAP POCKETS

Making the flap: Patterns often call for two layers of fabric and a layer of interfacing in a pocket flap. This can be extremely bulky in suit and coat fabrics, so it is best to experiment. Try a layer of the garment fabric, softly underlined, and a layer of matching lining fabric. Pin the garment fabric piece to the piece cut from lining, right sides together, fulling the garment fabric slightly. Stitch, trim and notch the seam. Turn the flap right side out. **Fig. 143.** The edge may be un-

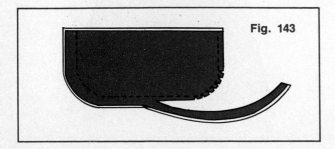

Fig. 143

derstitched by hand. (See Facings, pg. 617.) Top stitching may be added.

Faking the flap pocket: Flaps are easily used as decorations. In this case, the flap is constructed and stitched, right sides together with the garment along the pocket line. When stitching this seam, pull the lining of the flap tight so that the flap tends to turn over as soon as the seam is stitched. Trim the seam to 1/4 inch and slip stitch the flap over the raw edge. Top stitching is ideal for holding the flap down and adds a decorative touch as well. **Fig. 144.**

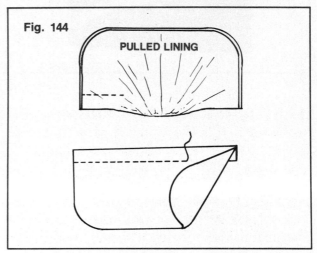

Fig. 144

PULLED LINING

Tips on real flap pockets: Because patterns vary as to the type of pieces given for the inside of the pocket, it is impossible to give exact methods here. The following method is understandable and can be used when a pattern does not provide concise instructions.

Lay the finished flap on first, right sides together with the garment. Pin and stitch it along the markings which indicate its placement. At each end of this stitching line, *it is very important that the needle drop exactly at the end of the flap,* not one stitch short or one over. Remember to back stitch about three stitches directly along the line. Cut the raw corners off the flap, as shown. **Fig. 145.** Lay the pocket pieces, in the order given in the pattern, right side down over the marked area and pin or baste them in place. **Fig. 146.** Turn to the wrong side of the garment and stitch along the visible stitching which holds the flap. Then stitch around the area indicated on the pattern, making about a 1/2-inch space for the opening,

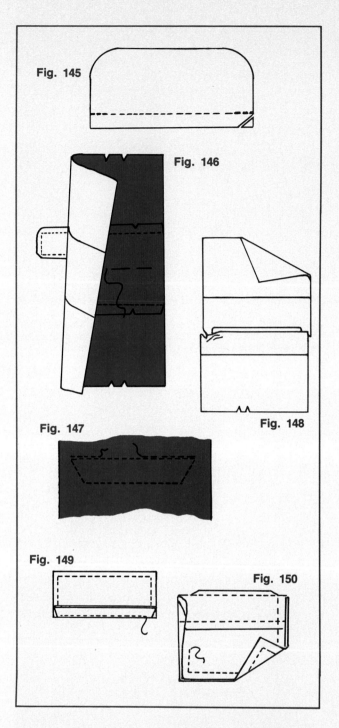

Fig. 145

Fig. 146

Fig. 147

Fig. 148

Fig. 149

Fig. 150

148. Do this step and then press it lightly. Press the seam open at the lower edge of the opening and stitch through the well of the seam by hand or machine to secure the lip or welt in place. **Fig. 149.** Finish the inside of the pocket as described in Buttonhole Pockets, page 596. **Fig. 150.**

FLIP LINING

Basic flip lining on sleeveless garment with front or back opening: Vests, sleeveless shifts and overblouses are all finished quickly and easily with a complete lining which eliminates the need for facings. Cut the lining by the same front and back pattern pieces used for the garment. Make all darts and seams in the garment and lining except the side seams and either front or back seam. (On a blouse or shift this would be the center back seam and on a vest the front opening.) *Three vertical seams must be left open.* **Fig. 151.**

Press both sections and lay them right sides together. Pin around armholes and neckline, matching all notches and seams. Full the outer garment slightly and pull the lining very tight. In the case of a vest, jacket or any garment with a button opening, continue neckline pinning down the edge of the opening. Stitch the pinned areas, trim and clip as for a Facing, page 617. **Fig. 152.**

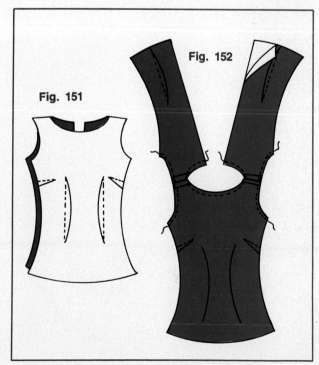

Fig. 151

Fig. 152

similar to that for a Bound Buttonhole, page 593. One way of insuring that the flap will cover the opening is *to slant the end lines in slightly,* as shown, so that the area is not a true rectangle. **Fig. 147.** Make a buttonhole cut on the pocket pieces and on the garment, not into the flap seam. Turn the pocket through to the wrong side. At this point, the pattern usually shows the lower edge of the pocket being folded up into the opening like a buttonhole — only with one lip. **Fig.**

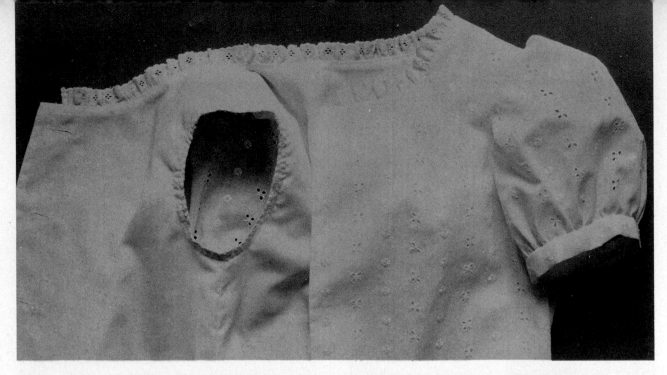

FLIP LINING FOR A GARMENT WITH SLEEVES. The armhole is finished around the edge with zigzag stitching and the sleeve is left unlined and sheer. Neck ruffle is incorporated like a collar between the garment and lining.

FLIP LINING IN VEST. All edges are finished before turning right side out. Side seams are stitched last, leaving only a small opening in lining side seam to be finished by hand.

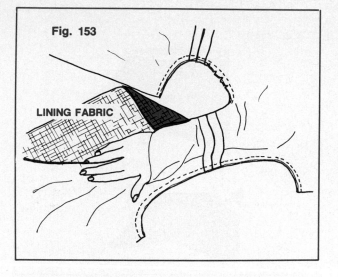

Fig. 153

LINING FABRIC

To turn the garment right side out, pull each divided piece (two sides of back or two sides of front) through its own shoulder. **Fig. 153.**

If worked slowly and gently, quite a lot of fabric can be pulled through. Thin fabrics can be worked through a shoulder no wider than $1\frac{1}{2}$ inches. Thick fabrics require about $2\frac{1}{2}$ inches. (For very narrow shoulders, an alternate method is described on page 626.)

If the garment is to have a zipper, sew the back seam of the garment fabric up to the zipper opening. Set in the zipper and sew the lining seam up to the zipper opening. Lay the side seams of the garment fabric right sides together and pin from the hem to armhole. Continue pinning the lining fabric right sides together from the armhole down to the hem. Keep garment and lining

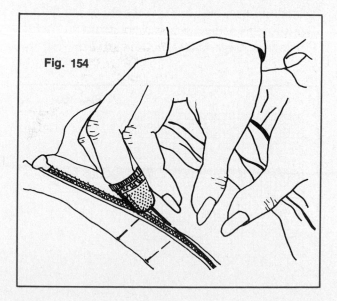

Fig. 154

separate. Stitch and press seams flat. Turn the lining under along the zipper and hand stitch it into place. **Fig. 154.** If necessary, the neckline and armholes may be understitched by hand.

The hems can be made separately, keeping the lining 1 inch shorter. **Fig. 155.** As an alternate method, press the garment hem in place and press the lining $\frac{1}{2}$ inch shorter. Trim the garment hem to $1\frac{1}{4}$ inches and the lining hem to $\frac{3}{4}$ inch. Lay them together, preferably on a flat surface such as the ironing board, and pin the turned edge of the lining in place $\frac{1}{2}$ inch above the turned edge of the garment. Match centers and seams and slip stitch the two together. **Fig. 156.**

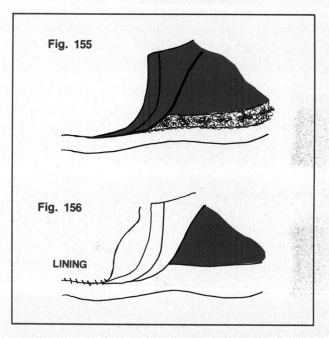

Fig. 155

Fig. 156

LINING

Special note for a man's vest: When joining lining and garment around the neck and armholes, it is possible to continue the stitching down the front and across the lower edge of the front. Also stitch across the lower edge of the back. The rest can be turned by pulling the fabric through and out the side of the back. Sew the back and front of the garment right sides together along side seams. Turn under lining side seams and slip stitch them together. This system is especially good for heavy leathers, fur fabrics and needlepoint vests, as all hems and facings are eliminated.

For garments with sleeves and collars: Making a flip lining in a garment which has a collar is exactly like facing a collar (see Collars, pg. 602).

The collar must be attached as soon as the shoulder seams are sewn and before the lining is attached at neckline and armholes.

Sleeves make the flip lining method even easier. No seams have to be left open. Stitch the garment together, all darts, side and shoulder seams. Sew the lining together separately. Seam them right sides together only around the neckline. Trim, clip and understitch. Turn garment right side out. Smooth the lining and garment fabric in place around the armholes and pin. These can now be treated as one layer and the sleeves set in as usual. Sleeves may be left unlined or may be flip lined from the bottom edge. Remember to cut the lining 1¼ inches shorter so that it will pull up the hem. The top of the sleeve and its lining may be treated as one layer or the armhole may be hand finished with the lining as in a tailored garment. (See Tailoring, pg. 676.)

Alternate flip lining method: This method can be used when the shoulders are very narrow or when there is no center front or back seam. Do not use it for very heavy fabric. Sew darts in the front and back of both lining and fabric but *do not sew shoulder seams.* Pin each piece and its lining right sides together around neckline and armholes and stitch. (On back piece, stitch only to the shoulder seam and backstitch for security.) Trim, clip, *turn the front only* right side out and understitch by hand. **Fig. 157.** Slip the shoulder pieces of the front inside the shoulder pieces of the back so that right sides of fabric are together. Be sure that the front completely fills the back. Stitch across shoulder seam, stopping and backstitching at each seam intersection. **Fig. 158.** Clip corners of back shoulder seams; *do not clip into front.* **Fig. 159.** Turn the back piece right side out.

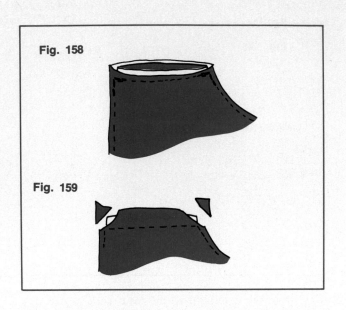

Fig. 158

Fig. 159

If the seam is too thick, turn back and trim one layer of fabric to ⅜ inch.

FRINGE

Purchased fringe: Fringe can be purchased and sewn on, preferably with two rows of zigzag stitching, so that it acts as a finish to the raw edge of fabric. It is available in cotton, rayon, wool and synthetics made to look like wool. Check the washing and cleaning specifications of both the fringe and garment fabric so that the two will be compatible.

Fringing an edge: The straight edge of loosely woven fabric can be attractively fringed, but should be staystitched for security. This is especially true if the item is to be washed. In the garment fabric, pull out one thread at the desired depth for the fringe; this may be from ¾ inch to 1½ inches. **Fig. 160.** Machine stitch along this

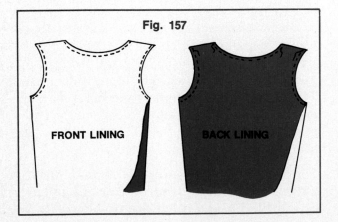

Fig. 157

FRONT LINING

BACK LINING

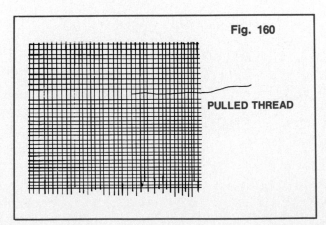

Fig. 160

PULLED THREAD

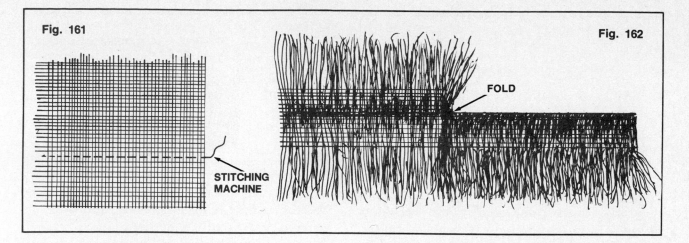

Fig. 161

STITCHING MACHINE

Fig. 162

FOLD

line, using about twelve stitches to the inch. Ravel all the threads from the edge back to this point. **Fig. 161.**

Self fringe: Sometimes it is desirable to use self fringe on an edge which is not straight or the fringe made by the previous method needs to look thicker. To do this, cut a straight piece of fabric the proper length for the edge to be trimmed and twice as wide as the desired finished width, plus 1 inch. If the edge is very long, the fringe can be made in sections. Ravel each edge back to the desired depth, leaving the 1 inch of fabric in the center. Fold along the center of the fabric strip and press. Apply the fringe between garment and facing or lining following the method for piping. **Fig. 162.** (See information on Edgings, pg. 608.)

FULLING

At times, it is necessary to ease one longer piece of fabric to a shorter one when the difference in

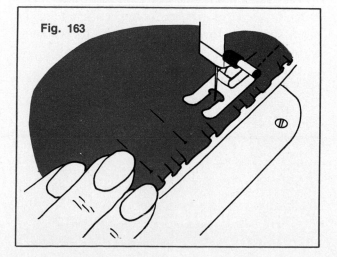

Fig. 163

length is not so great as to make an ease thread necessary. In this case, place the longer piece on top and gently push it along with the hands as it is stitched. This is called "fulling" one piece onto the other. It may help to divide the piece into even spaces and pin in the fullness at intervals. **Fig. 163.**

FUSIBLES OR BONDING AGENTS

Fabrics can be bonded together by using a thin webbing of dry glue, now available under several trade names, and a warm iron. When buying this material, ask for a fusible or a bonding agent.

GATHERS

Gathering can be done by hand or machine; in most cases, machine gathering is not only quicker, but also does a smoother job. There are ruffling, shirring or gathering attachments or settings for some sewing machines but they usually require a good deal of regulating and setting. They are really useful only if yards of ruffling for curtains or costumes is necessary. Check the sewing machine manual.

Gathering by machine: Set the sewing machine for its longest stitch, about six to the inch. Run two rows of stitching, about $1/8$ inch apart, along the edge to be gathered. A row of stitching should be on either side of the seam line. Take both bobbin threads (those threads on the underside of the fabric) in one hand and gently slide the fabric along until it is gathered to the desired length. Tie off the thread ends and adjust gathers until they look even. **Fig. 164.**

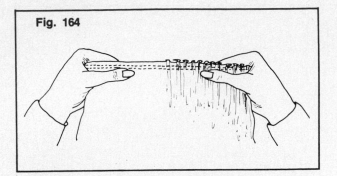

Fig. 164

Special tips on machine gathering: If the fabric is very heavy, it may be necessary to use heavy-duty thread sold in fabric shops. It may also help to loosen the tension on the machine slightly.

On very short areas to be gathered, stitch one row, turn the fabric and make one stitch between the rows; return for the other row. This method will leave only one set of loose ends. **Fig. 165.**

Gathering by hand: Gathering by hand can be

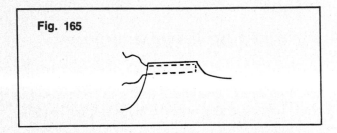

Fig. 165

done in much the same way as on the machine — two rows of stitching, ¹/₈ inch apart. Tie a knot in the thread and take one small backstitch so that the knot cannot be pulled through the fabric. Sew one row of fine, running stitches and leave thread and needle hanging at the end of the row. Sew the second row, then draw both rows to the correct length. Finish off tightly with several backstitches.

Attaching gathered piece to adjoining piece: Lay gathered fabric right sides together with adjoin-

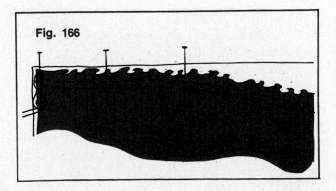

Fig. 166

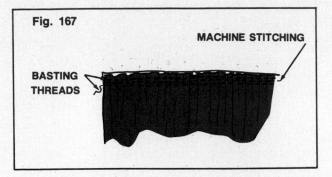

Fig. 167

MACHINE STITCHING

BASTING THREADS

ing piece and pin in place. Be sure that the gathers are distributed evenly. **Fig. 166.** With the gathered side up, stitch the seam exactly between the two rows of stitching. This way, the gathers can be easily controlled. **Fig. 167.** If desired, the row of gathering which shows on the outside of the garment can now be removed.

GLUE

Sometimes it is necessary to use glue to hold two pieces of fabric, fake fur or leather together. Check carefully to find a variety of glue which does not make stiff spots and which will not bleed through the fabric. Read labels, ask salespeople and, when all else fails — Test! On some areas, the newer Fusibles or Bonding Agents are practical. (See pg. 627.)

GODETS

A very graceful way to give fullness to a skirt is to insert triangular pieces of fabric called godets. These are generally used in six-gored and eight-gored skirts and are incorporated into the seams. When this system is used, sew the skirt seam down to the point where the godet goes in and backstitch to hold. Sew the godet into each side of the seam, stitching from the bottom up to this same point and backstitching again.

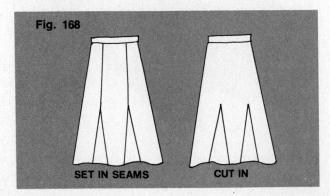

Fig. 168

SET IN SEAMS   CUT IN

Sometimes godets are installed in slashes in an otherwise plain skirt. See the section on Gussets, for the method of treating and reinforcing the slashes. **Fig. 168.**

GORES

Panels of fabric, usually in skirts, are called gores. Skirts can be described as four-gored or eight-gored. **Fig. 169.**

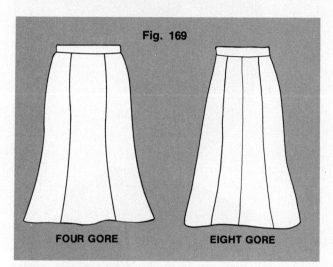

Fig. 169

FOUR GORE   EIGHT GORE

GRAIN

The grain of fabric is the direction in which the threads lie. One set, parallel to the selvage, is the length grain; the other set, perpendicular to the selvage, is the cross grain. When laying out a pattern, it is necessary to place the pattern pieces with the grain as directed on each. **Fig. 170.**

GRIPPERS

Large snaps which are hammered together onto fabric, instead of being sewn in place, are called grippers. They are available in metallic finish, colors, and with many decorative designs. These can be used instead of buttons on cowboy or sport shirts and on children's clothes. Directions for attaching them are to be found on the package. **Fig. 171.**

GUSSETS

Small geometric pieces of fabric called gussets are sometimes inserted into clothing, especially under the arm, to make the garment more com-

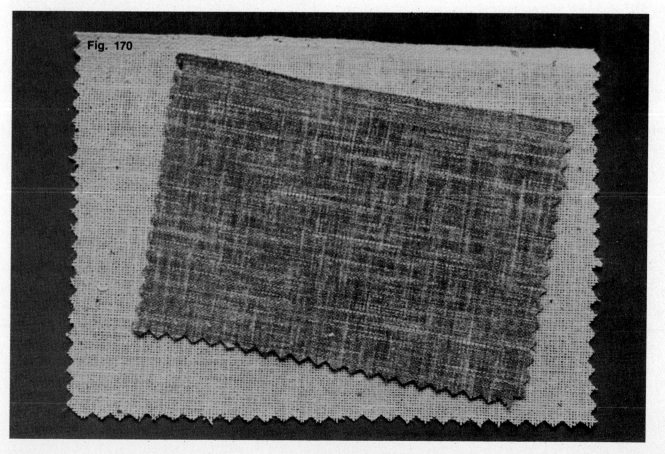

Fig. 170

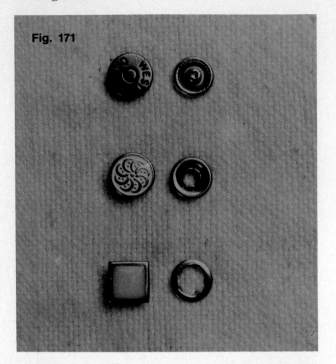

Fig. 171

fortable or longer wearing. Sometimes they are used in altering a bodice to give more room. (See Alterations, pg. 581.) There are two fairly standard-shaped ones which are given in patterns for kimono-sleeved garments. The triangle is the easier gusset to insert, the diamond is slightly harder.

Markings and reinforcement for all gussets: Transfer the symbols from the pattern to the fabric so that each corner can be easily identified. **Fig. 172.** Use different colors of tailor tacks described in Marking, page 643.

Cut a small bias piece of lining fabric, about 1 1/2 inches square, to cover and reinforce the point of the marked slash. Pin it in place on the right side of the fabric, as shown. Staystitch along the seam

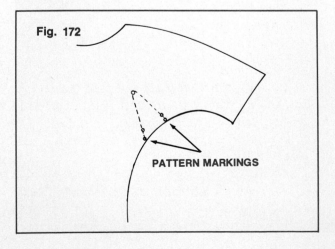

Fig. 172

PATTERN MARKINGS

lines of the slash, making one stitch across at the point to separate the lines. **Fig. 173.** Slash the opening and turn the bias piece to the wrong side. If the end puckers, the opening has not been slashed far enough to the point. **Fig. 174.**

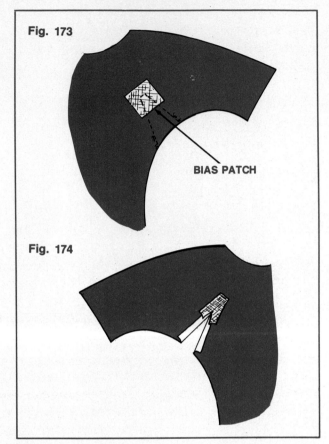

Fig. 173

BIAS PATCH

Fig. 174

Triangular gussets: Lay the seam line of the slash right sides together with the seam line of the gusset. The seam allowance on the gusset will be an even 5/8 inch on all sides. On the slash, the seam allowance will decrease toward the point and increase again along the other side. For this reason, the raw edges cannot be laid together. Pin the seam lines together, being careful to pull the bias piece out of the way. With the slashed piece up on the machine and following close to the staystitching line, stitch the seam. (The staystitching should be hidden in the seam.) The bias piece will serve as a seam allowance to hold when maneuvering the machine around the point. Stitch to the point; drop the needle into the fabric; lift the presser foot and turn the corner. Clear all the fabric out of the way, drop the foot and then continue stitching down the other side. **Fig. 175.**

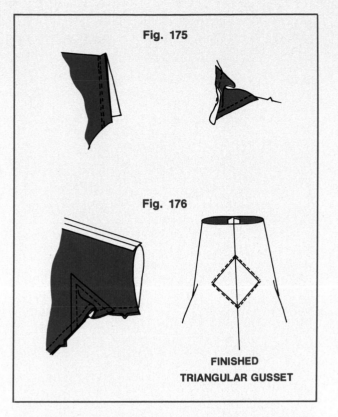

Fig. 175

Fig. 176

FINISHED
TRIANGULAR GUSSET

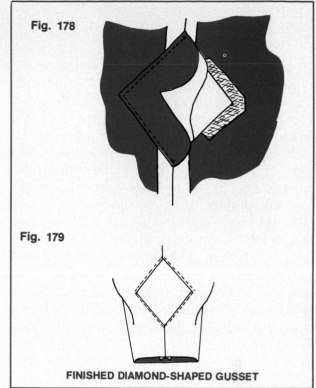

Fig. 178

Fig. 179

FINISHED DIAMOND-SHAPED GUSSET

Press the seams of the gusset away from the gusset and, if desired, top stitch $\frac{1}{8}$ inch from the edge for further reinforcement. When one triangle has been installed at each underarm of both the front and back of the garment, the underarm seams can be sewn together. **Fig. 176.**

Diamond gussets: Stitch side seams and underarm seams of bodice, stopping at the staystitching of the slash. Backstitch for security. **Fig. 177.** Pin diamond gusset in place, right sides together, along one slash, just as in the triangle gusset. Stitch along the slash, from side seam to under-

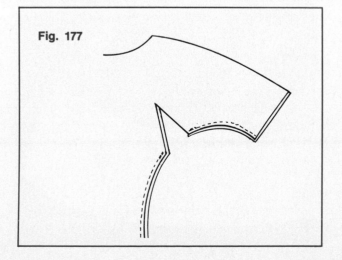

Fig. 177

arm seam, backstitch at each backstitched point on the seam. Repeat process for the other slash.

Never try to cross over the side and underarm seams in order to stitch the entire diamond in one operation. **Fig. 178.** Press seams away from gussets; trim out excess bulk at the intersections of seams. The entire gusset may be top stitched, if desired. **Fig. 179.**

HEMS

A customary way to finish a raw edge is to hem it by first turning under the edge to a depth of $\frac{1}{4}$ or $\frac{1}{2}$ inch, turning it again to the desired hem depth and then stitching it into place. The first turn can be eliminated by finishing the edge with seam binding, hem lace or any Finishes, page 620.

Hems on straight edges: A straight edge can be hemmed any depth without becoming difficult to handle. The only limiting factors are the weight of the fabric and the desired finished effect. Gathered skirts, which are cut in straight panels, frequently look better with a wide hem (at least 4 inches). If skirts are sheer, the hem can be as wide as 6 or 8 inches. The hem on the straight legs of pants or on a straight wool or corduroy skirt should be no more than $1\frac{1}{2}$ to 2 inches deep or it will appear too bulky. A narrow, skimpy hem tends to cheapen the appearance of skirts or pants.

It is preferable to mark the desired length of a straight garment and then turn up the same amount of hem all around so that the grain line around the lower edge will be even. If a skirt hangs unevenly (dipping in the back, for instance), it may be adjusted at the waist so that the grain line can be kept even at the bottom. (See Waistbands, pg. 683.) Once the proper length has been decided upon, lay the garment, wrong side up, on a flat surface such as an ironing board; measure and turn up the hem all the way around. The hem can be pinned as it is measured and then basted about 1/2 inch from the turned lower edge. On some garments the hems can be pressed down as they are measured. If the hem is too deep, measure and chalk the proper depth from the lower edge and cut off the excess. Finish the edge by any of the methods shown on page 620 and hem as described below.

Hems on curved edges: When hemming such curved edges as flared skirts, remember, *the deeper the curve, the narrower the hem.* A circular skirt can have only about a 1-inch hem; a simple A-line skirt can have about 2¹/₂ inches. If the hems are much deeper than that, it becomes necessary to gather — not ease — the upper edge of the hem to fit the skirt smoothly. The result is a rather clumsy appearance.

It is almost always necessary to have someone measure or "hang" a flared skirt on the wearer and mark the hemline carefully all the way around. A yardstick can be used for this, but a clip or chalk marker makes the job easier. **Fig. 180.** Lay the garment, wrong side up, on a flat surface such as an ironing board; turn the hem along the marked line and baste it in place, keeping the basting line about 1/2 inch above the turned edge. With a ruler and chalk, mark the desired hem depth. Just below the chalked line, machine stitch an ease thread. (See Ease, pg. 607.) Stop and restart at intervals to guard against handling too great a length of fabric on one thread; 24 to 36 inches is enough to cope with at a time. Trim off the raw edge 1/4 inch above the ease thread. Pull the ease thread gently so that the edge of the hem fits inside the skirt

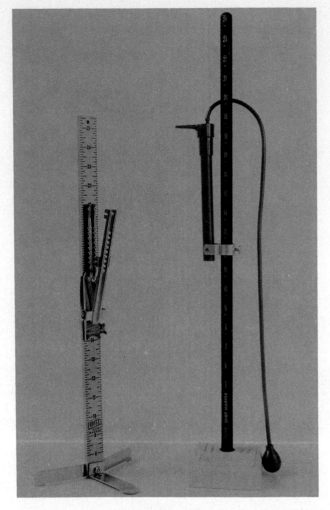

Fig. 180

smoothly *but not tightly.* Complete the edge with any of the Finishes on page 620; hem by any of the methods below. **Fig. 181.**

Methods of hemming: There are several stitches and techniques commonly used for hemming.

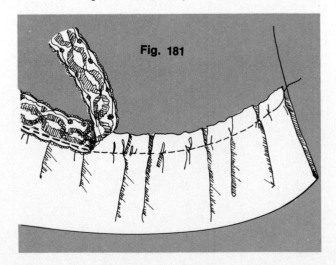

Fig. 181

These can be used alone or combined with a number of the Finishes described on page 620.

Whipping or overcast stitch: The standard stitch of hemming is this simple "up-and-over" one. It is generally used in combination with the turned edge or the lace or seam binding finish. The stitches should be very tiny where they enter the outer fabric, picking up no more than two threads of the fabric, and there should be a space of nearly 1/2 inch before the next stitch is made into the outer fabric. **Fig. 182.** Do not pull the thread too tightly. The work on a long stretch may go more quickly if the garment is pinned to a sofa arm or the edge of a cork table. Hold the hem toward the body so that it is stretched taut. Work along a 10 or 12-inch section this way and then move the fabric up and pin it again. Ladies of the 19th century used little metal hem clamps to keep the fabric stretched while they stitched the hems around their enormous skirts. **Fig. 183.**

Slip stitch variation: There is another method of hemming which looks very much like the overcast or whipping stitch, but is worked from right to left, picking up several stitches on the needle at one time. Slip the needle into the outer fabric, picking up one or two threads; bring it up through the hem, picking up stitches along the edge for nearly 1/2 inch; bring the needle down, up and over again. It is handled like the running stitch or slip stitch but goes over the hem edge instead of between layers. This stitch is most often used with the same finishes as the previous method. **Fig. 184.**

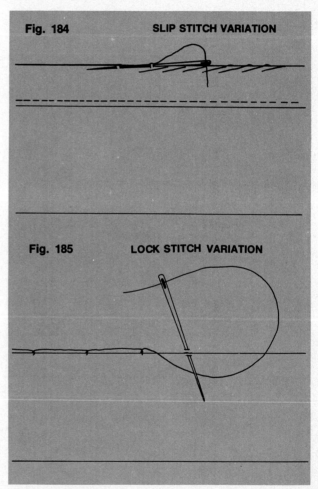

Fig. 184　　SLIP STITCH VARIATION

Fig. 185　　LOCK STITCH VARIATION

Lock stitch variation: Pants legs and children's clothes, which receive rough wear, can be hemmed with a lock stitch, which is a variation of the whipping stitch. Work it in the same manner as the whipping stitch, slanting the needle toward the body as the stitches are made. Anchor the fabric at the starting point, if desired. Each time the needle is brought up through the hem edge,

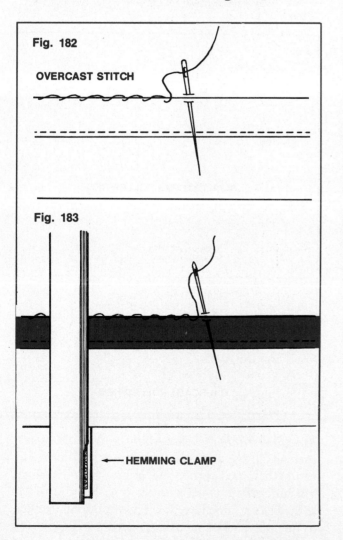

Fig. 182

OVERCAST STITCH

Fig. 183

← HEMMING CLAMP

throw the thread around to the left, passing under the needle so that the stitch will lock in the manner of a blanket stitch. **Fig. 185.**

French or tailor's hem with slip stitch: Hems on heavy fabrics, such as wool or velveteen, have a tendency to show through on the right side of the garment. It is possible to prevent this by making a French or tailor's hem and pressing very lightly. Finish the edge with stitching and pinking, zigzag stitching or as described in Method 3, Bias Binding, page 589. Baste the edge of the hem to the garment less than 1/2 inch below the finished edge. Hold the fabric with both the hem edge and the garment folded back so that you can slip stitch loosely between them — 1/8 to 1/4 inch down from the edge. Catch a thread or two of the outer fabric and then a thread or two of the hem edge, moving 1/4 to 1/2 inch along between the stitches. **Fig. 186.** Fasten the ends of the thread securely but do not pull the thread tight.

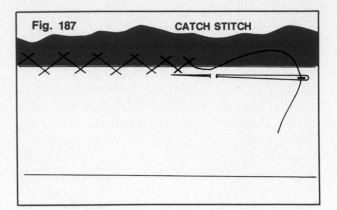

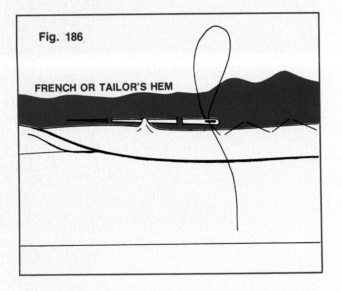

Catch stitch over raw edge: Some closely woven fabrics and most knits require no finish along the raw hem edge and can be hemmed attractively with a catch stitch. There is an added advantage on knits in that the stitch has enough give to stretch with the fabric. With the needle going from right to left, make a small stitch into the garment just above the edge of the hem. Move the needle to the right and down about 3/8 inch; make a small stitch from right to left in the hem. Continue in this zigzag fashion, remembering never to pull the thread too tightly. **Fig. 187.**

Hand-rolled hems: The very finest chiffons and batistes are sometimes finished with a tiny, hand-rolled hem. Literally roll the raw edge between your thumb and forefinger until it forms a tightly rolled edge, less than 1/8 inch deep. This roll can be slip stitched almost invisibly, **Fig. 188,** or overcast so that the stitching is a part of the decoration of the edge. **Fig. 189.**

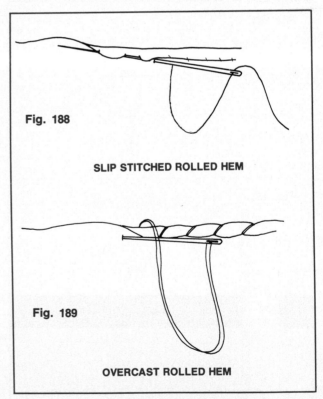

Machine-stitched hems: Many household items, such as cloths, napkins, bedspreads, curtains, etc, can be hemmed neatly and evenly with a straight machine stitch which shows along the edge of the hem. Set the machine stitch at about eight or ten to the inch and be sure that the tension is adjusted properly. It is preferable to stitch from the right side as most machine stitching, when properly adjusted, looks slightly smoother and better on the right side. A very narrow machine-stitched hem, about ¼ inch, is used on the lower edges of shirts and blouses and in a few other places and is often referred to as a shirttail hem.

Almost all zigzag machines have a special setting for blind stitch hems. It takes a little practice to learn to use them correctly, but it is well worth the time. The machine blind stitch can be used for lots of household sewing, for play clothes and children's clothes. The hem should be pressed in place and basted about ½ inch down from the top edge. Lay the hem on the machine and turn the fabric back so that the wrong side of it is in view and expose the upper edge of the hem. Stitch on the edge of the hem; the needle will swing over into the fabric every fifth stitch. **Fig. 190.** Decide on stitch lengths and widths to suit the individual project and fabric; check the machine manual and make samples each time.

Fig. 191

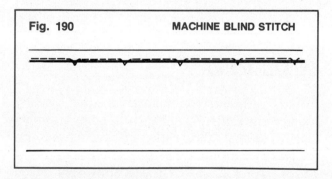

Fig. 190   MACHINE BLIND STITCH

HOOKS AND EYES

Though hooks and eyes were the forerunners of zippers, they have stayed around to supplement zippers and to do the little jobs for which they are best suited. Use them on waistbands, at the top of the zipper opening at the back neck and in all the small spots which are pulled open easily. The new wide, flat hooks for skirts and pants are especially satisfactory for waistbands. They are also easy to apply, sewing through a series of holes like snaps. **Fig. 191.**

In applying a conventional hook and eye (the small ones which come in silver or black), it is necessary to bring the thread over and over the two rings at the base of the hook and several times under the hook itself before fastening off tightly. **Fig. 192.** Always set the end of the hook slightly back under the edge of the garment when using it on neck edges and other points where the two sides of the fabric just meet. Make a small eye of thread in the opposite edge. (See Buttonloops, pg. 598 for the best system of making thread eyes.) **Fig. 193.** When using hooks and eyes on overlapping edges, the straight metal eye provided in the pack is better than the loop one. The loop eye is meant for use on neck edges, but the thread eye system is less obtrusive and holds better. The exception to this is the heavy coat hook. These may be metal or thread-covered and have only a loop eye.

Fig. 192

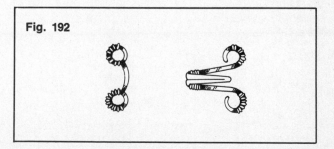

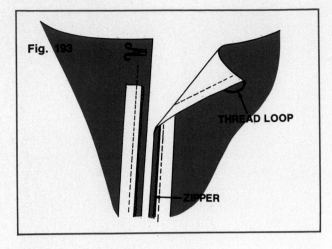

Fig. 193

THREAD LOOP

ZIPPER

INSEAM POCKETS

The simplest of all pockets are the ones which look like an opening in the seam, usually in a side seam or front panel seam. The only problem with pockets of this type is that if the skirt or pants are fitted too tightly, the pockets spring open and make an unattractive line across the hips. The best advice is, unless the hips are slim enough to stand this extra bulk, you should eliminate inseam pockets except on loosely fitted or gathered skirts.

To construct an inseam pocket, check the pattern and guide sheet. There will be an extra extension of fabric on each side of the seam at the place for the pocket. **Fig. 194.** Before cutting, check for correct pocket placement. The skirt pattern may need to be lengthened or shortened to bring the pocket to the right place. Cut out the pocket pieces from a matching lining fabric. Seam one

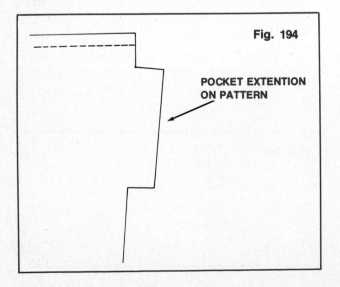

Fig. 194

POCKET EXTENTION
ON PATTERN

piece, right sides together, to each side of the extension and press the seams toward the lining piece. Pin or baste the seams of the garment right sides together and stitch. Follow the outline of the pocket so that it is incorporated into the seam. Press the pocket toward the front of the garment. **Fig. 195.** If possible, hand stitch the front edge of the pocket to a seam or facing to secure it.

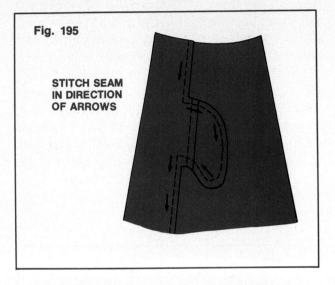

Fig. 195

STITCH SEAM
IN DIRECTION
OF ARROWS

INTERFACING

Collars, cuffs and front facings on jackets usually require extra stiffening. This is done by adding a layer of special fabric called interfacing between the two pieces of outer fabric. There are a number of fabrics, both woven and nonwoven, made especially for interfacing. Other fabrics, such as organdy and lawn, are sometimes used in lightweight garments.

Patterns and suggestions for handling interfacing are given in most patterns where it is required. Following is a list of general tips on interfacing which may be added to the pattern information. If woven interfacing is to be used, cut it on the same grain as the piece of garment to which it will be attached. Use nonwoven interfacing only in areas where a soft roll is not the desired effect; it is perfect for stiff areas such as mandarin collars, hat brims and belts. Be sure that the interfacing is not too heavy a material. Make a sample, if necessary, to be sure. Baste or pin the interfacing to the wrong side of its respective piece (usually under collar, garment neckline or jacket front) and incorporate it into the seams around that piece. Always trim interfacing to within $\frac{1}{8}$ inch of seam line after stitching. **Fig. 196.** For further information on handling interfacing in a tailored garment, see Tailoring Tips, page 676.

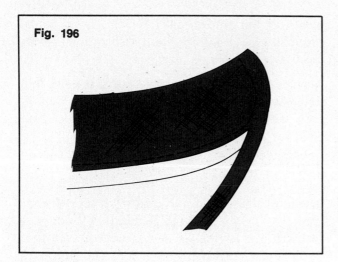

Fig. 196

IRONS

A good iron, preferably a steam iron, is an essential part of sewing equipment. (See pg. 610.) For the proper way to use an iron in sewing, see Pressing, page 660.

KIMONO SLEEVES

A so-called kimono sleeve is not like the kind used in an authentic Japanese kimono, but is a

Fig. 197   KIMONO SLEEVE

sleeve cut all-in-one with the body of the garment. **Fig. 197.** Such sleeves are more satisfactory on loose garments where there is not enough pull or strain on them to rip the underarm seam. If they are used in fitted garments in well-constructed patterns, they are usually made with a gusset to allow ease of movement. (See pg. 629.)

Kimono sleeves can be reenforced without gussets by using a piece of narrow twill tape or seam binding as a stay in the seam. The tape should be no more than $\frac{1}{4}$ inch wide, so, if seam binding is used, fold it in half and press it. (See Stay Tape, pg. 673.) Cut a piece of the tape about 3 inches long and hold it along the seam in the underarm curve so that the seam is stitched directly along the center of the tape. Clip the seam allowance in three or four places around the curve, but do not clip the tape. **Fig. 198.**

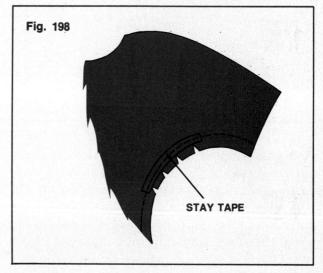

Fig. 198

STAY TAPE

KNITS

There is a special world of fabric for the home seamstress which has made her work easier and expanded her horizons — knits! Included are double knits, jerseys, stretch knits and warp knits of the lacy raschel type. Double knits are especially easy to cut and sew and most knits are easy to fit. Little finishing is required for any knit and several shortcuts are possible which would never work on woven fabrics.

When planning a knit garment, look for patterns which say "For Knits Only" or "Suitable for Knits." The *Knits Only* patterns have almost no darts, which eliminates a major fitting problem. In the areas where darts would normally be found, such as the side bust, there is a short area of ease between notches or markings to control the needed fullness. **Fig. 199.** Knit garments are frequently designed without waistlines because they cling to the figure easily and can be belted without looking bulky.

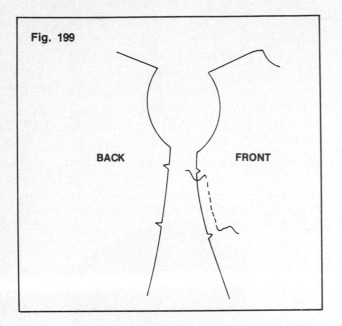

A great deal has been said and written about the correct thread for sewing knits, but the type of stitch used is more important than the thread. The point is to allow a bit of stretch in the seams so that each pull on the garment will not rip the seam stitching. Many of the new machines have a special knit stitch with a lot of "give." It is well worth getting out the machine manual and putting this stitch into practice.

Any simple zigzag stitch, set for a slight zigzag width and a normal length, will also give a seam some elasticity. If a machine will only work a plain straight stitch, be sure that the tension is not too tight to avoid stretching the fabric a little as the seams are stitched.

If a facing is required in a knit garment, it is frequently better to construct it of a thin woven fabric so as to stabilize the neck or armhole. Other ways of finishing knits are suggested under Edgings, page 608. Rib knit bandings and trims are available and are often coordinated to knit fabrics. These are easy to handle and give a very

professional look. Knits should be hemmed with the pinked French Hem or the Catch Stitch Hem. (See pg. 631.)

Because knits are usually easy to fit and often as stretchy as sweaters, the length of the zippers does not always have to be as long as in woven garments. If the zipper matches well, many knits, especially the thin ones, look nice with an open-faced zipper. (See pg. 685.)

Beginners can sew on double knits, but the thin jerseys and the stretch knits should be left to those with more experience. See Layouts, page 640, for suggestions on cutting.

LACE

The most delicate of all fabrics is lace and some special skills are required in handling both wide lace and lace edging. Some wide lace has finished or bordered edges so that if it is cut crosswise, there is no need to hem it. The coarser cotton laces are usually unfinished on the edges and should be handled like any other fabric. A

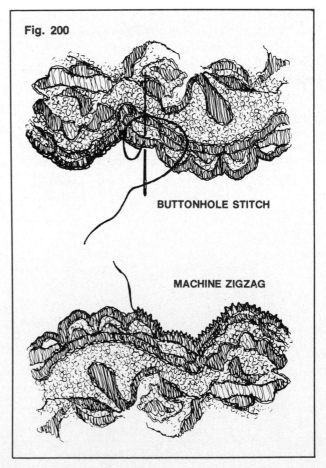

BUTTONHOLE STITCH

MACHINE ZIGZAG

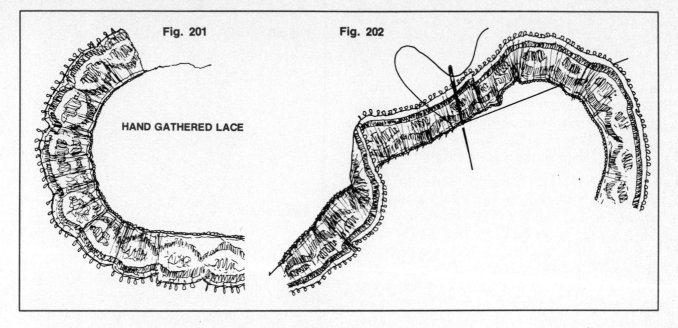

Fig. 201   Fig. 202

HAND GATHERED LACE

charming way to use the finished edge of lace is to appliqué it to another sheer fabric such as organdy. This can be done by hand with tiny buttonhole stitches or with a close, narrow machine zigzag stitch. **Fig. 200.** Cutout designs from lace can be appliquéd onto other fabrics. Lace may be underlined with a compatible fabric to make a more tailored garment, even an evening suit, or may be used sheer over a matching or contrasting slip or underdress. All these interesting choices mean that a good deal of prior planning is essential before starting a lace garment.

Lace edging: The use of lace edging as an inside finish for hems, seams and facings has caused manufacturers to produce a large line of inexpensive synthetic laces. Finer lace edging is still available for use on the outside of fine blouses, lingerie and baby clothes.

The better quality lace edgings have a line of thread in the straight edge which can be pulled gently to ruffle the lace. When planning for ruffled lace edging, measure the area to be trimmed and allow about twice enough lace to cover that length. Gather it to the desired length and adjust the gathers evenly. **Fig. 201.** Tie off the ends of the thread.

If the lace is to be applied to a finished edge, such as a collar or a faced neckline, hold the ruffle, right sides together, with the fabric and sew them together with a fine overcast stitch. Catch only a

thread or two in the edge of each stitch. After stitching, push the lace back so that it lies smoothly around the edge, then steam it lightly. **Fig. 202.**

Sometimes lace, especially insertion lace, is applied to an unfinished edge. It may be stitched, by hand or machine, along the indicated stitching line. The raw edge may then be hand rolled and stitched in place with an overcast stitch. Remember to roll the edge away from the lace insertion to avoid having it show through. **Fig. 203.**

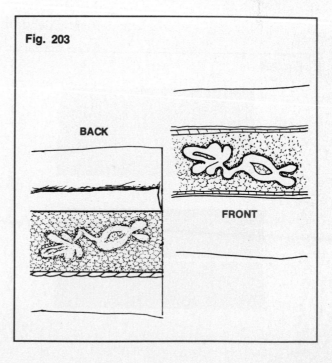

Fig. 203

BACK

FRONT

LAYOUTS

The worst sewing mistakes often occur in laying out the pattern and cutting the fabric! Nothing, short of the purchase of more fabric, can remedy such errors. A quick run down of all the things to consider when starting a project may help to prevent these tragedies. Use this list as a reference each time a new garment is undertaken.

Fabric: Check each piece of fabric for small flaws in the weave, spots of grease from machines or color inconsistencies. Many of these are not large enough to warrant returning fabric to the store but might be annoying if they appeared in the center front of a garment. With a pin, mark each spot which is to be avoided. When laying out the pattern, place the marked spot in an inconspicuous place or, if possible place it entirely outside any pattern piece.

Many fabrics have no distinct right and wrong side, so, choose the side with no flaws for the right side. Many fabrics are folded with right sides together to prevent a dirt line at the fold on the right side. Knits tend to have a very strong fold mark which, because they are so wide, can be avoided totally by refolding the fabric as shown, **Fig. 204.** Wools are almost always folded right sides together, but there are other ways of detecting the right side of smooth wools. Any fabric with a twill weave is woven so that when the piece is draped against the body, the diagonal line on the right side will run from the left shoulder to

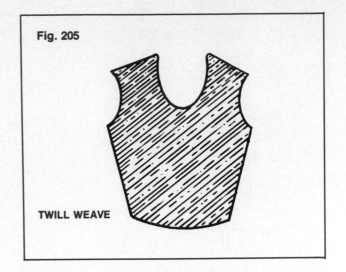

Fig. 205

TWILL WEAVE

the right hip. **Fig. 205.** Wool flannel has a smooth look on the right side, with the weave showing very little. On the wrong side, a strong cross grain shows in the weave.

After straightening the end or cross grain of woven fabric (see Fabric Preparation, pg. 617), lay the fabric, as the pattern suggests, on a large table, the floor or a cutting board. Most layouts require that the fabric be folded on the length grain or cross grain so that the pieces are all cut double. No matter which way the fabric is folded, the selvages should lie together and the straightened, cross-grain ends should lie together — everything squared. If this does not happen and there are two short corners, pull the opposing short corners to stretch the fabric somewhat. Try folding again to see if the fabric is squared; if not, pull and fold again. **Fig. 206.** Sometimes, the problem can be corrected by wetting a fabric to preshrink it. (See Fabric Preparation, pg. 617.) Sometimes, steaming it will help. *Bonded fabrics cannot be straightened. This quality makes them somewhat less than satisfactory.*

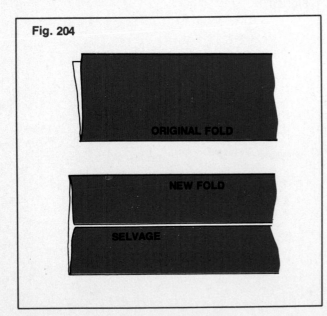

Fig. 204

ORIGINAL FOLD

NEW FOLD

SELVAGE

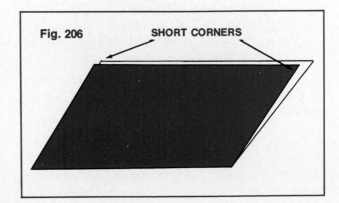

Fig. 206   SHORT CORNERS

General pattern layout suggestions: Sort the pattern pieces so that all the sections which belong on the garment fabric are in one pile and all of those which will be cut from lining or interfacing fabric are in separate piles. Do not trim off the margins; it is easier to cut evenly when cutting through both the paper and fabric. The margin may also be useful when altering patterns. (See Patterns, pg. 651.)

Any line labeled "Lay on Fold of Fabric" must have that edge of the pattern exactly on the lengthwise fold.

Most pattern pieces will be cut on the double fabric, either on the fold to make a whole piece, such as a blouse front, or not on a fold so that there will be two pieces, as for a blouse back with zipper. **Fig. 207.** It makes no difference whether the fabric is folded with right or wrong sides together, as two opposite pieces will be cut either way. *If, however, pieces are cut singly, remember to reverse the second one or the garment may have two left sides instead of one left and one right.* Cutting single pieces is dangerous; try to avoid it except in cases of a "Cut One" piece. "Cut One" pieces are the ones thus marked on the pattern pieces and they must be laid *right side up* (so you can read the print) *on the right side of the fabric.*

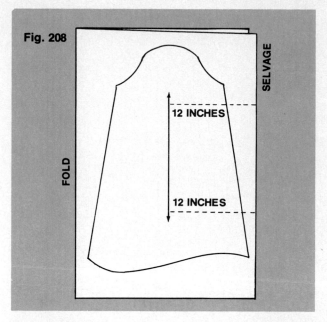

Fig. 208

12 INCHES

12 INCHES

FOLD

SELVAGE

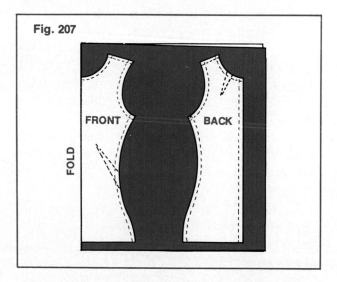

Fig. 207

FRONT   BACK

FOLD

The marked grain lines on pattern pieces must go along the length grain of the fabric, parallel to the selvage edge. For absolute accuracy, measure in at least two places from the selvage to each end of the marked grain line. **Fig. 208.** The pattern margins may overlap up to the cutting lines when they are laid on the fabric. Watch for and allow for pieces which must be cut twice (usually collars or cuffs). With a little practice, the beginner can soon make up her own layouts. Fabrics now come in so many odd widths that the garment often uses less fabric than the pattern layout calls for.

Layouts for stripes: Balanced stripes are relatively simple to deal with; unbalanced stripes must be laid out as a one-way design. When folding a fabric with a balanced stripe, be sure that all the stripes match through — dark on top of dark and light on top of light. (See Plaids, pg. 658.) The fold of the fabric should be directly down the center of a stripe. If this is done and the fabric pinned together carefully, all slanted seams should chevron effectively. **Fig. 209.** Be sure to get all center front or center back lines of

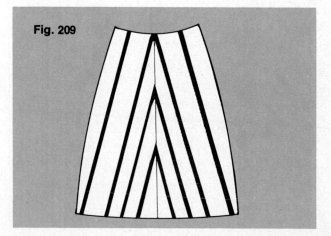

Fig. 209

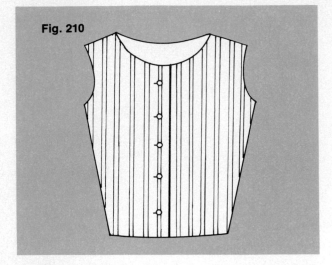

Fig. 210

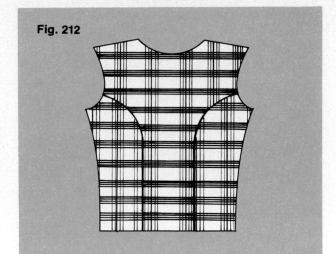

Fig. 212

the pattern directly on the center of a stripe, preferably a dark one. **Fig. 210.**

With unbalanced stripes, there will usually be a predominant color line. Lay the predominant color on a matching line when folding the fabric and the other stripes will fall into place. Choose a pattern with simple lines; one which is pictured in a bold stripe is usually safest. *Remember to lay all the pieces in one direction as with naps and one-way designs.*

Layouts for plaids: Follow the same rules for laying out balanced and unbalanced plaids that are given above for stripes. (For definitions of Plaids, see pg. 658.) However, plaids present one further problem — the horizontal lines of the

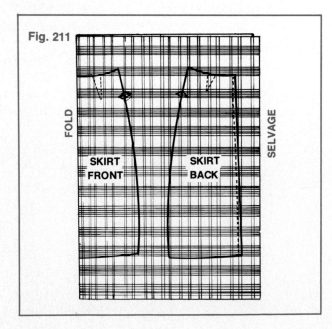

Fig. 211

FOLD

SELVAGE

SKIRT FRONT

SKIRT BACK

plaid must match as closely as possible. This can be done by placing corresponding notches on seams at exactly the same point in the plaid line. **Fig. 211.** When there is a curved seam, such as over the bust line in princess styles, the plaids can only match up to the place where the curve becomes obvious and has ease on one side. Beyond that point, be sure that the slippage of the lines is the same on both sides. **Fig. 212.** On long seams, double-check the plaids at all notches or marked points. Some hand-woven plaids are uneven and will never match exactly at all points.

Napped fabric and one-way designs: Many fabrics, because of texture or their printed or woven designs, have a definite "up and down." (For definitions of Napped Fabrics see page 646, for One-Way Designs, see page 648.) When choosing a pattern for these fabrics, make sure that it does not have a warning against the use of napped fabrics or one-way design. *The layout diagrams will include one-way arrangements. Use one of these or make up your own, but be sure to put the top of each piece of pattern in the same direction.*

When folding fabric for a one-way layout, fold lengthwise, but never crosswise. A crosswise fold makes the nap or design lie one way on one layer and exactly the opposite on the other. If the garment is to be cut as though the fabric were folded crosswise, cut the fabric across the center and turn one layer around. Lay it back on the other piece with either right sides together or wrong sides together so that the nap of each piece lies in the same direction. Proceed as you would if the fabric were folded crosswise. **Fig. 213.**

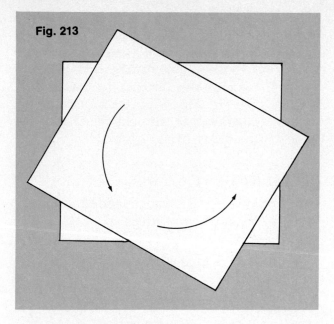

Fig. 213

Layouts for border designs: Woven or print borders on fabric can be attractively handled, but do require some imagination. Saris often have a wide border on one side and a narrow one on the other side. Both can be used to great advantage. The traditional use of a wide border is on a gathered skirt, cut crosswise so that the border falls around the lower edge. Borders can also be worked into bodices to give the appearance of a yoke and then worked correspondingly into the sleeves. **Fig. 214.** The narrow borders of saris can be used on shirt-sleeve cuffs and front bands. *To plan for borders, make some preliminary sketches, measure pieces, make trial layouts but do not cut until all the pieces are fitted onto the fabric.*

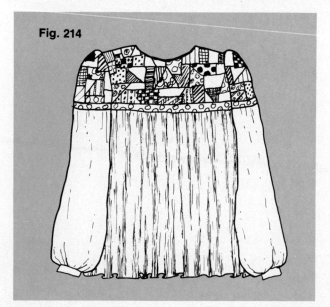

Fig. 214

Novelty designs: Large prints, bias-printed plaids and other novelty designs do not require a great deal of matching but do require some forethought. If this is a first attempt at using a bias-printed plaid, buy a pattern which is specifically shown in such a plaid. (There will be a note to that effect on the envelope.) Bias-printed plaids work very badly in patterns which have pieces to be cut on the bias. Too many seams are not suitable for bias-printed plaids because it is nearly impossible to make them match in the manner of straight plaids. A few casually matched lines look fine, but a multitude of them can be nothing but confusing.

Very large, all-over floral prints should be treated as any other fabric — no matching and very little planning. Try not to place one enormous rose on exactly the wrong spot on the back of a skirt. Make a point of putting the best colors near your face. If the print is in a panel treatment, it is often best to use a pattern with very few seams to give proper play to the design in large uncut areas.

LININGS

The term "lining" has a variety of definitions. There are the linings inside coats and jackets, which are used to finish the inside and to give warmth and durability. For extra warmth, interlinings are sometimes used between the lining and the outer garments. (See Tailoring Tips, found on page 676.)

Dresses can have Underlinings, (see page 682). These are sometimes called construction linings and add body and shape to the garment. Dresses may also be finished with Flip Linings (see page 623), which hide seams, do away with the necessity for a slip and often make scratchy fabrics bearable to sensitive skin.

MARKING FABRIC FROM PATTERN

Patterns have all sorts of markings to denote where pieces fit together, where ease is needed and where buttons and buttonholes are to be placed. These marking should be transferred to the fabric so that they can serve as guides for the assembly of the garment. There are several ways in which this can be done, but the method which damages the fabric least and best serves the purpose is the Tailor Tack, see page 675. This marking is made with thread and is well worth the little extra trouble that it takes to learn to make them correctly. Once they're in place, they mark both sides of the fabric — both layers have been cut together so that there should be no further trouble in assembling the pieces.

Chalk can be used to mark fabric, but the accuracy is dubious because the pattern must be lifted and then, each layer must be marked separately. Chalk also brushes off easily while the garment is constructed so that the marks do not remain clear.

Dressmaker's carbon and a tracing wheel should be used by the directions on the package, if it is used at all. The carbon will not mark on heavy woolens and other rough-textured fabrics and sometimes will leave permanent marks on light, sheer fabrics. However, it is extremely useful in working with muslin shells or "fitting patterns" and with appliqué and some household sewing, such as slipcovers.

Very light pencil can sometimes be used on the wrong side of the fabric, but, like chalk, this requires lifting the pattern piece. It is not advisable to use a pencil because the mark is nearly impossible to remove.

Notches: Around the edges of pattern pieces there are notches, numbered to correspond to notches on adjoining pieces. These are sometimes single notches and sometimes in groups of two or three to make it easy to identify front and back seams on skirts, pants, etc. The quickest and most efficient way to handle them is to clip in sharply about ¼ inch for each notch. Cutting out around them often makes it hard to distinguish the groups of two from those of three and, in heavy wools or loosely woven linens, the notches will ravel quickly. **Fig. 215.** While the garment is still in the cutting-out stage, also clip the ends of the folds (always center front or back).

MEASUREMENT CHART

(Minimum ease allowance added to body measurements when needed)

Bust . . . .
    (+ ease of 3 inches) . . . .

Waist . . . .
    (+ ease of 1 inch for waistbands) . . . . . .

Hips — 4 inches below waist . . . .
    (+ ease of 2 inches) . . . .

Hips — 7 inches below waist . . . .
    (+ ease of 2 inches) . . . .

Shoulder to point of bust . . . .

Shoulder to waist front . . . .

Shoulder to waist back . . . .

Across upper back (between armholes) . . . :

Across upper front (between armholes) . . . .

Around upper arm . . . .
    (+ ease of 2 inches) . . . .

Around forearm . . . .
    (+ ease of 1½ inches) . . . .

Around wrist . . . .
    (+ ease of 1 inch) . . . .

Shoulder to elbow . . . .

Shoulder (around elbow) to wrist . . . .

Finished skirt lengths (short) . . . .
    (long) . . . .

Pants Special Measurement:

Around thigh at fullest part . . . .
    (+ ease of 2 inches) . . . .

Finished length
    from waist along finished seam . . . .

Crotch (from waist front to back
    between legs, with ease allowed
    to feel comfortable) . . . .

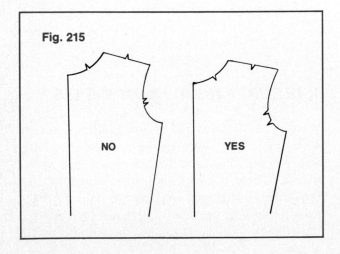

Fig. 215

NO   YES

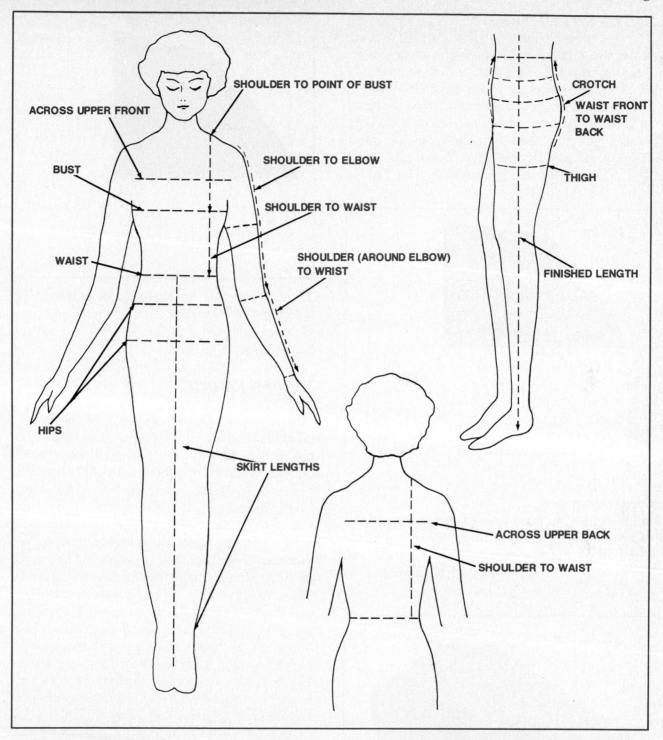

ACROSS UPPER FRONT

SHOULDER TO POINT OF BUST

SHOULDER TO ELBOW

BUST

SHOULDER TO WAIST

WAIST

SHOULDER (AROUND ELBOW) TO WRIST

HIPS

SKIRT LENGTHS

CROTCH

WAIST FRONT TO WAIST BACK

THIGH

FINISHED LENGTH

ACROSS UPPER BACK

SHOULDER TO WAIST

MEASURING

The first step to custom dressmaking is to record your own body measurements and refer to them often. To measure properly, wear the undergarments which are most flattering to the figure and the shoes which are frequently worn so as to stand properly. *Do not measure over outer garments — over a slip only.*

The chart shows all the important measurements. For some of these the help of a friend will be necessary. Note the circumference measurements, both with and without the added ease which is necessary for movability. (See Pattern Alteration, pg. 652.)

MITERED CORNERS

When two hems come together at a corner, as on curtains and table mats, it is often necessary to miter the ends together to prevent bulk. Press the turned edges for both hems; then, press the hems in place to the point where they meet at the corners. Pinch the hems together from the outer edges to the turned inner edge. This forms a visible crease slanted across each hem. **Fig. 216.** If

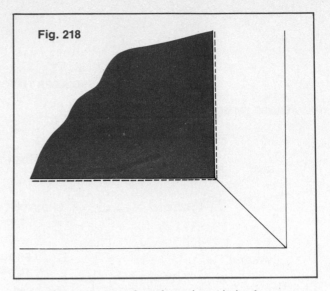

Fig. 218

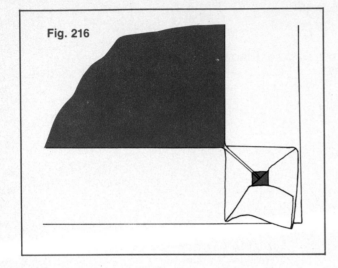

Fig. 216

you wish, mark this hem on the wrong side with chalk or pencil. Lay the hems, right sides together, so that these marked lines meet and pin the lines together for a seam. Stitch along the lines, from the turned edge to the corner and backstitch for security at each end. **Fig. 217.**

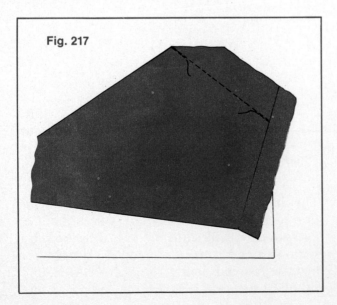

Fig. 217

Trim the excess so that there is a ¼-inch seam remaining. Cut away the corner as shown and press the seam open. Turn the corner right side out and hem as usual. **Fig. 218.**

NAPPED FABRICS

Fabrics which can be stroked like fur in one direction, but not in the reverse, are called napped fabrics. They are made by applying a nap or pile to the surface of the woven or knit fabric. The most common examples are velvet, velveteen, corduroy, wool doeskin, wool broadcloth and velour. Take a piece of any one of these and hold it up in the light with first one end up and then the other. The shading is quite different, the fabric appearing darker in one direction than the other. Wool looks best and wears longer with the nap stroking down like a fur coat. The cottons and most synthetic fabrics, such as velveteen, corduroy and the like, look better with the nap running up, giving a darker and richer appearance. *The first rule of sewing napped fabrics is that the nap on all sections must run in the same direction, regardless of the direction chosen.* (See the information on Layouts, page 640.)

NECKLINES

Necklines are a primary consideration of any garment. A neckline should be selected which will compliment a particular figure type. Read carefully the sections on Collars, page 602 and Facings, page 617. These are helpful in giving a professional finish to this important area.

NEEDLES

One item of equipment which is of primary importance to seamstresses are needles for hand sewing. These range from little "Shorts" and "Sharps" to long "Milliners." The sizes run in reverse order — the smaller the number, the larger the needle. Size 7 or 8 is thin enough to handle well and still fairly easy to thread. For people who have difficulty seeing the eye, "Darners" which have a long eye, may be easiest to thread. There are also needles with a slot in the top of the eye so that the thread can be slipped into it. These are never as fine as the #7 or #8, but are a boon to people with poor eyesight.

Sewing machine needles: The sizes of sewing machine needles run exactly opposite to hand sewing needles and the numbering is somewhat erratic. The smallest available is a size 9, then they run 11, 14, and 18. The ones used most often are #11 and #14. There are some specialty needles, such as a ball point, for sewing on knits. It is best to buy sewing machine needles at a sewing machine store. If the model number of the machine or style number of the needle is uncertain, take an old needle and match it. Insert the new needle in exactly the same position of the old one. Be sure to push the needle all the way up and turn the screw tightly. (See Sewing Machine Maintenance, pg. 668.)

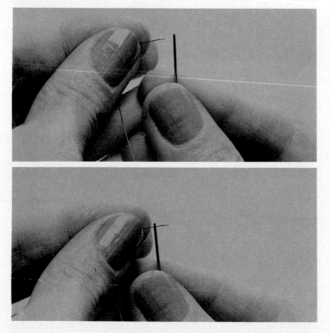

Fig. 219

Tricks for threading: Cut the thread end with sharp scissors, moisten the end and press it between your thumb and forefinger to make it smooth and straight. Hold the thread between the thumb and forefinger of the left hand (right hand for left-handed people) so that barely 1/4 inch of thread is visible. With the other hand, push the needle gently onto the thread. **Fig. 219.** When the thread has started through the eye, take hold of the end of it and pull it through. *Remember, push the needle onto the thread, never aim the thread at the needle.* When using light thread, hold the entire operation against a dark surface and vice versa.

NO-BAND WAISTLINES

A professional finish for the top of slacks and skirts, especially those which hang low on the hips, is a smooth, fitted facing of bias fabric. This can be substituted for the band or finish in any pattern which does not have gathers or heavy pleats at the waistline.

Stitch and press all seams, darts and the zipper; then, try on the garment. Mark the upper edge exactly where it is to be finished, either at the waist or an inch or two below. To locate the exact point, tie a string around the waist and then, place pins along it. Run an ease thread around the marked line, and pull it to the exact measurement of the waist. Trim the seam allowance to 3/8 inch.

Cut a piece of lining fabric on the bias, 3 to 4 inches wide and 6 inches longer than the measurement of the eased line. Turn the end of the bias in 1/2 inch and fold the bias along the center. **Fig. 220.** Lay the bias piece on the right side of the garment, raw edges together, and pin along the eased seam line, fulling the edge of the bias. (See Bias Facing on a curve, pg. 590.) When the zipper is reached at the other end, cut off any excess bias allowing 1/2 inch to turn in.

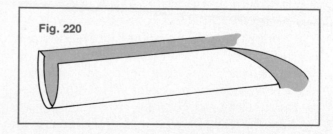

Fig. 220

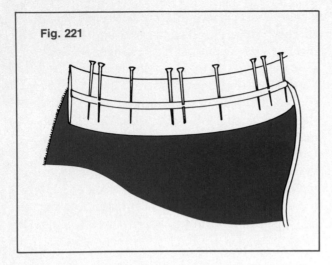

Fig. 221

Cut a piece of stay tape (see pg. 673) the exact length of the eased line and lay it along the seam line on top of the bias. Pin it in a few places and stitch all layers together along the center of the tape. **Fig. 221.** Clip the seam at 1-inch intervals all around but do not clip stay tape. Turn the bias facing over the seam and understitch. By hand, tack the folded edge of the bias facing to the zipper, darts and seams. **Fig. 222.**

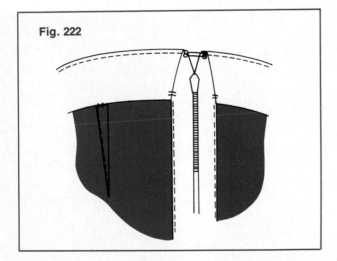

Fig. 222

NOTIONS

A term found on the backs of pattern envelopes and in department stores is "Notions" or "Sewing Notions," meaning all the little odds and ends which are needed to complete a garment. In department stores, it also means the necessary small equipment such as pins, needles and tape measures. Read the Notions list on the pattern envelope carefully because it gives the number of buttons, the length of zipper and other pertinent information for each view of the garment.

ONE-WAY DESIGNS

Some fabrics, especially those used in home decorating, have prints which can only be used in one direction — just as a picture cannot be hung upside down. With decorator fabrics, this also creates what is known as a motif repeat — the picture repeating every 12, 18 or 24 inches. Extra fabric allowance must be made for the average sized one-way designs and even more for large motif repeats. For clothing, there is usually a napped fabric or one-way design yardage given in the yardage chart on the back of the envelope. In the case of the large, one-way motif repeats in decorator fabric, it is necessary to do some planning and arithmetic to arrive at the total number of yards needed to complete a project.

In the smaller prints used for clothing, check carefully to see whether a print has a disguised one-way design. For instance, if there are four kinds of flowers in the print, two of them may always go in one direction, never the reverse. Han-

NONAPPARENT ONE-WAY DESIGN

APPARENT ONE-WAY DESIGN

dle this as a one-way design. (See Layouts, page 640.) The best advice is: *if in doubt, treat any fabric as a one-way design when cutting.*

PANTS

Making pants is a special type of sewing in which fitting is of primary importance. Sewing the sections together is no problem once a pattern has been altered to fit. There are some special patterns on the market which have complete fitting directions. (Note the pants section in Pattern Alterations, pg. 652.) The first step in fitting pants is to construct a muslin shell from the altered version of your pattern. Press it and try it on. A few more corrections may be needed. Adjust the muslin and transfer the alterations of the pattern. *Keep the master pattern and use it as reference when altering other pants patterns.* Once a pattern is fitted, most seamstresses will use this pattern for all successive pants, unless styles in leg shapes and length change a great deal or very full evening pants are called for. Even shorts can be made by cutting off moderate legged patterns. The seat and hip sections will fit the same no matter what sort of leg is used.

Tips on assembling: *Make each leg separately.* (The side seam may be basted for an extra fitting until the crotch seam is sewn.) Clip about every 3 inches along the thigh curve of the inseam and press it open. **Fig. 223.** It is easier to position the crotch seam on the sewing machine if *one leg is*

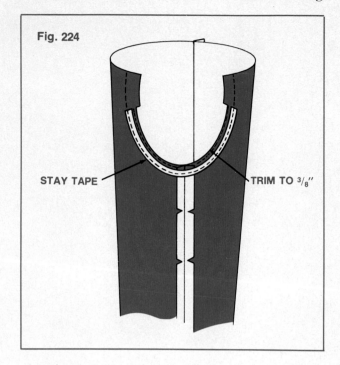

Fig. 224

STAY TAPE — TRIM TO 3/8″

turned right side out and place inside the other leg which is wrong side out. Lay a stay tape along the curved, lower part of the seam, usually in the area from notch to notch. Stitch through the center of the tape; then, make another row of stitching, 1/8 inch inside the seam. **Fig. 224.** Trim the curved part of the seam to 3/8 inch. Do not trim the upper straight part of the seam, but press it open down to the taped area.

PATCHING

If clothes wear out in one spot, get burned or stained in a small area, patches are about the only remedy. When making garments, save at least a small piece of the fabric from each garment for just this purpose. Otherwise, matching is nearly impossible and in many cases, the best idea is put on a very obvious decorative patch.

Matching patches: When cutting a patch of matching fabric, be sure that the grain line and the print match the area to be covered. In lightweight materials, it is best to turn under the edges of the patch and appliqué it in place with a small blind stitch. (See Stitches, pg. 674.) In heavier fabrics with a coarse weave, it is sometimes possible to place the patch under the hole and weave or darn the two fabrics together. In either method, trim away the excess loose fabric.

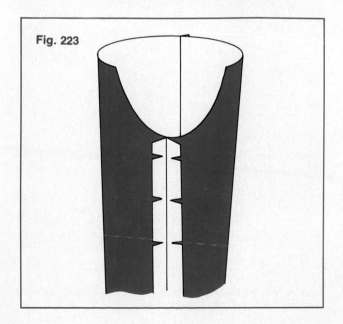

Fig. 223

Fig. 225

Decorative patches: A zigzag sewing machine is really handy for items such as decorative patches. On children's clothes, jeans, play clothes and many other garments, it is a simple process to apply imaginative cutouts. To dress up a good, cotton wrap skirt or linen dress, machine appliqué a flower cut from a print fabric or use one of the cotton lace flowers which can be purchased. **Fig. 225.** (See Appliqué Chapter.)

PATCH POCKETS

One of the best methods of giving a dull garment a little life is to add patch pockets. They may be large and bright, in contrasting colors, a turned bias on a plaid, embroidered or decorated with braid. A zippered pocket can be created by cutting off the top of the pocket and inserting a zipper between the two pieces. Another idea is to add a flap which buttons onto the patch pocket. **Fig. 226.**

Tips on patch pockets: Hem the upper edge of a patch pocket by turning it right sides together

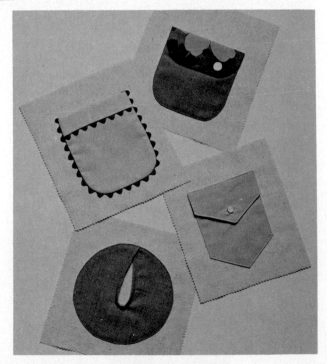

Fig. 226

PATCH POCKETS give free rein to imagination and add decorator touches to plain garments.

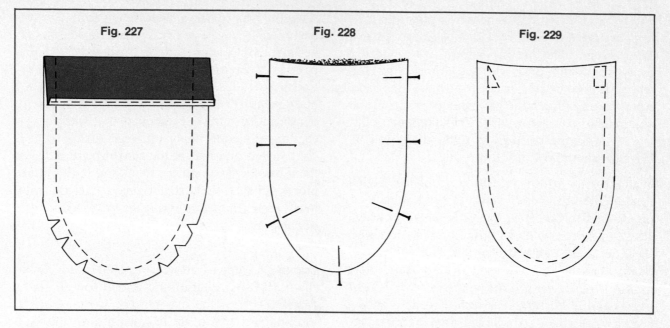

Fig. 227   Fig. 228   Fig. 229

along the hemline and seaming the ends like a facing. First, finish the raw edge with zigzag stitching or a ¹/₂-inch turn-under. If the pocket is curved, continue the stitching on the seam line all the way around the pocket. Doing this makes it easier to turn the edge under smoothly. Notch out some of the fabric around the curves and press the edges under. **Fig. 227.**

When pinning a patch pocket in place, do not pull it tight; let it stand away from the garment slightly along the top edge. **Fig. 228.**

Most patch pockets are top stitched in place with a line of machine stitching about ¹/₈ inch from the edge. If a rectangle or triangle of stitching is made at each upper corner as a reinforcement, there is less chance of ripping the pocket from the fabric. **Fig. 229.**

On tailored garments, patch pockets are sometimes lined and applied to the garment by hand with a blind stitch. (See Tailoring Tips, pg. 676.)

PATTERNS

Choice and size: Patterns come in a large range of sizes and figure types. It may take some experimenting to find the one most suited to a particular figure. Even with the best choice, most people need to do a little altering. For those over 21, it is best to use Misses' or Women's sizes, as these have the most appropriate clothes and the largest variety. Even if a Junior size fits better, it may be

necessary to learn to alter a Misses' pattern to achieve the desired effect.

In general, it is a good idea to consider bone structure when choosing pattern size. For those who are small boned and have added weight, a pattern size which may sound as though it is a bit too tight will look better. The bust and hips are easily altered, and the shoulders and neckline will look neater. Only a fairly large-boned person will find that is a good idea to buy a slightly larger, rather than slightly smaller pattern.

Look at the number of seams and darts when deciding whether a pattern will work for a figure type. For instance, if the pattern has no seams and no darts, it will not be suitable for an hourglass-shaped figure. The rule is, *the more darts, the more shape.* A skirt with eight darts can accommodate a small waist and round hips much better than one with only four darts. **Fig. 230.**

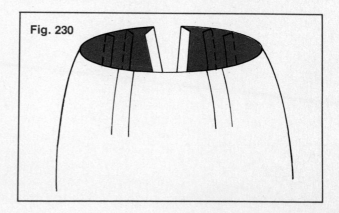

Fig. 230

First steps in fitting: When first attempting to alter a pattern to fit, start with a basic pattern and some muslin. Cut out the pattern as is, marking every seam and dart with carbon and tracing wheel. Allow extra fabric on all the side seams when cutting. Stitch the garments together on the original lines, using a large machine stitch, and try it on. If the garment is tight, there will be enough seam allowance to let out.

Watch for the following fitting problems: Tightness in the bust, hips, waist, across the back or upper arm; too great or too little length in waist, sleeve or skirt; too much fullness in the neck and shoulder area, bust, waist or hip. Alterations can be made in the seams as long as an inch or less is needed. *No seam should be taken in or let out more than* ½ *inch from the seam line.* This adds a total of 1 inch to a seam and of course, allowance would have to be made in cutting to let out that much. *The one exception to this is the side seams on the hips* which can be altered in even larger amounts.

Altering the pattern before cutting: For the beginner, it is wise to trace a pattern piece to experiment on it rather than cutting the original pieces. Materials include tissue paper, transparent tape, a felt tip pen and above all, the body measurement chart and a tape measure. In measuring a pattern, remember that with the exception of sleeves and pants legs, the garment is constructed one-half at the time. Measure across the hips of a skirt and the front and back pattern pieces. Then double that figure to get the total measurement. *Measure only from seam to seam, skipping over the darts.*

Standard types of alteration: Here are a few of the most usual alterations. If one sounds like a familiar problem, experiment by measuring, altering and trying out in muslin until the technique is established. Fortunately, once fitting problems are recognized and a method is devised for correcting them, the same basic alterations are easily made on all patterns.

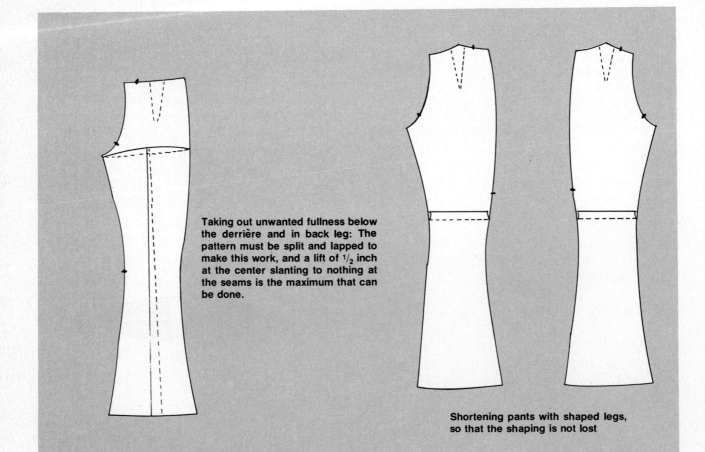

Taking out unwanted fullness below the derrière and in back leg: The pattern must be split and lapped to make this work, and a lift of ½ inch at the center slanting to nothing at the seams is the maximum that can be done.

Shortening pants with shaped legs, so that the shaping is not lost

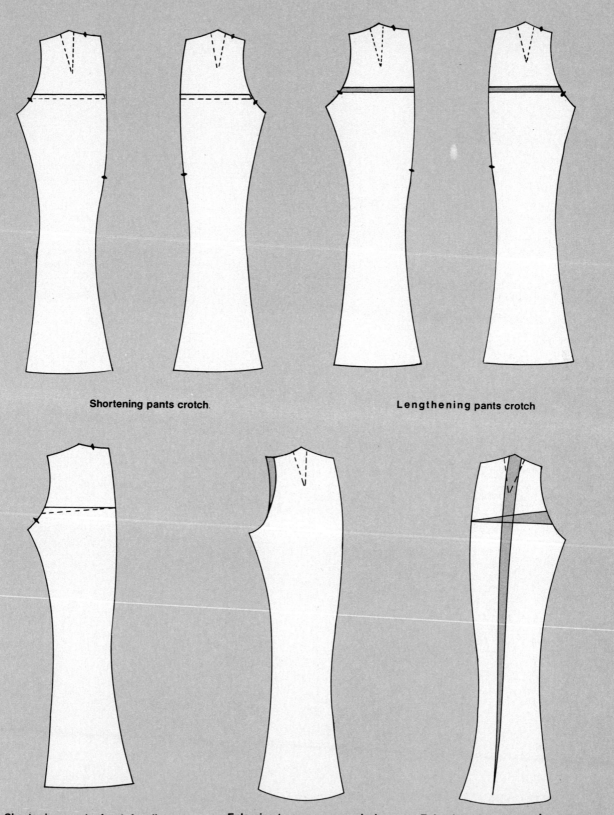

Shortening pants crotch.

Lengthening pants crotch

Shortening pants front for figure with very flat tummy

Enlarging tummy area on slacks

Enlarging hip and derrière area on slacks

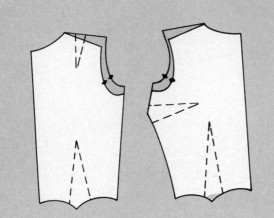

Raising shoulder and armhole for square shoulder

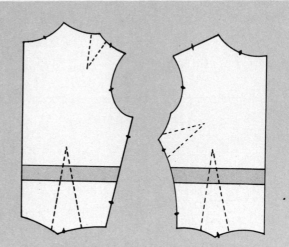

Lengthening waistline more than the 1/2 inch allowable at the lower edge

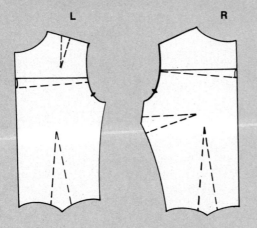

Shortening back for erect figure. (L) Shortening upper front for slightly stooped figure, 1/2 inch to nothing at armholes. (R)

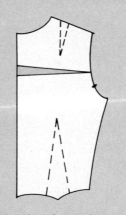

Lengthening back for round shoulders, 1/2 inch slanting to nothing at armholes.

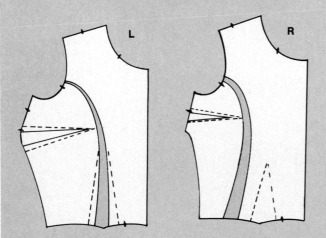

Enlarging bust while keeping waist the original size. (L) Enlarging bust and waist. (R)

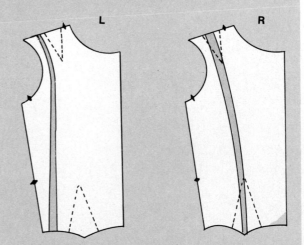

Widening lower back and waist, bringing pattern together again at shoulder. (L) Widening upper back area. (R)

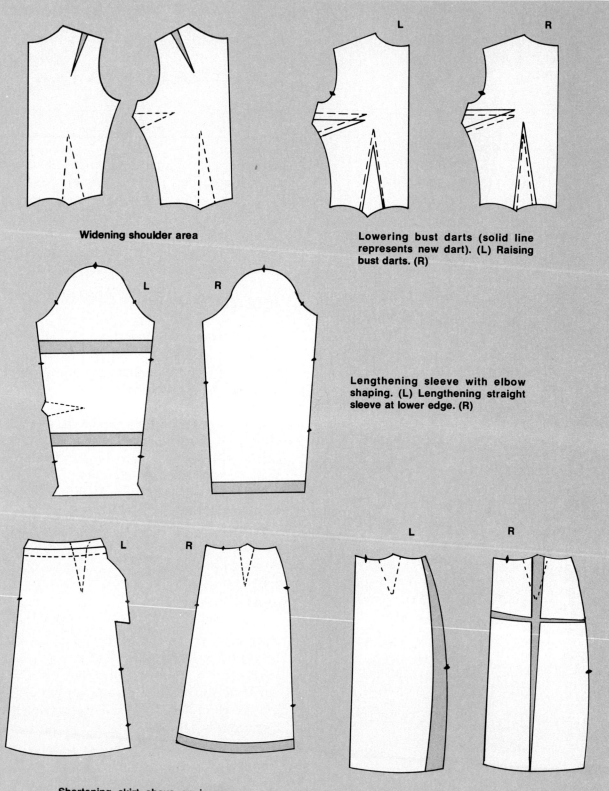

Widening shoulder area

Lowering bust darts (solid line represents new dart). (L) Raising bust darts. (R)

Lengthening sleeve with elbow shaping. (L) Lengthening straight sleeve at lower edge. (R)

Shortening skirt above an inseam pocket to raise pocket; use the same technique for raising pleats or other style lines. (L) Most skirts can be successfully lengthened or shortened at lower edge, as shown. (R)

Enlarging hips on side seam. (L) Enlarging skirt back for larte behind: 1/2 inch at center slanting to nothing at side seams. (R)

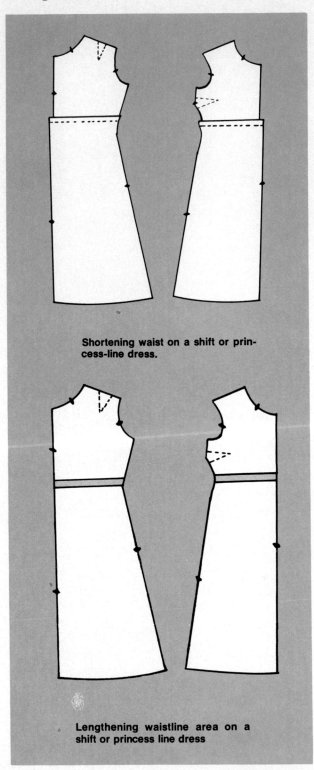

Shortening waist on a shift or princess-line dress.

Lengthening waistline area on a shift or princess line dress

PICOT

Tiny loops or points along the edge of ribbon or lace are referred to as picot edges. The same effect can be achieved on fabric by using the machine hemstitch disk or attachment on your

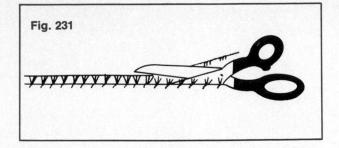

Fig. 231

sewing machine and then cutting along the openwork just beyond the stitching. **Fig. 231.** Check the sewing machine manual. It is also possible in many communities to have hemstitching done on factory-type machines for a nominal fee. Picot of this type is an excellent finish for sheer fabrics such as chiffon and for bias ruffles.

PILLOW FORMS

A wide variety of pillow forms to use in making decorative pillows are now available in foam rubber, polyurethane foam, polyester filled and kapok filled. The choice is really a matter of personal taste. The synthetics seem to wear well; the kapok is more fragile, but wonderfully soft. Standard or stock shapes may be purchased and many places will cut the foam forms into individual shapes and sizes. Before beginning a piece of needlework for a pillow, it is wise to obtain the form so that the pattern will be the correct size. It is generally better to make the cover slightly tight for the form so that it will fit without any wrinkles.

PINS

Regardless of the type fabric, always use the best in pins! The ones sold in this country as "silk pins" are the best made here, but if the opportunity to obtain Swiss pins arises, do so. There are also good ones made in France, England and Germany, but the Swiss variety is tops.

Pin basting: Modern machines are made with a flexible presser foot to allow for sewing over pins which have been placed perpendicular to the seam line. **Fig. 232.** This is called pin basting or French basting and is an ideal way to hold fabric together for stitching. This short cut may be used on any seam which does not need to be basted for fitting. It is especially good for holding together

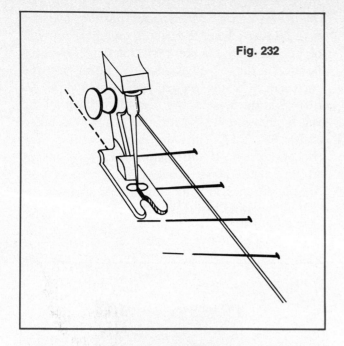

Fig. 232

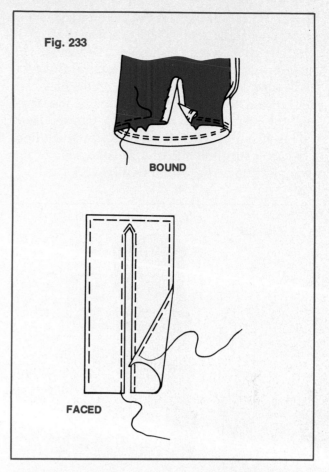

Fig. 233

BOUND

FACED

the horizontal lines of plaids or for fabrics, such as corduroy, which tend to shift during stitching.

Warnings on pin basting: Be sure that the sewing machine does have a hinged foot before stitching over pins. Use fine pins without the colored heads, as these heads will make the pin stand up from the fabric too far and the foot will not run smoothly over it. Never let the head of the pin go in so far that it is under the presser foot. Place the pin with the head toward the raw edge of the seam. Pick up just enough of the fabric with the pin to hold the two layers together at the seam allowance, 5/8 inch from the edge.

PIPING

See Corded Piping, page 604, and Edgings, page 608.

PLACKETS

Before the invention of zippers, all garments were closed with elaborate snap or hook and eye plackets. It now seems unnecessary to discuss the snap plackets used for closing dresses. However, one form of bound placket remains in use on shirt sleeves and occasionally, on the skirt portion of children's dirndl dresses. A simple, faced placket is sometimes used on shirt sleeves, though it is far less satisfactory than the bound one. **Fig. 233.** The same type of placket is used to enable a

zipper to be inserted in a part of a garment where there is no seam to accommodate it.

Bound Placket: Staystitch around the opening, starting about 1/4 inch from slash mark at raw edge and slanting toward the slash mark at other end. Take one stitch across and slant back to 1/4 inch from the mark at raw edge. Slash all the way to the end where the one stitch was taken across. **Fig. 234.**

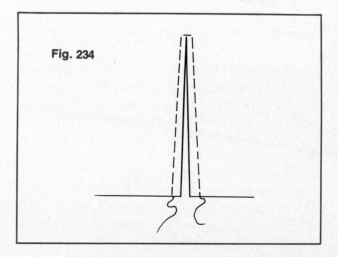

Fig. 234

Use fabric cut on the bias for the binding as it is easier to handle and ravels less. Cut a strip of binding twice as long as the slash and about 1¼ inches wide. Pin it, right sides together, along the slash edge. Make a ¼-inch seam on the bias strip and a seam along the staystitch line on the slash. Lay the piece on the machine so that the slash side is up and stitch, following the staystitch line. **Fig. 235.** Turn the bias and finish by any of the methods under Bias Binding. **Fig. 236.**

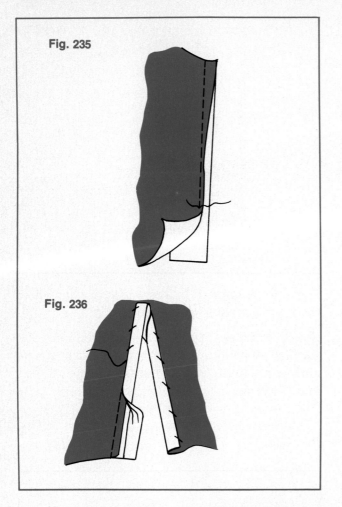

Fig. 235

Fig. 236

Faced placket: Cut a facing piece large enough to extend at least an inch on each side and at the end of the placket. (If it is too large, it can always be cut down later.) If this type of placket is used on a sleeve or at the neck for a button opening on a medium-weight fabric, it is usually cut from the same fabric and on the same grain as that portion of the garment to which it will be sewn. If it is used to make a zipper opening, it is better to cut it on the bias of a lightweight lining fabric which is compatible to the garment.

Lay the facing piece, right sides together, over the slash line and seam the pieces together. As with the bound slash, the seam will start ¼ inch from the slash at the raw edge, slant to a point, sew one stitch across at the end and slant to a point ¼ inch from the slash at the raw edge. Slash all the way to the end where the one stitch was taken across. **Fig. 237.** Turn the facing to the wrong side and press. If the material shows signs of raveling at the point, work a small area of buttonhole stitches in matching thread around the end or machine top stitch very close to finished edge. **Fig. 238.**

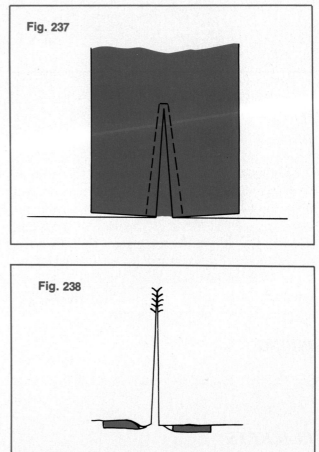

Fig. 237

Fig. 238

PLAIDS

One of the oldest ways of decorating fabrics is to weave yarn-dyed color into it. When color is woven in both directions, it produces either a check or an even more elaborate plaid. One of the traditional and still popular forms of plaid is the Scottish tartan, which was originally wool but now is made from cotton or synthetics.

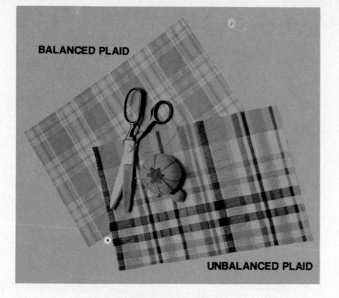

BALANCED PLAID

UNBALANCED PLAID

There are two kinds of plaids — balanced and unbalanced. A balanced plaid has identical lines on each side of the center of the squares and identical lines at top and bottom of the squares. Because of this, the plaid looks the same in either direction and can be cut with no consideration of a distinct up and down. The unbalanced plaids do not have repeating lines and are definitely one-way designs. For a balanced plaid, it is wise to buy a little extra material to allow for matching the plaids. The larger the plaid, the more fabric will be necessary to allow for matching. (One-eighth to 1/4 yard is usually enough.) Unbalanced plaids should be bought by the one-way design allowance on the pattern envelope, plus a little extra for matching plaids, as with the balanced plaids.

PLEATS

Fullness can be added to a skirt without any appearance of bulk or extra weight by the use of pleats. The vertical line of hard-pressed pleats is as slimming as vertical stripes and much more graceful than a straight skirt. Careful calculating of measurements and accurate stitching are necessary to make pleated garments fit well, so they are not for absolute beginners! Specific types of pleats in various groupings are given in patterns. It is necessary to mark carefully with Tacks and follow the directions for assembly. It is wise to baste everything for an initial fitting when dealing with a pattern with a number of pleats and seams in the skirt.

One way of making a pleated skirt without a pattern and also avoiding most of the fitting pitfalls is to pleat enough fabric to go around the hips, adding a little ease. Sew this onto a yoke, about 5 inches long, which has been cut from the top of a basic skirt which fits. **Fig. 239.** For knife pleats,

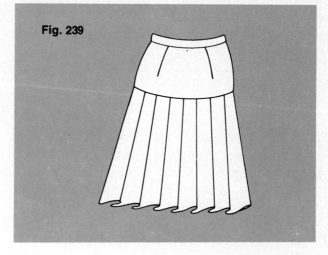

Fig. 239

allow fabric width three times the hip measurement. Allow the desired finished skirt length from the yoke down, plus hem. The ironing board makes an ideal working area, as pleats can be pinned to it and pressed without moving them. **Fig. 240.** Fold the fabric and fold it over an inch, or the desired pleat width. Fold the next pleat to meet the under edge of the first one. Continue until all the fabric is used. Hide any necessary seam by sewing it in the back edge of a pleat. **Fig. 241.** Plaids, stripes and other fabrics with obvious grain lines are the easiest to handle. Do not press the pleats all the way into the hem area until the hem is stitched in place.

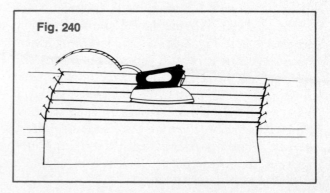

Fig. 240

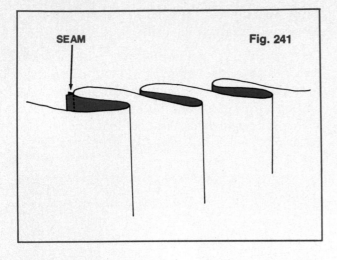

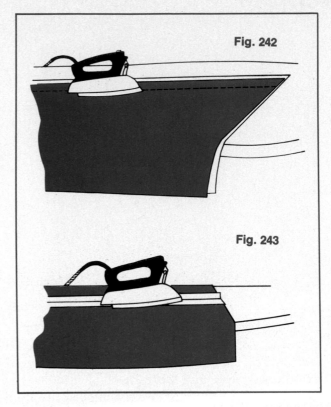

PRESHRINKING

Fabric should already be preshrunk when it is purchased, but it may still have a 1% or 2% residual shrinkage. Check all tags and labels for information. If there is any residual shrinkage listed on the label or if there is any doubt, preshrink by the methods described in Fabric Preparation.

PRESSING

It is almost as important to press well as it is to cut and stitch well if the finished product is to look truly professional. The first rule: Use a light touch and a steam iron which works well. An ideal steam iron is one which is small enough to go into all the corners. Taking care of all sewing equipment is a necessity, if it is to remain in good condition; but, it is especially important that the steam iron be kept clean and in perfect working order.

What to press and when to press it: Press each dart and seam before another seam is sewn across it. As soon as a seam has been stitched, press it, holding it taut and in the same position in which it was stitched. All the fabric should lie right sides together. **Fig. 242.** Then, lay the garment piece right side down on the ironing board and press the seam open flat. **Fig. 243.** It often helps to open the seam with a free hand just ahead of the iron. There are a few seams, such as those around an armhole, in the back edge of a pleat, etc. which are not pressed open flat. If in doubt, always refer to the pattern instruction chart for special pressing instructions.

Almost all darts are pressed down or toward center front or center back. **Fig. 244.** Double-ended darts must be clipped three or four times at the deepest part. **Fig. 245.** On very heavy fabrics, darts can be split open and pressed like a seam to within ¼ or ½ inch of the point. Then press the point in the direction it would normally go. **Fig. 246.** *It is always safe to split darts in knits or underlined fabrics, but, if there is any doubt about fabric*

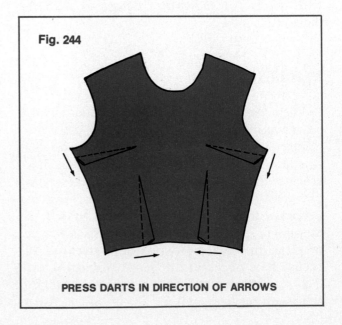

Fig. 244

PRESS DARTS IN DIRECTION OF ARROWS

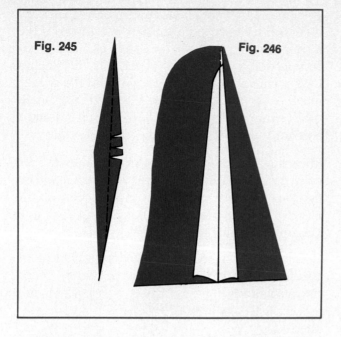

Fig. 245   Fig. 246

raveling, make a test dart on a leftover scrap and split it.

Special pressing tips on special fabrics: Velvets and other deep-piled fabrics should be pressed with the right side down on a special "needle board" made for this purpose. A less expensive alternative is to put a leftover piece of the velvet face up on the ironing board and lay the velvet to be pressed face down on it. The same technique can be used with rough-textured fabrics, using a terry towel on the board to keep from pressing the texture flat or slick.

Some few silk or synthetic fabrics are better pressed with a dry iron; the steam makes a mark or track on peau de soie, for instance. If in doubt, test on a sample piece.

On any delicate fabric, avoid pressing the seams or darts down so hard that they make a mark through on the right side. In extreme cases it may be necessary to put strips of brown paper or non-woven interfacing under the edges of the seam when pressing it.

Final shaping on finished garments: The press mitt is especially useful in giving a finished garment the proper curves. Use it for the bust line and the curve of the hips. Use a transparent press cloth over the fabric and steam through it very lightly, gently "persuading" the garment to take the desired shape.

RAGLAN SLEEVES

The most versatile and comfortable of all sleeves is the raglan. It is easy to put together and there are practically no fitting problems involved. Do not sew the sleeves together and do not sew the side seams of the bodice. Seam the front of the sleeve to the front of the bodice and the back of the sleeve to the bodice back from neck to side seam line and backstitch. **Fig. 247.** By not sewing to the raw edge of the fabric at the underarm, a ready-made clip is created which will enable the garment to turn right side out smoothly. The armhole seams are largely on the bias, so it is wise to include some stay tape as the seam is stitched.

Clip the armhole seams in the curves and press them open flat. **Fig. 248.** Baste the shoulder seam (or dart, as the case may be) and the side seam for fitting. **Fig. 249.**

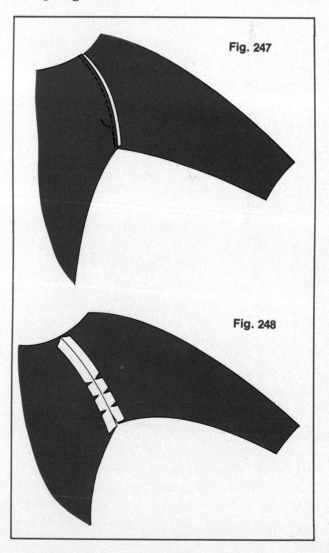

Fig. 247

Fig. 248

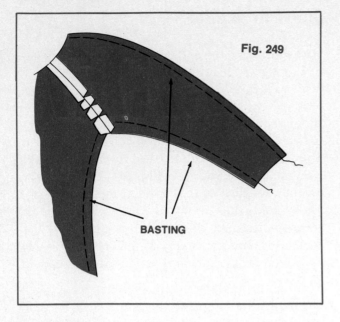

Fig. 249

BASTING

RICKRACK

One of the least expensive and most versatile braid trims available is rickrack. For more information, see Braid, page 591.

RUFFLES

Ruffles can be cut either on the straight grain or on the bias. If the straight grain is used, cut across the fabric, selvage to selvage. The advantage of cross grain over length grain is that it gathers more softly and any necessary piecing of seams can be done along the selvage, which will not ravel. Bias ruffling is very soft and graceful and easy to handle, as well as yielding an interesting design effect in plaids, checks and stripes.

Planning ruffling: Strips of fabric should be cut to desired finished width, plus ¹/₂ inch on each side for the hem or seam. The length should be at least 1¹/₂ times that of the area to which the ruffle is to be attached. For lighter fabrics, the length of the ruffle can be increased, up to 3 times the fullness for very sheer organzas or chiffons. For average-weight fabrics, the ideal length is twice the finished piece. Bias ruffling should never be skimpy as it will flatten out entirely.

Methods of gathering ruffling: For small amounts of ruffling, use two rows of machine stitching as described in Gathers, page 627. If yards of ruffling for curtains and household items is needed, check to see if the sewing

machine has a ruffling attachment. Read the direction for setting the amount of fullness on the attachment and then test on a strip of fabric identical to that being used. A piece about 20 inches long is enough to use as a gauge. Once the attachment is set for twice the fullness (the 20-inch piece would gather 10 inches) or other desired amount, the ruffles will take very little time.

Finishing the edges: Fabric cut on the straight grain can be finished with a narrow hem made by hand or machine. If the sewing machine has a narrow hemming attachment, try it out for large quantities of ruffling.

Bias fabric is not as easy to hem as straight grain but there are other ways to treat it. Again, check the machine for fancy zigzag edges which are especially suited to bias. Picot edges are another alternative.

One very good way of treating bias ruffles is to cut the fabric twice the desired ruffle width plus seams and fold it down the middle so that one edge is automatically finished. Run the gathering threads along the raw edge through the double layer of fabric. **Fig. 250.** This technique can be used on straight fabric also if it is thin enough.

Applying ruffles: Many ruffles are applied as edging. It is easy to add ruffles to a neckline which needs a little help or to a straight sleeve which should be longer. Apply the ruffle, following the directions for Edgings, page 608. **Fig. 251.** When trying on a dress in the fitting stage, consider such uses of self fabric ruffles as a way of rescuing an otherwise plain garment.

When ruffles are to be applied to the surface of fabric, pin them in place, right sides together with the fabric turned up opposite to the way they will lie when finished. Stitch along the seam line of the ruffle between the rows of gathers. Stitch again, using either straight or zigzag stitching, about ¹/₄ inch closer to the raw edge. Trim off the remaining raw edge close to this last stitching. Press the ruffle down over its stitching and, if desired, top stitch it about ¹/₈ inch from the folded edge to keep it in place. **Fig. 252.**

An attractive treatment of ruffles for surface application is the double-edged ruffle. Both edges are hemmed or finished as desired and the gathering is run down the center or slightly to

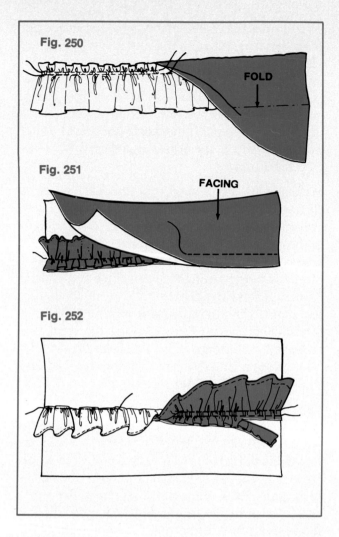

Fig. 250 — FOLD

Fig. 251 — FACING

Fig. 252

SCALLOPS

An attractive finish for household items, children's clothes and casual wear is a scalloped edge. Scallops can be finished with a facing or with a close satin stitch on a zigzag sewing machine.

Planning scallops: Any edge which is to be scalloped must be measured and then, that figure must be divided to determine how many scallops of an exact width will fit along it. For instance, if the project is a cafe curtain which measures 36 inches along the lower edge when it is finished, six 6-inch scallops or nine 4-inch scallops will fit perfectly on that edge. The depth of the scallops should be decided at this point. Then, on the wrong side of the fabric, mark two lines; mark the scallop widths along the top line. **Fig. 254.** Make a cardboard pattern with a compass or use a plate or other available circle to draw the scallops between the markings.

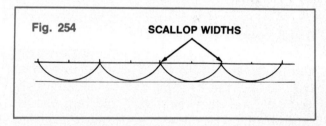

Fig. 254 — SCALLOP WIDTHS

one side of center. The ruffle is applied to the surface with one or two lines of machine stitching along the gathering line. **Fig. 253.** Narrow rickrack or braid can be stitched along this line for added effect.

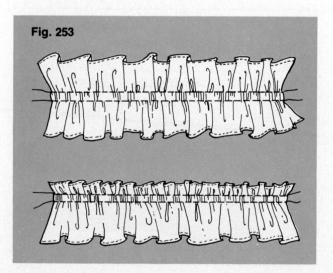

Fig. 253

Facing and finishing scallops: Cut a facing wide enough to reach an inch or two above the top line of the scallops. Pin it, right sides together, with the edge of the fabric and stitch along the scallop lines. Use a fairly small machine stitch, about twelve to the inch, and make one stitch across at the bridge between the scallops. Trim the seam to $1/8$ or $1/4$ inch, depending on how much the fabric ravels. Notch all around and clip the corner between the scallops. **Fig. 255.** Turn right side out and use a pointer and curver or the rounded handles of scissors to round each scallop into shape. Press gently along the edges, using the fingers to

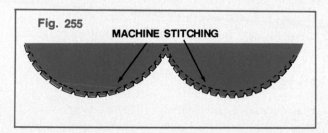

Fig. 255 — MACHINE STITCHING

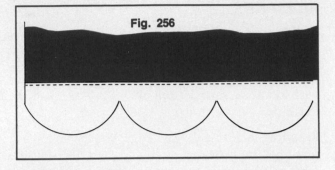

Fig. 256

work out any points which form. The facing may be finished on the machine or by hand. **Fig. 256.**

Finishing scallops with zigzag: Very firm fabrics can be finished by using a close satin stitch around the edge, through only the one layer. If the fabric is light or loose woven, lay a facing, wrong sides together, with the main piece and work through both layers; or a thin interfacing may be used between the layers for added stiffness.

SCISSORS

Scissors and shears are so essential to good sewing that they should represent one of the largest equipment expenditures. The most important type is the bent-handled cutting shears. Make sure they are sharp and when they become the least bit dull, have them properly sharpened by an expert. If high quality shears of best steel are purchased, they will last a lifetime and through many sharpenings. Avoid using them for any purpose other than sewing.

Other sizes and types of scissors, such as buttonhole, pinking and embroidery scissors are also handy to have.

SEAMS

For the beginner, sewing perfectly straight seams appears to be more difficult than it really is. When first learning to sew on a machine, it is wise to practice sewing both straight and curved seams. It takes a very little time to become proficient enough to begin making simple items. Skill will increase with each additional project.

TYPES OF SEAMS

Plain seams with plain or finished edges are the type which are used most. A great many fabrics do not ravel and can be left raw along the edges. Most patterns allow ⅝ inch for the width of the seam allowance. Sewing machines have a ⅝-inch line marked on the face plate to guide the fabric. If the machine is too old to have this guide, measure and mark the line with fingernail polish or transparent tape. If the fabric does ravel or if a pretty finish on the seams is desired, see page 620 for Finishes.

French seams are used on very fine fabrics such as chiffons and on baby clothes and lingerie. These are not as difficult to do as they seem and they add to the over-all looks of a garment. If the pattern allows ⅝-inch seams, start by placing the two pieces of fabric wrong sides together and make a ⅜-inch seam. **Fig. 257.** Trim this seam to slightly less than ¼ inch and press it all one way. Fold fabric, right sides together, along the seam line and press the stitched edge. Stitch on the original ⅝-inch seam line (¼ inch from the stitched and folded edge). **Fig. 258.**

Fake French seams are very useful when sewing ruffles to the edge of curtains or other items which will not be faced or lined. Begin by following the directions for regular French seams — wrong sides of the fabric together. Make a ¼-inch seam. Press the seam away from the ruffle and toward the flat fabric. **Fig. 259.** Fold the flat fabric over the seam so that the right sides of the fabric and the ruffle are together. With the ruffle uppermost on the machine, stitch through ruffle and fabric as close as possible to the first stitched seam. In this way the seam is still enclosed without doubling the thickness of the ruffle. **Fig. 260.**

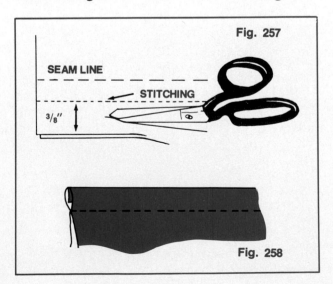

Fig. 257

SEAM LINE

STITCHING

3/8″

Fig. 258

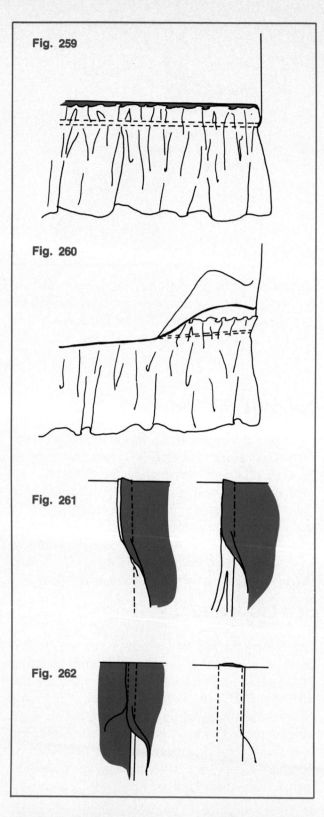

Fig. 259

Fig. 260

Fig. 261

Fig. 262

seam in one direction and trim the under layer to $1/4$ inch. **Fig. 261.** Fold the upper layer over the trimmed layer and pin, press or baste into place. (The width from the seam line to the folded edge should be just under $3/8$ inch.) On the right side of the fabric, top stitch through all layers of the seam $1/4$ inch from the seam line. If a double row of stitching is desired, top stitch again near the original seam line. **Fig. 262.**

Trimming or grading seams: Seams which are to be *pressed open flat should not be trimmed*. Edge seams or encased seams, as they are sometimes called, should be trimmed or graded in most cases to prevent bulk. Grading, usually done on thicker fabrics and in tailoring, means trimming one layer shorter than the other to form a sort of bevel for a smoother edge. Interfacing in any seam should be trimmed almost to the stitching itself. If the seam is to be graded, one layer will be cut to about $1/4$ inch and the last layer to $1/2$ inch. Sometimes it is necessary to leave at least one layer the full length so it can be incorporated in top stitching. **Fig. 263.** Check the pattern direction sheet if top stitching is shown.

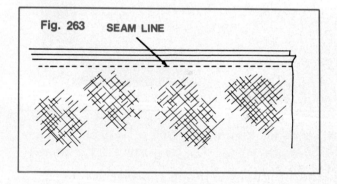

Fig. 263   SEAM LINE

TREATMENT FOR CORNER SEAMS

When it is necessary to stitch around a corner, be sure to drop the machine needle into the fabric exactly at the turning point, then lift the presser foot and pivot on the needle. If the corner is an outside one at a right angle, such as on the lower edge of a jacket, the corner seam should be cut straight off, almost to the stitching, before the piece is turned right side out. **Fig. 264.** If the point is sharper than a right angle, as on some very pointed collars, it will be necessary to trim the seam along each side. **Fig. 265.** If the fabric ravels easily, it may be useful to make one stitch

Flat-felled seams are used for added strength and a tailored appearance on sport clothes. There are several ways to make them, but the surest way to achieve a smooth effect is to first make a plain seam with the fabric right sides together. Press the

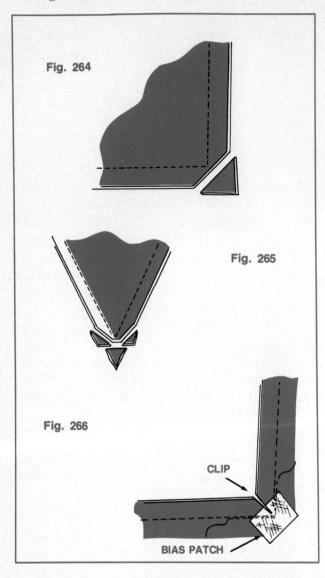

Fig. 264

Fig. 265

Fig. 266

CLIP

BIAS PATCH

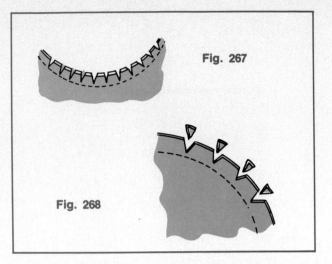

Fig. 267

Fig. 268

across the end of this type of very sharp point. (See Collars, pg. 602 for further suggestions.)

If the corner is an inside one, such as on a square neck, it may be helpful to lay a small bias piece of thin fabric on the seam as it is stitched to prevent raveling. Stitching around the corner a second time, exactly on the first stitching but with a slightly smaller stitch, will also reinforce the corner. Clip directly to the stitching at the corner before turning the piece right side out. **Fig. 266.**

TREATMENT FOR CURVED SEAMS

The rules for treatment of concave and convex curved seams are simple. A concave curve, such as a round neck, must be clipped at intervals of about $1/2$ inch to enable the seam to "give" enough for the piece to be turned smoothly right side out. **Fig. 267.** A convex curve, such as a

scallop or Peter Pan collar, must have narrow notches of fabric removed every $1/4$ to $1/2$ inch so that the seam will not fold over and form lumps when the piece is turned right side out. **Fig. 268.** Test the theory with pieces of paper or firmly woven cloth for a clearer understanding.

SELVAGE (also Selvedge)

A narrow, woven edge on fabric which prevents fraying is called a selvage. It is not necessary to trim off this edge when using the fabric on the straight grain. Leaving it on along zipper seams is especially advantageous, as it keeps the fabric from raveling and jamming the zipper. On draperies and other areas with long, straight seams, a selvage edge may seem to pull slightly so, clip it sharply every 6 inches to prevent puckering.

SEWING MACHINES

For those who are just beginning to sew, it is a good idea to rent or borrow a sewing machine for a period of time to discover general likes and dislikes. That will, at least, provide a point of reference when choosing a rather expensive piece of equipment. For most people, a sewing machine is a one-time investment so, it is advisable to purchase a good one which will bring enjoyment rather than one which will not last.

If an old machine is available, take it to a good repairman and have it put in working order to use for a while. The beginner will need nothing more than a machine which sews forward (and possibly backstitches) evenly. It should also have an adjustment for the stitch length.

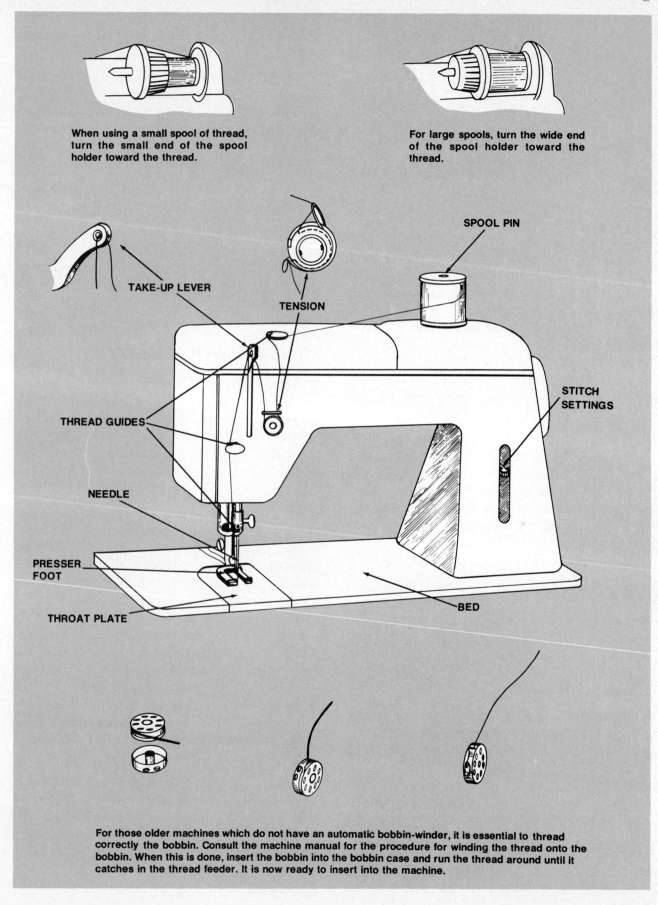

When using a small spool of thread, turn the small end of the spool holder toward the thread.

For large spools, turn the wide end of the spool holder toward the thread.

SPOOL PIN

TAKE-UP LEVER

TENSION

STITCH SETTINGS

THREAD GUIDES

NEEDLE

PRESSER FOOT

THROAT PLATE

BED

For those older machines which do not have an automatic bobbin-winder, it is essential to thread correctly the bobbin. Consult the machine manual for the procedure for winding the thread onto the bobbin. When this is done, insert the bobbin into the bobbin case and run the thread around until it catches in the thread feeder. It is now ready to insert into the machine.

The day will come when a shiny, new machine, with a variety of interesting stitches and tricks is needed. The factors to consider before buying are: Will it be used for heavy-duty work, slipcovers, deck furniture, etc? Will it be used for children's clothes and the type of things which look well with machine embroidery? Will there be enough space to leave the machine set up or will it have to be put away for periods of time? Should it be portable so that it can be taken to a summer cottage or for extended periods away from home? Will its function be to mend a few simple rips and tears?

If a heavy-duty machine which also makes good buttonholes and does embroidery is desired, think of the machine as a major investment and to be prepared to pay for the best. Research carefully, shop, try out, ask friends and read consumer reports. After purchasing such a machine, be sure to take advantage of any help in learning to use it properly. Have any problems corrected before the service contract or warranty runs out.

For less demanding sewing, there are several good medium-priced machines which will do the basic zigzag stitch, make buttonholes and blind hems. These even come in portable form for the traveler or small apartment dweller. So-called "bargain machines" are almost never a bargain! They are especially frustrating to a young child learning to sew; children are better off with a good used machine.

USE AND MAINTENANCE

A sewing machine, like a car, performs better if the owner uses it carefully. Read the manual and do some practice sewing. The most important factor is to thread top and bobbin correctly! Learn to do this so that it is automatic.

Be sure that the needle is inserted correctly and change it when there is any reasonable doubt that it is sharp. There is a long groove on one side of the needle and the thread always enters the eye from that side. Machine needles may thread from the front, left or right, depending upon the model. Again, check the manual for exact instructions. Further information on types of needles can be found under needles, page 647. The machine should be oiled sparingly, but often, following the directions in the manual. For

several days after oiling, remember to wipe the area of the face plate and needle before beginning to sew.

If the machine is complex, start by using it for straight sewing to become accustomed to the position of the stitch gauge, backstitch and tension. Then, referring to the manual, experiment with the various zigzag stitches, built-in buttonholers, stretch-knit stitches, etc.

A complicated machine should be used only by the person who is thoroughly familiar with all its operations.

When a machine is not in use, it should be covered to keep out dust and dirt. Clean it often, especially after sewing on fuzzy fabrics. The vacuum cleaner is ideal for cleaning the bobbin area under the face plate.

PROBLEMS TO RECOGNIZE

If the stitch looks rough and loopy, the tension needs adjustment. "Rough" on the underside or bobbin side means that the tension should be tightened. "Rough" on the top side means that the tension should be loosened. Move the tension only one number or $1/8$ inch at a time and check again.

There are several factors which cause the thread to break — the needle positioned backwards or not pushed all the way up into the shaft; the tension is too tight; the spool is backwards on a machine which has a horizontal spindle (causing the thread to catch in the notch in the end of the spool); or, some part of the mechanism for zigzag, etc. has not been locked fully into place. Check all of these items and if the thread still breaks (and it is not a left-over spool from years past), completely rethread the machine and the bobbin to make sure that the thread is not caught at some point. If this doesn't work, it is a good idea to have a service man check the machine.

If the top thread does not pick up the bottom one to form a stitch, the needle may be in backwards or threaded incorrectly; the machine may need oiling and cleaning; or, the thread may be of a synthetic type which the machine rejects. If this happens once in a while, but becomes steadily worse over a period of time, it is probably because the timing mechanism needs setting. In this case, the machine is ready to go in for general repairs and a thorough cleaning and adjusting by a professional.

SHIRRING

Decorative gathering which is run in several rows is called shirring. It is used around waistlines, on puffed sleeves and on yokes. The best way to make it smooth and even is to sew the gathering lines with a large machine stitch. Mark the rows with chalk, using a ruler or notched cardboard to keep them even. **Fig. 269.** Be sure the bobbin is full before beginning!

After the shirring is pulled to the correct size and smoothed out evenly, it can be made more stationary by working an embroidery stitch over each line. A chain stitch or featherstitch is especially suitable. Such areas as cuffs or waistlines are often stayed by putting a band of lining fabric underneath and catching it in place by hand. **Fig. 270.**

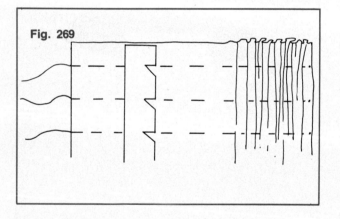

Fig. 269

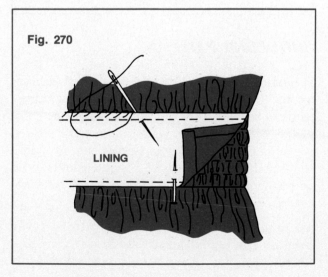

Fig. 270

LINING

SHIRT TAILORING

Shirts have a very special tailored look which depends on a few tricks of assembly — flat-felled seams and pressing as each stage is completed. One advantage of shirt tailoring is that everything is all machine finished — hems, buttonholes, collars, cuffs and facings.

Flat-Felled Armholes: See Seams, page 664, for flat-felling. Remember that only a true shirt pattern which shows flat-felled armhole seams can be finished with a flat fell around the armhole. Any other armhole seam is too curved. Shirts are assembled in a special order so that the armhole seam is made and finished before the side seam is stitched.

Set in the sleeve in the usual manner. Press the seam toward the body of the shirt. Clip the trimmed layer of the seam along the curve, almost to the stitching. Clip the long layer of the seam along the curve to a depth of about 1/4 inch. **Fig. 271.** Turn under the edge and baste, stretching the fabric slightly to make it lie flat. Machine stitch and press lightly.

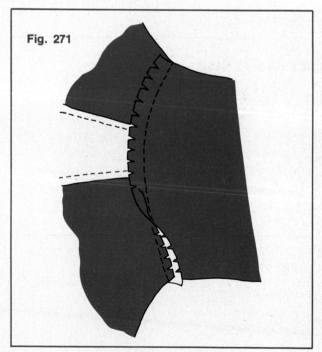

Fig. 271

YOKES

If a shirt has a yoke, it is usually lined with self fabric if the shirt is lightweight. In the case of a heavy wool or corduroy shirt-lining fabric is best. The cuffs and neckbands on heavy shirts are also somewhat easier to handle if the inner layer or facing is made of a light fabric. Be sure that all the fabrics used, including interfacings, are compatible and equally preshrunk.

BUTTONHOLES

Machine-made buttonholes are especially suited for shirt tailoring. The buttonholes in a banded shirt always run up and down, and in a plain front shirt, they run either way. **Fig. 272.** In a man's shirt, buttonholes are always in the left side.

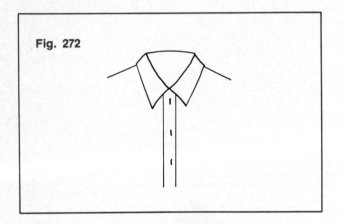

Fig. 272

SLEEVE FINISH

A few patterns for men's shirts still include a rather complex and very attractive sleeve-slash finish with a wide overlap. There will be complete directions in the pattern; remember to transfer all pattern markings clearly to fabric and to turn and press on the exact lines indicated. **Fig. 273.**

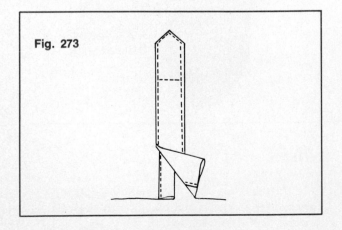

Fig. 273

Easy fake sleeve placket: If it is necessary slash placket altogether on a shirt-type sleeve, make two marks about 1¼ inches apart in the area where the slash is indicated. Run a row of stay stitching along the seam line for about 2½ inches, sewing beyond these marks at each end. **Fig. 274.** On the marks, clip up to the stay stitching. Turn up the 1¼-inch section on the wrong side of the sleeve. Hem it by hand or machine, anchoring the raw ends firmly. **Fig. 275.** Attach the cuff with the overlap end at one mark and the underlap extension starting at the other mark, as shown. **Fig. 276.** Finish the cuff in the usual manner and press.

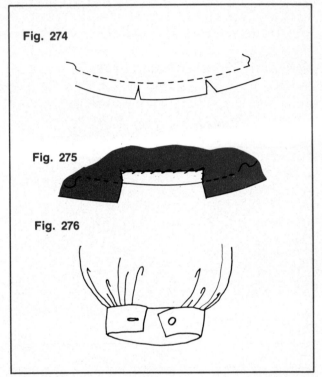

Fig. 274

Fig. 275

Fig. 276

SHOULDER PADS

Shoulder styles, like all other aspects of fashion, change from time to time and the seamstress tends to think that shoulder pads have gone completely out of use. However, most well-tailored coats and suits with set-in sleeves have at least a slight padding. People with shoulder deformities will find padding very useful to correct the appearance.

To make a full-size shoulder pad, use the diagram as a pattern. It can be made as small as is necessary. Build the pad in layers with a firmly woven interfacing on top and a firm, thin lining fabric on the bottom. In between, put as many layers of cotton batting as needed, usually from three to six. Put several strips of 1-inch wide batting along the armhole edge between the other layers. When the layers are complete, hold the pad rolled over the hand with the interfacing uppermost and working first along the armhole edge, catch stitch all layers together with rows of large stitches. **Fig. 277.**

If the pad is to go into a tailored, lined garment, it should be securely basted in place along the armhole seam with double thread. If it is to go into an unlined garment, first fold a bias piece of matching lining fabric over the raw pad at the armhole edge and stitch around the curved side. **Fig. 278.** Bind the raw edge if desired. Then, hand tack it into place in the garment; thus, making it removable for washing or cleaning.

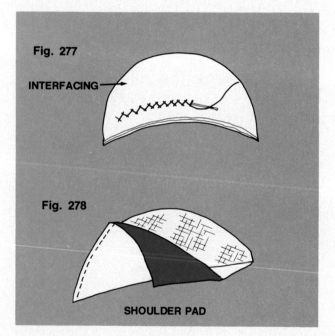

Fig. 277

INTERFACING

Fig. 278

SHOULDER PAD

SLASHES

It is often necessary to make a sharp slash into fabric to create a neck or sleeve opening, or to permit a piece such as a Gusset, page 620, or a Godet, page 628, to be inserted. To make it possible to slash to the end of the marked area and still have a tiny piece of fabric strong enough to stitch on, it is necessary to stay stitch along the seam lines, making one stitch across at the end of the slash. **Fig. 279.**

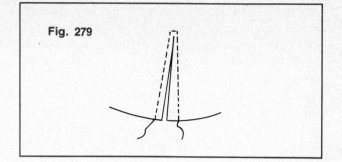

Fig. 279

SLEEVES (Set-in)

The classic sleeve and the one which takes the most care in handling for a professional effect is the set-in sleeve with the smooth shoulder line. The only trick is in using an ease thread properly. On the sleeve pattern piece, there will be markings, usually notches, with a notation saying to ease between these marks. Run a machine ease thread exactly along the seam line in this area. (Some patterns suggest that the ease be broken off for a space of about 1 inch at the crown of the sleeve and started over. If the ease thread is run all the way across and not pulled in that area at the top, there will be half the number of loose thread ends to deal with.)

Before pulling the ease thread, pin the sleeve right sides together with the armhole, carefully matching underarm, shoulder mark and notches. **Fig. 280.** There will be about $1/2$ to $3/4$ inch of fullness along each side of the sleeve cap. Turn the fabric so that the sleeve is uppermost; pull the ease thread gently from each end until it fits into the

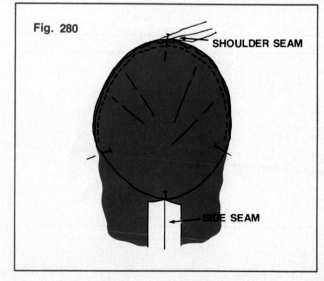

Fig. 280

SHOULDER SEAM

SIDE SEAM

armhole. Do not try to ease the inch at the top where the sleeve is almost straight grain; it eases with very little effort along the sides where it is bias. Distribute the ease and pin the sleeve to the armhole at intervals of about 1 inch. **Fig. 281.** The sleeve may either be basted in and then stitched or it can be stitched as is with the pins in. Pull the fabric slightly to each side across the line of stitching to hold the fabric flat and taut as it runs under the needle. This will help prevent puckers from forming as it is stitched.

Check to make sure that the sleeve is in smoothly. Make another row of stitching 1/8 inch in toward the raw edge from the first one, still holding the fabric as smooth as possible. Trim a scant 1/4 inch from the raw edge of the armhole all around. Press along the seam with the sleeve still in the same position in which it was stitched. *Do not flatten the seam from outside.* **Fig. 282.**

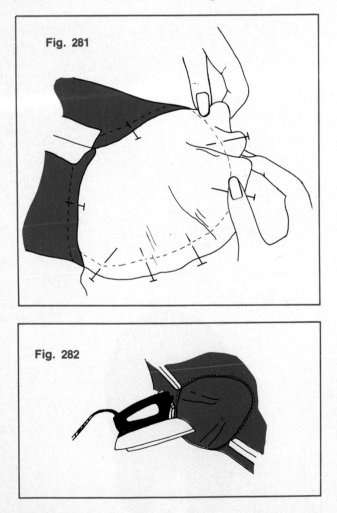

Fig. 281

Fig. 282

Puffed sleeves: Puffed sleeves are handled exactly like any other set-in sleeves, except that they

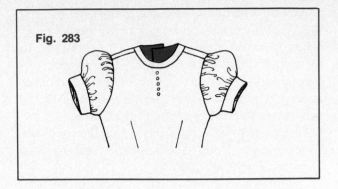

Fig. 283

are easier. Run two rows of machine stitching for gathers and pull them up after the sleeve is pinned in at the four marked points. Machine stitch over the gathers, keeping them distributed evenly. No pressing is needed. **Fig. 283.**

SNAP FASTENERS

A smooth fastening for small areas can be achieved with snaps which come in a variety of sizes. The ball half of the snap should go on the overlap side of the closing and the socket half on the underlap. **Fig. 284.** Sew the ball half in place using a whipping stitch. Sew through each of the four holes in the snap, catching the facing and interfacing of the garment, but not sewing through the surface layer of fabric. Push the ball down hard on the underlap piece so that it makes a slight mark in the fabric where the socket half is to be sewn. Sew the socket in place through all four holes and all layers of fabric.

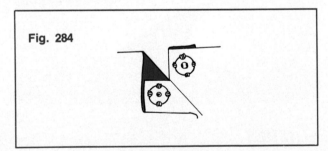

Fig. 284

STAY STITCHING

One way to control areas of fabric which might stretch or fray is to stay stitch with a single line of machine stitching. Do this as soon as the pattern is removed from each piece of fabric, being sure not to stretch the area while stitching. When stay stitching very sheer, hard-to-manage fabrics, cut a strip on tissue paper to size, mark the line to be

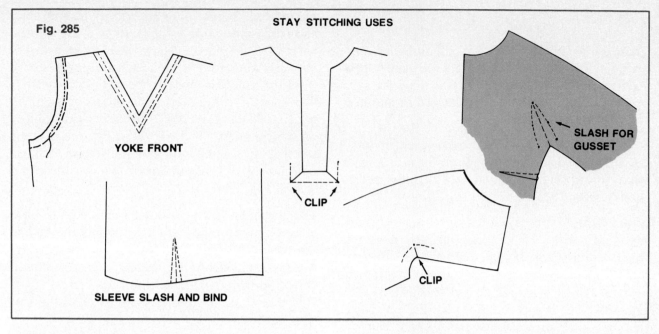

Fig. 285 STAY STITCHING USES

YOKE FRONT

SLASH FOR GUSSET

CLIP

CLIP

SLEEVE SLASH AND BIND

stitched and lay it on the fabric. Stitch through the tissue and fabric and then, tear away the tissue. The stitching should always be just inside the seam (toward the raw edge) from the seam line so that it will be hidden in the seam. Below are examples of places where stay stitching is useful. **Fig. 285.**

STAY TAPE

If a more permanent means of reinforcement than stay stitching is necessary, stitch narrow tape along the seam line at the time the seam is made.

This is useful in places where there is considerable strain on the garment or where the seam is eased or gathered to a specific measurement.

Use ¼-inch cotton twill tape (be sure that it is preshrunk), ¼-inch linen tailor's tape or ribbon seam binding folded along the center to a width of ¼ inch. Hold it over the pinned or basted seam and stitch through all layers at once. It is easier to keep the tape centered over the seam if it is guided by hand rather than being pin basted in place. Below are examples of places where stay tape is useful. **Fig. 286.**

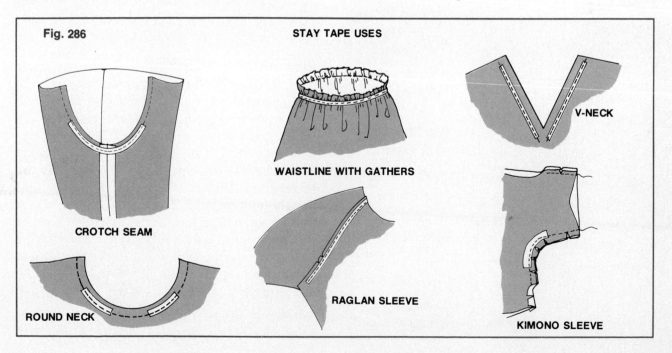

Fig. 286 STAY TAPE USES

CROTCH SEAM

WAISTLINE WITH GATHERS

V-NECK

ROUND NECK

RAGLAN SLEEVE

KIMONO SLEEVE

STITCHES

There are several hand stitches commonly used in dressmaking and tailoring. There are many more used in embroidery which may at times, be applied to clothing. These are discussed in another chapter.

Running stitch: This is the basic, even in-and-out stitch used to join two layers of fabric in a seam. If it is long and easy to pull out, it is called basting. **Fig. 287.**

Slip stitch: A running stitch done between two layers of fabric, rather than through them, is called a slip stitch. If a piece of fabric has been turned under, overlapped and pinned to another piece of fabric, it can be slip stitched into place. **Fig. 288.** This is a good way to handle patterned fabrics where an exact match of the design is desired.

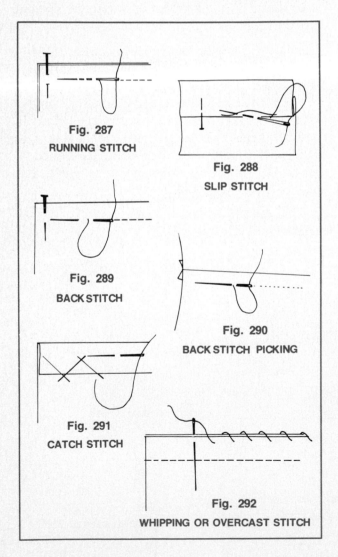

Fig. 287
RUNNING STITCH

Fig. 288
SLIP STITCH

Fig. 289
BACK STITCH

Fig. 290
BACK STITCH PICKING

Fig. 291
CATCH STITCH

Fig. 292
WHIPPING OR OVERCAST STITCH

Backstitch: When more security is needed in a seam than the running stitch will give, use a backstitch. Put the needle down through both layers of fabric and bring it up as for a running stitch. Take the needle back half the length of that stitch and insert it; bring it up again the same length as the first stitch. **Fig. 289.** A backstitch picking is used for zippers which are set in by hand. Take a stitch about $1/4$ inch long underneath and then, go back on top only about one or two threads of the weave. **Fig. 290.**

Catch stitch: When hand stitching needs to have some elasticity, especially in knits and bias fabric, use the catch stitch. This is done by inserting the needle from right to left, then bringing the thread down, moving slightly to the right, crossing the first thread. Take another small stitch to the left, then up and over to the right. **Fig. 291.**

Whipping or overcast stitch: The stitch used most on hems and also over raw edges to prevent fraying is the whipping or overcast stitch. Put the needle under the fabric from right to left, perpendicular to the edge being stitched, bring the thread up over the fabric and take the next stitch like the first one, $1/4$ to $1/2$ inch away. **Fig. 292.** You may work along the edge, either toward or away from yourself.

Lock stitch: This stitch is like the whipping stitch except that the thread is not allowed to go over the edge but is held to the left so that it is under the needle. **Fig. 293.** This forms a lock around the next stitch as the thread is pulled up.

Blind stitch: A blind stitch can only be done where there are several layers of fabric to hide the under part of the stitch or where that part of the stitch will be entirely on the wrong side of the fabric. It is used to hold down a folded or finished edge, such as the lining in a tailored jacket or the edge of a patch pocket. Bring the needle up through the folded edge, over the edge and directly into the other fabric, making the tiniest possible stitch. Run the needle under that layer of fabric for about $1/4$ inch and bring up through the folded edge again. The stitch pattern continues in, up, over, as invisibly as possible along the edge. **Fig. 294.**

Buttonhole stitch: The raw edges of buttonholes are encased with a very tight, closely placed stitch

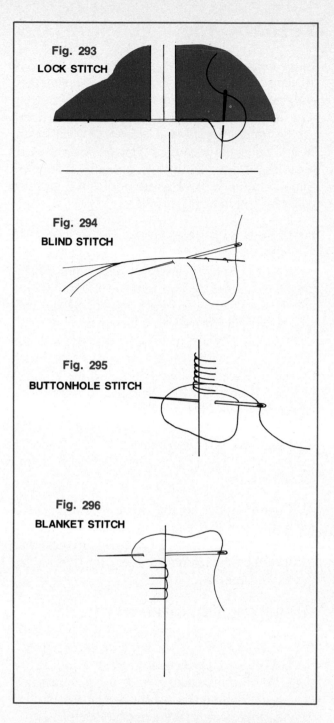

Fig. 293
LOCK STITCH

Fig. 294
BLIND STITCH

Fig. 295
BUTTONHOLE STITCH

Fig. 296
BLANKET STITCH

worked farther apart than the buttonhole stitch and deeper into the fabric than either buttonhole or lock stitch. It is often worked over an edge like a buttonhole stitch, but the thread goes under the needle only once, as in lock stitch and forms a simple loop, not a "purl." **Fig. 296.**

TAB FRONTS

An attractive tailored opening, used in shirts and shirtwaist dresses, is the tab front. It can be made in any one of several different ways and the accurately marked pattern pieces and directions are in the pattern. **Fig. 297.** However, following are a few tips for additional help. Mark the fabric from the pattern piece very carefully. Mark the garment front from the pattern piece and stay stitch around the lower corners before clipping or stitching. As accuracy is the key to success on a tab front, measure as each stage is begun to keep everything to its exact dimensions. Trim and press with care.

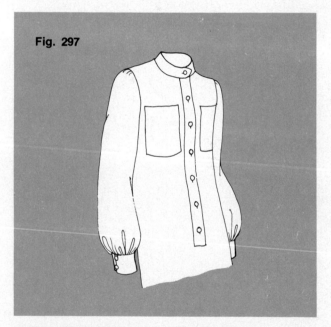

Fig. 297

which creates a hard-knotted or "purled" edge which wears well. Put the needle behind the cut edge of the fabric and perpendicular to it, bring it up about $1/8$ inch from the edge through a loop of the thread which is thrown completely around the needle. Pull the stitch up tight so that the loop forms the "purl" at the edge of the buttonhole. **Fig. 295.**

Blanket stitch: The blanket stitch is similar to both the lock stitch and the buttonhole stitch. It is

TAILOR TACKS

Thread loops, called tailor tacks, made by hand through both the paper pattern and both layers of fabric are the most accurate way of transferring markings. Choose thread colors which contrast with the fabric — a different color for each type of symbol on the pattern such as large dots, small dots, etc.

Use a double thread in the needle and no knot in the end. Lay the cut-out piece with the pattern still pinned to it on a flat surface. Take a small stitch down and back up through the fabric and the pattern at marked point. Leave an end of about 2 inches, take another small stitch across the first one and pull up to leave a loop of about 1 inch. Cut off thread to leave another 2-inch end. **Fig. 298.**

When all the markings are completed, unpin the pattern and tear it gently off each tack, holding the thread tightly in the other hand. This will leave a small hole in the pattern, but makes the tailor tack more secure than if the loop is cut. Now, pull the fabric layers apart to the length of the loop and clip the threads between. There will be identical markings on both pieces of fabric. **Fig. 299.**

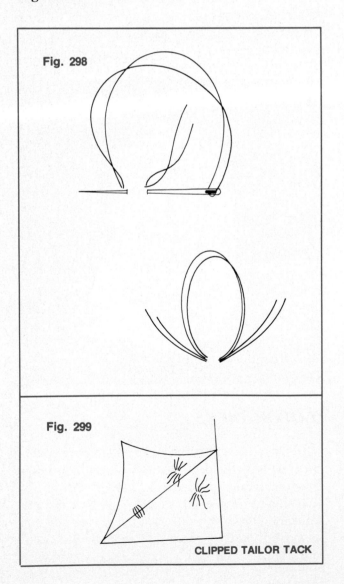

Fig. 298

Fig. 299

CLIPPED TAILOR TACK

TAILORING TIPS

In the tailoring of a lined garment such as a coat, all the sewing knowledge should be remembered and carried out even more carefully. Marking and fitting are even more important when there are so many layers and pieces to deal with. Bound buttonholes and all types of pockets are of great importance in tailored garments. There are some differences and some additional tips on tailoring which are found here.

PATTERN FITTING

A coat or jacket which will go over other clothes must have extra ease allowance in it. Don't panic and buy a larger size; when measuring the pattern, it will be apparent that the pattern has more inches in it already than a dress pattern in the same size. A jacket should have a 4 to 5-inch bust allowance and a coat should have 5 inches or more. Remember that the hip of a coat or long jacket must go over a skirt or perhaps a long sweater. It will need, at the very least, 3 inches more than the hip measurement. Add an extra $1/2$ inch to the "across shoulder back and front" measurements.

Add about 1 inch to the sleeve measurement at the upper arm and expect the entire sleeve to be wider in shaping as it goes down to the wrist. Most of the other standard alterations should remain the same.

SHAPING A TAILORED GARMENT

If a coat or jacket is to keep its shape, it will probably need underlining or interfacing, or both. Another alternative is to use a lightweight canvas interfacing throughout the entire garment as a combined interfacing and underlining.

If the fabric is firm enough, or the shape of the garment needs to be a bit softer, the underlining may not be necessary. Strips of interfacing cut on the bias may be used in the hem edges. Cut these strips 1 inch wider than the hem is to be. Lay them in the body of the jacket and in the sleeve so that they extend $1/2$ inch into the hem and $1/2$ inch above the point where the hem edge will meet the garment. Pin them in place and catch stitch loosely along each edge. Turn the hems up

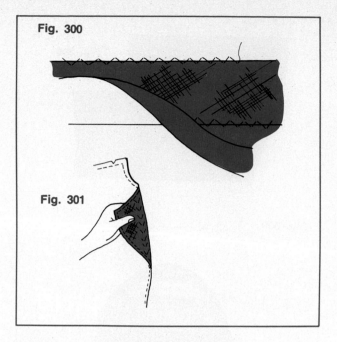

Fig. 300

Fig. 301

against the strips and Hem (see page 631) them into place. Let the stitches catch the interfacing strip only. **Fig. 300.**

When putting interfacing into tailored collars or lapels, keep the area rolled in the shape that it will be when worn. The interfacing will go in the *under collar* and the *body (not the facing)* of the jacket. This means that the pieces will be rolled over the hand with the interfacing uppermost. Starting at the neck edge of the collar and the "roll line" of the lapel, work loose rows of catch stitching until the space to the edge seam has been filled. **Fig. 301.** This will make the collar and lapel take the desired shape. **Fig. 302.**

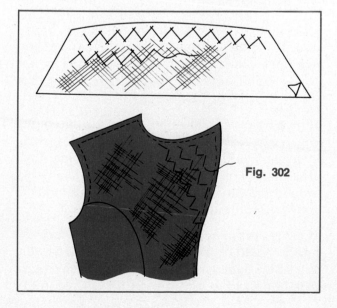

Fig. 302

SPECIAL TAILORED COLLAR CONSTRUCTION

Stitch the under collar to the jacket and the upper collar to facing, being careful to match all marks and notches. Keep seams exactly ⅝ inch. **Fig. 303.** Stop stitching and backstitch at the mark nearest the front edge of the collar (usually, but not always, the center front) leaving free the seam allowance on the front end of the collar. **Fig. 304.** Trim interfacing along seam and clip out

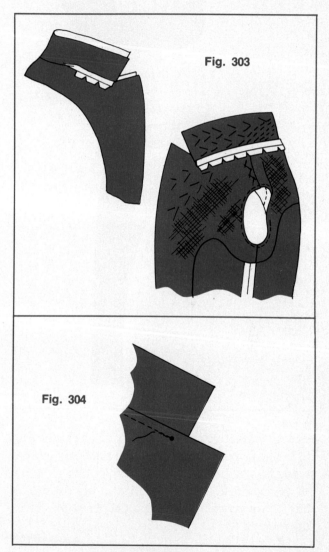

Fig. 303

Fig. 304

bulky corners at seam intersections. **Fig. 305.** Clip curves and press seams open flat. Be sure to clip jacket and facing to the exact point of backstitching. **Fig. 306.**

Starting at the center back of the collars, pin the two pieces right sides together, being especially

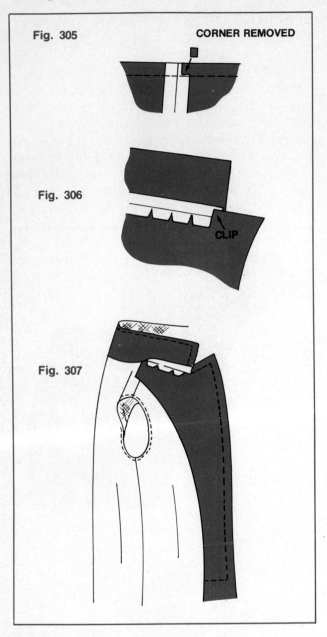

Fig. 305   CORNER REMOVED

Fig. 306   CLIP

Fig. 307

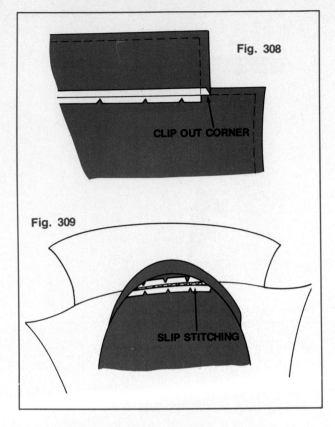

Fig. 308   CLIP OUT CORNER

Fig. 309   SLIP STITCHING

careful to match the ends of backstitching. **Fig. 307.** The upper collar on a good tailoring pattern is slightly larger than the under collar to allow for proper roll. In heavy fabrics, this difference may be increased by taking a deeper seam across the back of the under collar.

Stitch the seam all the way around the jacket front and the collar — from hem edge to hem edge — pivoting at the point of the backstitching at collar ends. Be sure to keep collar seams and lapel seams separated from each other at that point. Grade seams and clip corners, including the left over intersection corner at the lower front edge of the collar. **Fig. 308.** Turn jacket right side

out, understitch collar and lapels by hand. Slip stitch the two pressed-open neckline seams together loosely. **Fig. 309.**

COAT AND JACKET LINING CONSTRUCTION

The edge of the body lining of a tailored garment may be attached to the edge of the facing by hand with a blind stitch. Turn under the seam allowance on the edge of the lining and beginning at the center back and matching seams and markings, pin it to the $5/8$-inch seam line on the facing. Blind stitch catching only the facing, not the interfacing or jacket. **Fig. 310.**

It may be easier and smoother to pin the lining edge right sides together with the facing edge, matching markings carefully, and machine stitch all around. **Fig. 311.** Clip the seam on the lining around the curve at the back neck and press the entire seam toward the lining.

If the garment has a raglan or kimono sleeve, the lining should be tacked to the body with a swing tack at the underarm. Make a $1/2$-inch long swing tack by directions for Thread Carriers, (pg. 600),

Fig. 310

Fig. 311

Fig. 312

BASTING

and anchor it firmly to garment and lining in the sturdy seam intersection at the underarm.

If the garment has a set-in sleeve, the body lining of the jacket should be attached before the sleeve lining is set in.

After the shoulder pad, (see pg. 670) is sewn in place and the lining is sewn to jacket, baste the lining armhole to the jacket armhole. Keep the raw edges together and match all markings and seams. **Fig. 312.** The lining will seem slightly smaller than the jacket but the two must be kept together and the basting must be just inside the seam from the line of stitching which attaches the sleeve to the jacket. Trim a scant ¼ inch off the raw edge all around the armhole and clip the seam along the lower curve between the notches. **Fig. 313.** Turn under the seam allowance on top of the sleeve lining and baste it to itself near the turned edge. **Fig. 314.** Clip along the lower curve between the notches to relieve the tension. Pin the sleeve lining in place, matching the seams and markings and blind stitch it exactly on top of the basted line, catching deeply into all layers for added strength. **Fig. 315.**

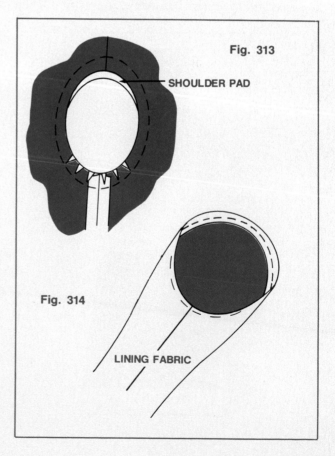

Fig. 313

SHOULDER PAD

Fig. 314

LINING FABRIC

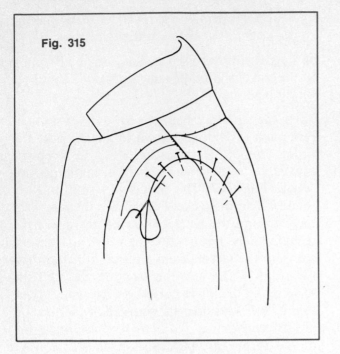

Fig. 315

HEMS AND FINISHES

With the facing lying away from body of garment, hem all the way across it and then fold the facing flat into place. **Fig. 316.** Slip stitch the lower edges together. In a heavy jacket, it may be

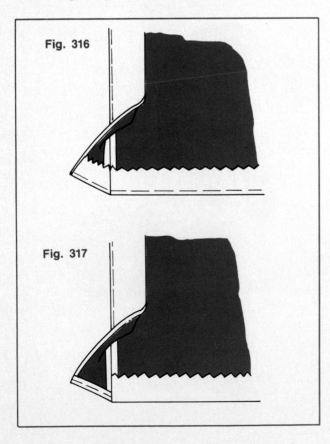

Fig. 316

Fig. 317

desirable to trim the hem in the facing to $^5/_8$ inch to avoid bulk in the hip area. **Fig. 317.** With matching thread, whip the raw edge of the facing down to the hem.

Mark the lining at the point where it appears below the finished jacket or sleeve edge. Turn it up $^1/_2$ inch above this marking and pin to hem. **Fig. 318.** Baste $^1/_2$ inch above the folded edge of the lining. Fold lining back along basting and slip stitch it to the hem, allowing this ease in lining length so that it will not pull. If soft pleats were allowed in the center-back and shoulder front of the lining, stitch them down about $1^1/_2$ inches by hand with a decorative catch stitch or feather stitch. **Fig. 319.** Give hems and pleats a very light steam pressing. Any tailored garment will be improved by having a good tailor or cleaner give it a proper hand pressing. However, if it has been pressed properly during the construction stages, the collar rolled correctly and the lapels are straight, it will need very little extra work.

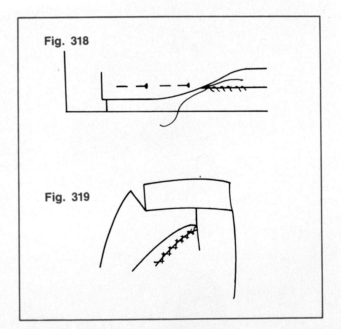

Fig. 318

Fig. 319

THIMBLES

There is more than just vanity involved in wearing a good silver thimble in the proper size. They are usually the most delicate and the easiest to handle of any kind of thimble available. Purchase one and form the habit of wearing it on the middle finger of the right hand (left, for those who are left-handed).

Its usefulness will rapidly become apparent, as it will help avoid wearing out the end of a finger.

THREAD

An in-depth discussion of thread seems almost useless, as the types and the fibers used seem to change constantly. Suffice to say that there are both cotton and synthetic threads, suitable for machine and hand sewing, now on the market. They are available in regular and heavy-duty weights in a variety of brands. Try various ones; thread selection is largely a personal choice. A good mercerized cotton still seems to knot less in hand sewing and cause less trouble in most machines. Silk thread is especially nice for hand finishing on silks and wools.

TOP STITCHING

A very tailored look can be achieved with top stitching done on the sewing machine and often with a heavier, more showy thread. Like so many simple-looking touches, it requires considerable practice. If it cannot be stitched almost perfectly, top stitching should be left out altogether.

Edge stitching is the easiest form of top stitching because the width of the presser foot is used as a guide against the edge to keep the rows even. **Fig. 320.** Many machines now have three needle positions so that when the edge of the foot is on the edge of the garment, the needle can be $1/8$, $1/4$ or $3/8$ inch from the edge. This is especially helpful as a top stitching guide. For wider widths, the fractional marking on the face plate of the machine can be used as a guide.

When top stitching is done along interior seams at a greater width than the presser foot, a strip of medium-weight paper can be used as a guide.

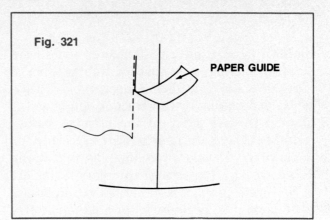

Fig. 321

PAPER GUIDE

Typewriter paper is an ideal weight. Cut it in a strip about 8 inches long and $1/2$ inch wide or however wide the stitching line is to be. Hold one edge of the paper against the seam and stitch along the opposite edge but, not through the paper. **Fig. 321.** Move the strip along as needed. An added benefit of this method, which makes it advantageous for edge stitching on soft fabrics, is that it prevents the fabric from pulling and creeping under the presser foot.

Top stitching should be done with a long machine stitch, about eight to the inch. If it is to be very showy, use silk buttonhole twist on the top of the machine; it is necessary to use it in the bobbin unless the stitching is along an edge which turns back so that both sides are visible. With the heavier thread, use a size 16 or 18 needle.

TUCKS

An interesting, decorative treatment for fine fabrics is tucking, which also is used like pleating or shirring for controlled fullness. Fabric can be tucked before the piece is cut so that an entire shirt front or sleeve, for instance, will be decorated with rows of stitched-down tucks. This is done easily along the grain line of gingham or striped dimity or by drawing faint parallel lines and using the presser foot to gauge the tuck width. Some sewing machines have a tucking attachment which helps in gauging width and distance.

If a pattern has tucks, measure and mark them very carefully to arrive at exactly the controlled fullness required. Sometimes, especially on very sheer fabrics, tucking by hand with a fine running stitch is easier than by machine.

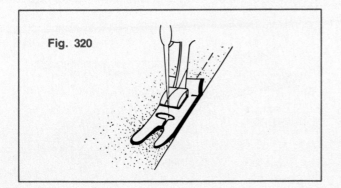

Fig. 320

UNDERLINING

Problem fabrics and very structured styles need the help of completely attached linings to make them have and keep their proper shape. This is called underlining or construction lining and is applied to each piece of the garment before assembly. There are fabrics made especially for underlining. These are very thin, but very strong and come in a large range of colors. Some are crisp for giving shape to princess lines and other fitted clothes; some are soft, for holding the easy shape of shifts and chemises in very soft fabrics. Underlinings have several side benefits: they help to prevent wrinkling; keep seams from pulling and splitting; and make wearing a slip unnecessary.

After cutting and marking the fabric pieces, use the same pattern pieces to cut the lining. Mark notches and centers on lining; it is not usually necessary to make other markings on both layers. If the lining is sheer, tailor tacks on the outer fabric will show through the lining clearly enough. It may be preferable to mark the lining with dressmaker's carbon and a tracing wheel and make only such markings as button and pocket placement on the outer fabric.

Lay the lining piece on a flat surface with outer piece wrong side down on top of it. Pin around the edges, being careful to keep the lining tight and the outer layer a little bit full. Machine stitch the layers together all around, except across the hem. **Fig. 322.** There is usually less slipping if the

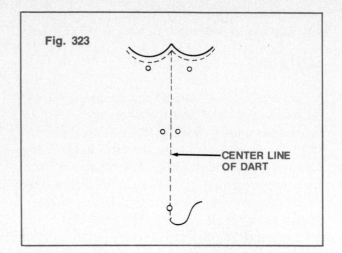

Fig. 323

CENTER LINE OF DART

garment is stitched with the smooth, firm lining fabric uppermost on the machine. Keep the stitches long (about eight to the inch) and inside the seam allowance — about 3/8 inch from the raw edge. Pin and stitch along the center line of each dart to just beyond the end point; the last stitches can be removed after the dart is made. **Fig. 323.** Once the lining is in, forget it and handle the pieces as though they were one layer.

UNDERSTITCHING

Facings are held firmly in place with a row of stitching through the facing and seam, but not into the outer layer of the garment. This is called understitching and is described in detail in Facings (see pg. 617).

VELCRO

A nylon tape fastener, called Velcro, is made of two strips which lock together. This sewing aide is easier to use than zippers in slipcovers and other home sewing, as well as outer wear and children's play clothes. One strip is soft and velvety and the other has small sharp hooks like a

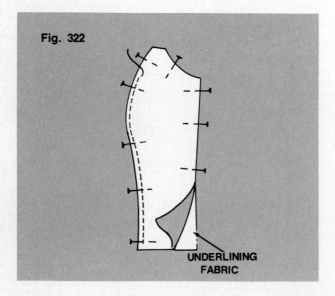

Fig. 322

UNDERLINING FABRIC

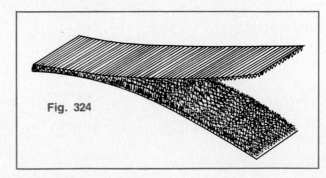

Fig. 324

burr so that they mesh together with an amazing amount of staying power. **Fig. 324.** The strips can be quite simply stitched by machine or by hand to overlap and underlap surfaces. Use a small 1-inch piece in place of a hook and eye on a skirt band. Replace zippers in fly-front pants and jackets with a strip the length of the opening. A few small pieces on slipcover arms and backs will hold matching protectors in place. Velcro has many varied uses. All that is necessary is a little imagination.

WAISTBANDS

Pants and skirts are frequently finished with stiffened waistbands which are easily seen and therefore, should be carefully fitted and finished. It is usually easier to fit them well if they are worked by correct measurements, rather than by a pattern. The stiffening can be made of grosgrain belting, grosgrain ribbon (always preshrink these before using) or of measured strips of interfacing, preferably nonwoven. This is one good use for iron-on interfacing.

Cut the fabric twice the desired finished width, plus two seam allowances and 3 inches longer than the waist measure. Cut the stiffening to the finished width and 3 inches longer than the waist measure. With chalk or light pencil, mark three lines on the wrong side of the fabric to represent the two seam lines and the exact center of the band where it will be folded. Lay the interfacing along the wrong side of the fabric, between the center fold line and one seam line. Machine stitch it in place along both edges. **Fig. 325.** This side of the band will go toward the body so the stitching will not show.

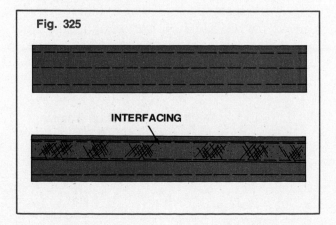

Fig. 325

INTERFACING

To be sure that the skirt or pants hang right, try on the garment with the seams stitched and the zipper in. Stand in front of a mirror and adjust the garment until the side seams hang straight. Place a string around the waist and mark along the string with pins. (It's easier if a friend will help, but it can be done alone.) This pinned line will be the seam line; stay stitch around it and trim the seam to $5/8$ inch. On many people, the waist dips in the back and correcting it at this point makes hemming a skirt a lot easier.

Fold the band and try it on. Mark the point where the $5/8$-inch seam allowance at one end, the overlap end, meets the underlap end. Pin the seam allowance on the unlined side to the marked seam on the top of the skirt or pants. The underlap and overlap markings should come at the top ends of the zipper. **Fig. 326.**

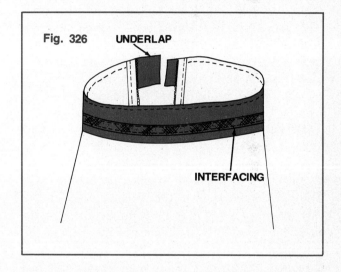

Fig. 326   UNDERLAP

INTERFACING

After the band is stitched into place, it is a good idea to trim the seam on the band slightly and clip the seam on the garment every 2 inches. Turn the band back, with right sides together, along the fold line and stitch across the ends. **Fig. 327.** Grade those seams in heavy fabrics and turn the band right side out. Fold under the seam

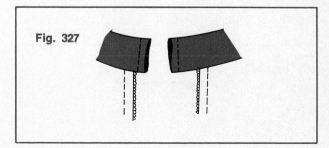

Fig. 327

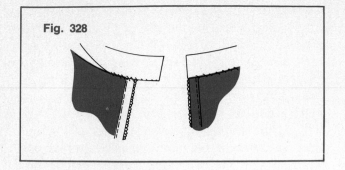

Fig. 328

allowance on the inside of the band and blind stitch it to the seam thickness just above the stitching line. **Fig. 328.**

WELT POCKETS

Types of welt pockets may vary from one pattern to another but certain problems and cures remain constant. The welt itself must be properly made, seams trimmed or graded (see Seams, pg. 664) and pressed to minimize bulk. The placement and the inside pieces, as well as the welt, must be carefully marked from the pattern after cutting. Each pattern will have fairly specific instructions for the pocket included in that pattern.

TIPS FOR ALL WELT POCKETS

Lay the welt in position right sides together with the garment and pin it in place. Machine baste along the seam line on the welt. At each end of this stitching line, it is very important that the needle drop exactly at the end of the welt — not one stitch short or one over. Backstitch for about three stitches directly along the line. Cut the raw corners off the welt, as shown. **Fig. 329.** Lay the pocket pieces, in the order given in the pattern, right side down over the marked area and pin them in place. Turn to the wrong side of the garment and stitch along the visible stitching which holds the welt. Turn exactly at the end of the backstitching to continue around the area indicated on the pattern, making an opening space about ¹/₂ inch wide as on a buttonhole pocket.

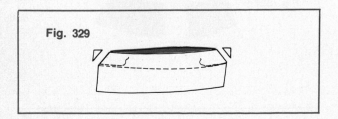

Fig. 329

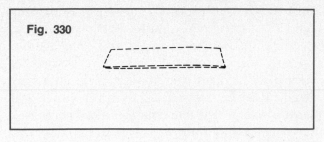

Fig. 330

One way of insuring that the welt will cover the hole is to slant the end lines in slightly, as shown, so that the area is not a true rectangle. **Fig. 330.**

Make a buttonhole cut on the pocket pieces and on the garment, but not into the welt seam. Turn the pocket through to the wrong side; the welt will stand up over the hole of its own accord. **Fig. 331.** Finish the inside of the pocket as described in Buttonhole Pockets, pg. 596. Blind stitch the ends of the welt in place.

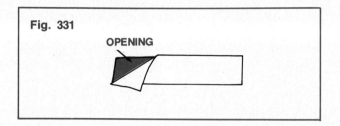

Fig. 331

OPENING

ZIGZAG

A type of stitching which somewhat revolutionized the world of sewing machines in mid-20th century is the zigzag. This means that the needle can move left and right, making a zigzag pattern of stitching useful for finishing, reinforcing and stitching on stretchy fabrics. **Fig. 332.** It has made blind hemming and buttonholes simple to do on home sewing machines. The more elaborate zigzag machines now include many pattern stitches based on the zigzag mechanism.

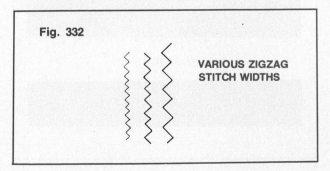

Fig. 332

VARIOUS ZIGZAG
STITCH WIDTHS

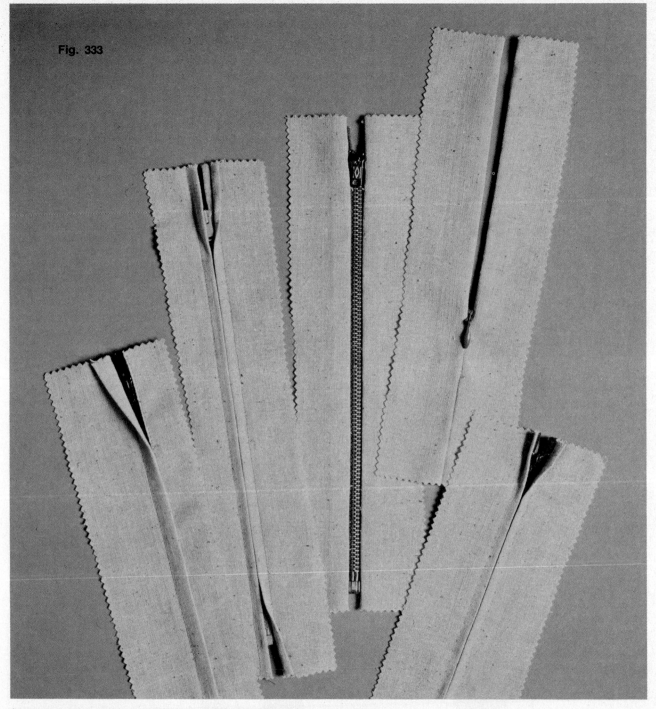

Fig. 333

ZIPPERS: from the left, overlapped, centered separating (jacket type), open faced separating, invisible, centered hand applied.

ZIPPERS

There are a number of ways to set zippers into garments. **Fig. 333.** The centered method or slot seam zipper is favored for fine dressmaking and may be finished by machine or by hand. The overlap is used primarily in skirts and pants and other sports clothes. The open-faced method is used in banlons and other lightweight knits and is useful in cushion covers, but the zipper color must match the fabric. Zippers can be applied either by the slot or open-faced method where there is no seam by making a Faced Placket, see pg. 657. Fly-front zippers for pants require extra pieces of fabric for facing and underlap, which will be given in the pattern. There will also be explicit instructions in the pattern and these vary considerably so that there is very little general instruction which can be given here. Just be sure to buy the correct length zipper and to transfer all markings accurately from pattern to fabric.

It is possible to cut off many types of zippers, practically all of the nylon or synthetic types, from the lower end. Overcast the coil firmly first and then, cut off the remaining zipper about ¹/₂ inch below the overcast area.

Any zipper installed in a seam should be put in before the waistband or neck facing is applied. It is best to leave an opening 1 inch longer than the zipper to allow for the ⁵/₈-inch seam to be taken at the top plus a little room to keep from crowding the zipper. If a zipper is crowded into too short a space, the fabric usually stretches to accommodate it and causes the zipper to ripple and bulge. The measurement of the zipper given on the package means the actual working part of the zipper — the teeth — not the tape. For a 7-inch zipper, leave an 8-inch space. Sew the seam up to that point and press it open flat; then, proceed with a centered zipper or an overlap zipper. See special instructions for the other types.

If a zipper crosses a waistline seam which is to be pressed all one way, a rather bulky seam intersection at the zipper makes for an unattractive installation. This can be prevented by clipping the seam (one layer only) as shown, 1¹/₄ inches back from the end of the seam, so that the seam can be pressed flat in the zipper area. **Fig. 334.**

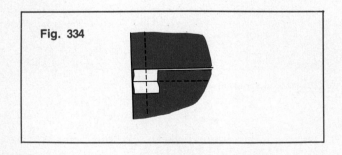

Fig. 334

CENTERED OR SLOT SEAM ZIPPER

There are three basic steps involved in installing a centered zipper. Since it is the most versatile type and very easy, it should be learned first.

Baste the zipper opening closed along the seam line with largest machine stitch. Press the basted seam open flat.

To insure correct placement of zipper, regardless of whether the final outside stitching is to be done by hand or machine, machine stitch one side of the zipper to one side of the seam. Open the zipper and lay it face down on the seam with the teeth running exactly along the basted seam line, starting 1 inch from the raw edge of the garment piece. Using the zipper foot on the machine and working from the bottom up, stitch one side of the tape to one layer of the seam — *not through to the right side of the garment.* **Fig. 335.**

Final stitching or top stitching is done on the right side of the fabric and can be done by hand or by machine. If the machine is used, stitch across the bottom below the teeth, turn ¹/₄ inch from the seam line and stitch up the side. Keep the stitching ¹/₄ inch away from the zipper, checking to insure that the fabric does not pull under the zipper foot. The zipper foot must always be away from the teeth of the zipper. When the first side is completed, slip the zipper foot over to the other side of the needle (most modern zipper foot attachments are reversible) and repeat the process, including the stitching across the bottom to add strength. **Fig. 336.**

For zippers in delicate fabrics, which are to be finished by hand, use the backstitch. This makes a very neat secure stitch and is much prettier on some fabrics than machine stitching. **Fig. 337.**

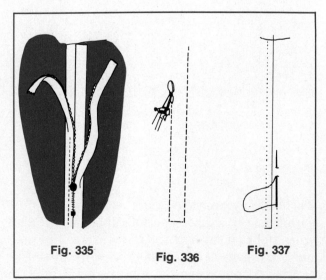

Fig. 335   Fig. 336   Fig. 337

OVERLAP ZIPPER

The side seams of skirts and pants, and sometimes the front seam (in place of a real fly front) are usually closed with an overlap zipper. In very heavy fabrics, a centered or an invisible zipper may make a flatter, smoother hip line.

On the underlap piece, run a row of machine stay stitching ½ inch from the raw edge. On the overlap piece, stay stitch on the ⅝-inch seam line. **Fig. 338.** Turn the fabric under along these lines and press. Lay the turned edge of the underlap side close to the teeth of the zipper and with

zipper foot, stitch very close to the turned edge. **Fig. 339.**

Bring the overlap piece into place, just covering the stitching on the underlap. The overlap may be basted in place by hand or on short zippers, it is possible to guide it by hand as it is stitched. Stitch across the bottom, below the teeth; turn the zipper foot ⅜ inch from the seam line and stitch up the side, staying ⅜ inch away. **Fig. 340.** Again, be careful that the fabric does not pull under the machine foot. The overlap may be finished by hand instead of machine, using the backstitch.

INVISIBLE ZIPPER

There are a number of invisible zippers available from different companies. Each company makes its own special zipper foot and they are not interchangeable. Very good directions come with each brand of zipper.

Most invisible zipper directions suggest that the entire seam be left open until the zipper is inserted and then stitch it up to the point of the zipper. On very stretchy fabrics, it may be better to stitch the seam, leaving an opening exactly the length of the zipper teeth. The zipper will still be set down 1 inch from the raw edge, but there will be a 1-inch tail of zipper hanging below the opening on the underside. By stitching the seam together first, margin of error is limited somewhat and will stand less chance of stretching the fabric on one side of the zipper.

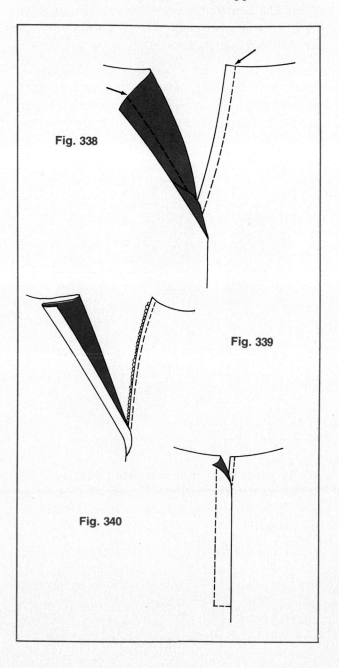

Fig. 338

Fig. 339

Fig. 340

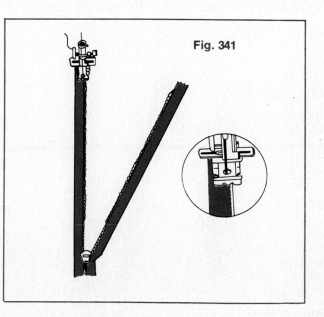

Fig. 341

The invisible zippers are stitched exactly the way a seam is made, with zipper tape and fabric right sides together. The zipper foot is slotted so that it runs along the teeth, making it possible to stitch very close to the teeth without getting close enough to jam the mechanism. **Fig. 341.** Make one or two practice runs, using a large machine stitch so that it can be pulled out and done over until the method is perfected. On difficult fabrics, such as velvet, it is always wise to put the zippers in with a large stitch first. Then, when it is correct, simply stitch over the same line with smaller stitches, leaving the large ones in place.

OPEN-FACED ZIPPER

A zipper applied in this way will have the teeth totally exposed so they must either match the fabrics or be of a decorative type. The large decorative ones — brass, plastic, etc — are generally used in jackets. This means that there is no seam to be sewn first. The teeth are usually very wide, so it will be necessary to take more than a 5/8-inch seam to compensate for this. If the open-faced zipper is used in a fine jersey or knit velour, use a lightweight synthetic one, for which it will be necessary to allow less than a 1/8-inch extra seam.

This method is really a matter of seaming a zipper in place, with the tape and fabric right sides together. Work with the zipper uppermost and use the zipper foot to stitch close to the teeth. **Fig. 342.** Allow a little more room between the stitching and the teeth than on the invisible zipper or, the stitching may jam the mechanism.

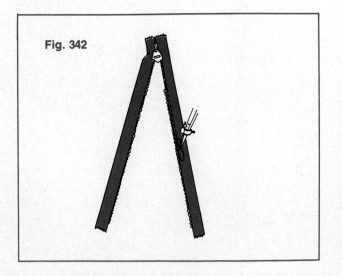
Fig. 342

ZIPPER IN A SLASHED PLACKET

It is possible to install a zipper where there is no seam by making a Faced Placket (see pg. 658). When the placket is completed and pressed, the zipper can then be installed by the centered or open-faced method. The only difference is that in the centered method, it is best to baste the zipper in place by hand on the outside of the fabric, without basting the opening together. Hand basting will be useful in the open-faced method, also.

FINISHING FACINGS OVER ZIPPER

When the zipper has been installed in the back neck of a garment, the facing should then be stitched around the neck.

Remember that the 5/8-inch seam has already been taken on the garment, but the 5/8-inch allowance on the end of the facing has not been used. The facing will stick out 5/8 inch beyond the

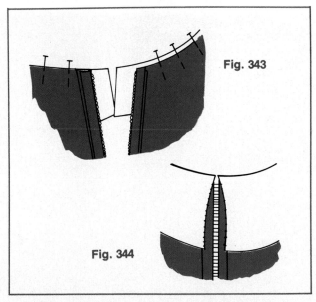
Fig. 343

Fig. 344

zipper when it is pinned in place. **Fig. 343.** *If it does not extend exactly this far, the neckline of the garment may be stretched, resulting in a homemade appearance!*

Finish the facing with understitching and cut off any zipper tape above the understitching. Turn the end of the facing under, 5/8 inch at the neck edge, slanting back to 3/4 or 7/8 inch at the lower edge of the facing. Pin it in place on the zipper tape and blind stitch it into place. **Fig. 344.**

SEWING PROJECTS

SEWING PROJECTS

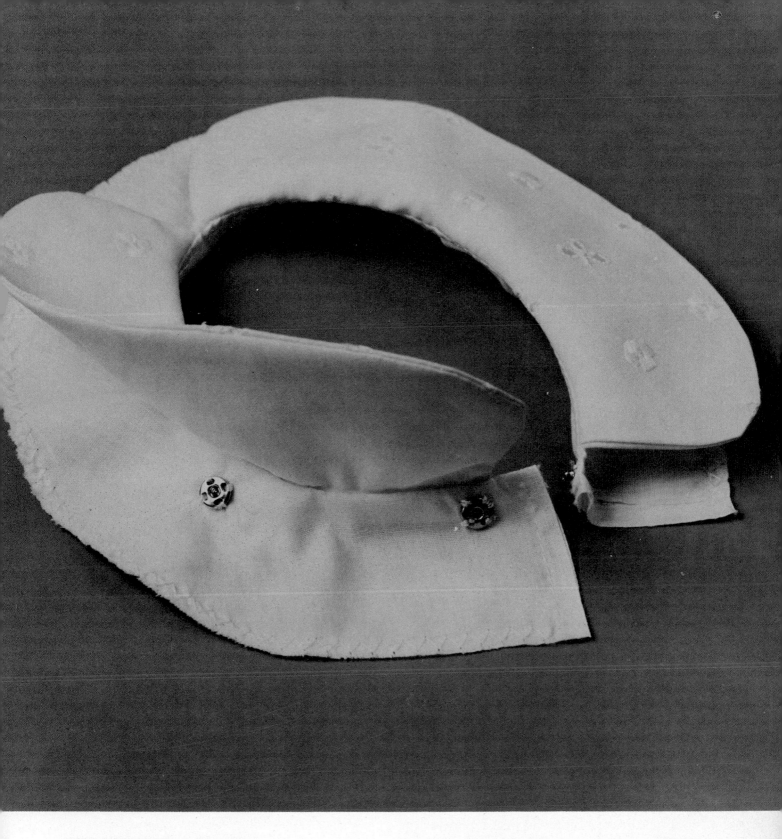

DETACHABLE COLLAR

It is sometimes convenient to have a detachable, washable collar on a dark dress. When the pattern has a **collar** and a **facing,** this can be done very easily. Make the dress and face the neck with a lightweight fabric without inserting the collar.

Cut two complete facings from the pattern. Make up both facings, make up the collar and insert it between the facings and stitch. Zigzag the outer edges together and sew a **snap** at the back neck to fasten the ends together. Sew snaps at the shoulders of dress and collar, as shown, to hold the collar in place.

SAFETY BACKPACK

Courtesy of Parents' Magazine

Every school child needs a place to carry school equipment. This easy to see backpack can be made of any sturdy sailcloth, but waterproof types are even better. The straps are fastened with overall buckles that allow for adjustment in length. The flap is fastened down with decorative **Grippers.**

The traditional octagon-shaped STOP sign can be replaced by all sorts of other traffic signs. You might try YIELD or PLAY AREA or SLOW. International signs, only beginning to be used here, have marvelous symbols instead of words. You can get a pamphlet of them from AAA.

Necessary Supplies: 1¹/₈ yards of 45-inch canvas or poplin fabric, bright yellow, ¹/₄ yard of contrast fabric (red, orange or black), 2 strap buckles, 6 grippers.

Use a ruler and chalk or pencil to mark out the several rectangular pieces for the bags (measurements given in inches):

Back and flap pieces	13¹/₄ x 29¹/₂
Front piece	13¹/₂ x 14¹/₄
Side inset	4¹/₂ x 37¹/₂
Cross brace	13¹/₄ x 3¹/₄
2 shoulder straps	3³/₄ x 25
4 short straps	3³/₄ x 4¹/₂

(⁵/₈-inch seams allowed on all)

Draw a traffic sign design about 8 or 9 inches square on contrast fabric. Allow 3 inches for hem at end of flap and pin design in place in center of flap. Set a simple zigzag stitch on machine to maximum width and fine length. Work zigzag over the lines drawn. Trim excess fabric away very close to stitching. Use bent-handled shears with the very fine point.

If fabric tends to buckle and pucker a great deal, try enclosing the working area in a large embroidery hoop. Or put a layer of lightweight Pellon® under the flap and trim it afterwards.

Fold all straps, right sides together, lengthwise and seam along side and across one end. Trim corner and turn with a new pencil or knitting needle. Press and top stitch ¹/₈ inch from edge.

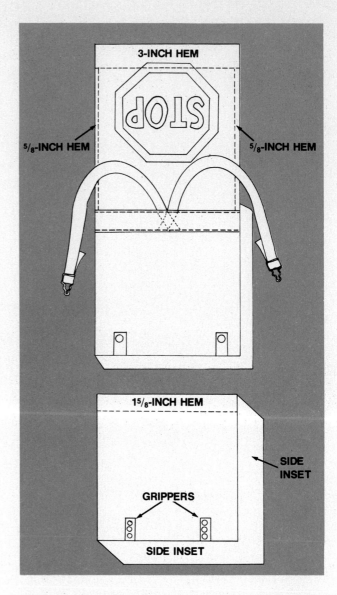

Fold seam allowances under along each side of cross brace. Set raw ends of shoulder straps in place at top center of back. Pin cross-brace piece over strap ends as shown and top stitch cross-brace in place. Make cross designs with stitching over strap ends for reinforcement.

Pin two short straps to lower edge of back and two to the lower edge of front. Hem upper edge of front 1⁵/₈ inches. Hem each end of side inset ⁵/₈ inch. Mark side inset at 12-inch intervals along both sides. Clip ¹/₂ inch deep at these points. Seam inset to front and back, matching clips to corners. Stitch with inset uppermost on machine to make turning the corners easier.

Backstitch firmly for strength at ends of inset and as stitching crosses short straps. Hem flap ⁵/₈ inch at sides and 3 inches at end.

For further strength, stitch the seams on the inside, then turn the bag right side out and press. top stitch about ⅛ inch from edge through 4 thicknesses. Work with the flat front or back uppermost in the machine and stop stitching and start over at each corner to avoid difficulty in turning corner.

Attach buckles and grippers as shown.

CAPE COD CURTAINS

Kitchens, bedrooms and bathrooms are brightened with ruffled tiebacks and kept private with the café panel underneath. The same directions can be used to make two tiers of cafés or the ruffled tiebacks alone. These cafés are hung on a spring rod inside the frame, but they can be made wider to hang on regular rods.

Cafés: Measure the desired width and divide it by two. Cut each panel one and one-half times this divided width, plus 4 inches for hems. Cut each panel the desired finished length, plus 8 inches for hems. Back the top edge — 6 inches deep — with a thin, firm **interfacing.** Turn under ½ inch along that edge and machine stitch it. Fold 5½ inches (to edge of interfacing), right sides together with the curtain. Plan and lightly draw a series of inverted **scallops** with ½-inch bridges between. The scallops should be about 6 inches wide and not more than 2½ inches deep. The first bridge at each end should be 2 inches from the side edges of the fabric. Example: A curtain cut 43½ inches wide will be finished 39½ inches wide with seven ½-inch bridges and six 6-inch scallops.

Make a strip of folded fabric (like **carriers**), finished ½ inch wide and long enough to make enough 3-inch pieces to fit one into each bridge. Fold each 3-inch piece, wrong sides together, and slip it into the curtain top at the bridge position. Stitch, clip and trim as shown and turn right side out.

Turn under ½ inch around the other three edges and machine stitch. Fold and press 1½-inch hems around these three sides, **mitering** the lower corners. Hem by hand or machine using a blind stitch.

Ruffled tieback curtains: Measure the desired width of the curtains and divide by two. Plan each panel twice this width. (Remember that the **ruffle** width is part of this total width.) Plan the finished desired length including ruffle and add 3 inches for hem at the top. For most standard-size windows, a 5-inch to 8-inch wide ruffle will be properly proportioned. The length of the ruffle should be about twice the length of the side and bottom edge to which it is to be attached. Piece and **gather** ruffles and apply with a **fake French seam.** Hem the plain edge of the curtain from the top through the ruffle with a 1-inch hem, preferably machine blind stitched. Hem the top with a ½-inch turn-under and a 2½-inch finished hem. Machine stitch the lower edge of hem and machine stitch along center of the hem to form 1¼-inch **casing** and 1¼-inch **heading.**

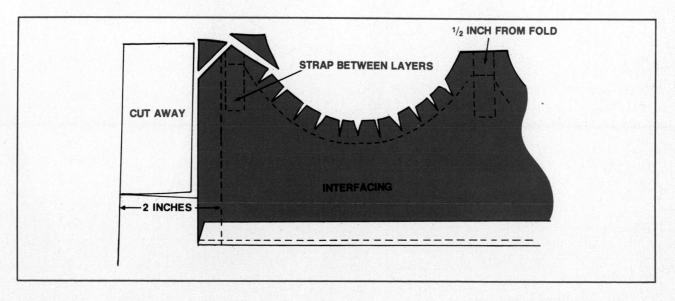

CUT AWAY

2 INCHES

STRAP BETWEEN LAYERS

½ INCH FROM FOLD

INTERFACING

CUDDLE BALLS

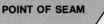
POINT OF SEAM

FULL-SIZE PATTERNS
ADD 1/4-INCH SEAMS

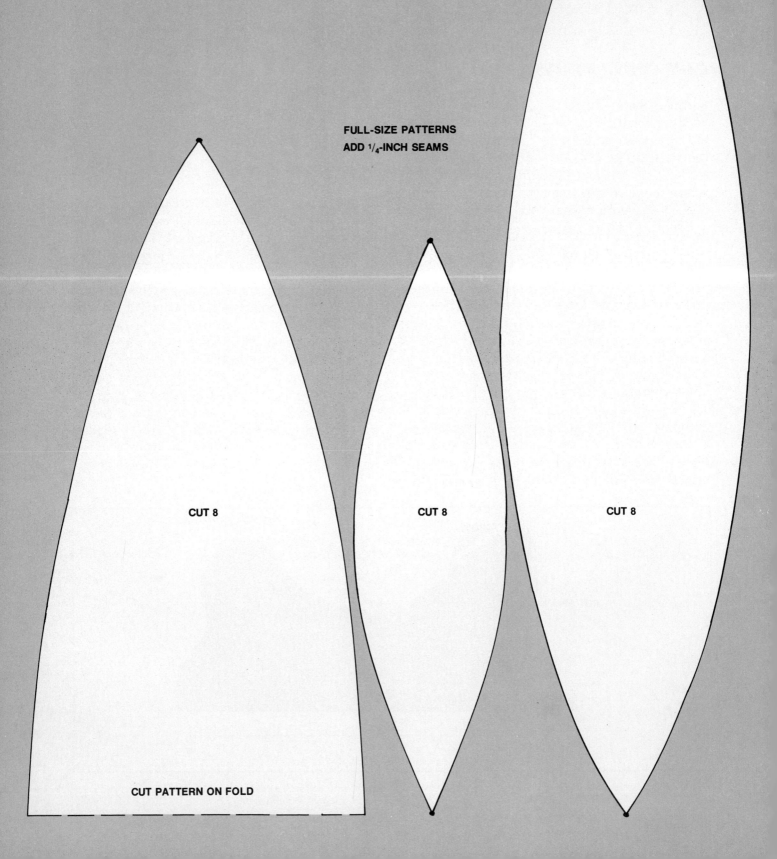

CUT 8

CUT 8

CUT 8

CUT PATTERN ON FOLD

CUDDLE BALLS

Make a large colorful ball for the baby, or a medium-sized ball for a toddler ready to play catch or a small felt one decorated with sequins for Christmas. Here are full-sized patterns for all three. The photograph shows the largest size.

The large ball takes ½ yard of 45-inch fabric and the middle-sized one takes ⅜ yard of 36-or 45-inch fabric. Either are also effective in patchwork scraps and the small one can be made from bits of felt. Four yards of **rickrack** or other **piping** is needed for the large ball and 3 yards for the medium ball. Stuff with polyester.

Trace desired size pattern onto fabric, adding ¼-inch seam allowance; cut out 8 pieces from this pattern. Seam four pieces together, right sides together, putting in piping, if desired. Stitch only to the point of the seam and backstitch as each two sections are joined. Join the 2 half balls together except for a 3-inch opening in one side for turning and stuffing. Finish by hand.

GIANT RUFFLED PILLOW

Make a great, floppy pillow for the bed, seat or floor, using two 38-inch squares and lots of color coordinated scraps. Make the ruffling one and one-half times the finished length for each row. There will be fifteen rows. Divide the distance from the center to one side by fifteen and mark the lines lightly on the right side of one square of fabric. The rows will be roughly 2½ inches apart.

Decide upon a method for cutting, finishing and applying the **ruffles**; there are several ways, each giving a slightly different effect. Finished ruffles should be about 3 inches wide so that they will overlap. The first ruffle, in the center is pulled together like a rosette; it may be finished with a large covered button if desired. Special tip: If the fabric used to make the squares seems too light-weight to hold the ruffles, back it with a light **interfacing.**

Make a knife-edged **pillow form** in muslin and **zip** the finished case over it so that it can be removed for laundering.

MAN'S TIE

Making a man's tie is easy, fun and inexpensive. It can be done entirely by hand in about three hours. Use a light-to-medium-weight, non-crush fabric such as silk or synthetic surah, Thailand silk, fine wool tweed, Viyella (a cotton and wool mixture), wool or synthetic challis, batik or cotton satin. Before deciding on a fabric, fold it into a bias strip to see how the texture and design will look. Many fabrics on the bolt seem suitable, but at second glance, will not work for a particular project. The yardage needed for one tie is ⅝ yard of 36-inch or 45-inch fabric; for two ties, ¾ yard of 45-inch or ⅞ yard of 36-inch fabric. Use ⅝ yard of medium-firm, woven interfacing which is compatible in color to the tie fabric. Precut tie interfacings are available at some notions counters. (See pages 700-701 for patterns.)

Make a pattern by joining the wide-end upper section **A** with the wide-end lower section **B** by adding 18 inches in between. Use a yardstick to line up the 18-inch piece. Be sure to trace the seam lines, fold lines and the grain line and all other markings. Repeat by making a pattern for the narrow end sections, **C** and **D**.

Lay the wide-end pattern **(AB)** on the right side of the fabric, placing the grain line on either the length or cross grain; in either case the tie will be on the bias. Pin in place to cut. Arrange the narrow end pattern **(CD)** on the fabric the same way before cutting. Pin in place, then cut. Cut the lining fabric by just the pattern for the lower section **(B and D)** of each end. Cut the interfacing to fit just the center section of each end of the tie pattern, that is, to fit between the fold lines, and cut it straight across at the bottom — 2 inches from the points of each end. Lay the interfacing on the wrong side of each tie piece and baste in place. Join the straight ends together, matching the X s. Fold under a ⅜-inch seam on one long edge and around the points, as indicated on pattern. Press in place. Fold ½ inch under on corresponding edges of the lining pieces and press. Lay the lining pieces wrong side down on the points of the tie (they will come to within ⅛ inch of the folded edges of the tie points). Pin in place and slip stitch or blind stitch the folded edges of the lining to the tie.

Fold the tie along both fold lines and press very gently. Turn under the seam allowance and slip stitch the seam edge over the raw edge, being sure to stitch through into the interfacing enough to secure it but do not stitch into the right side of the tie.

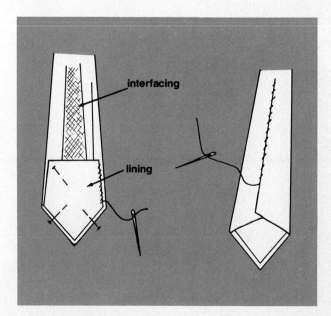

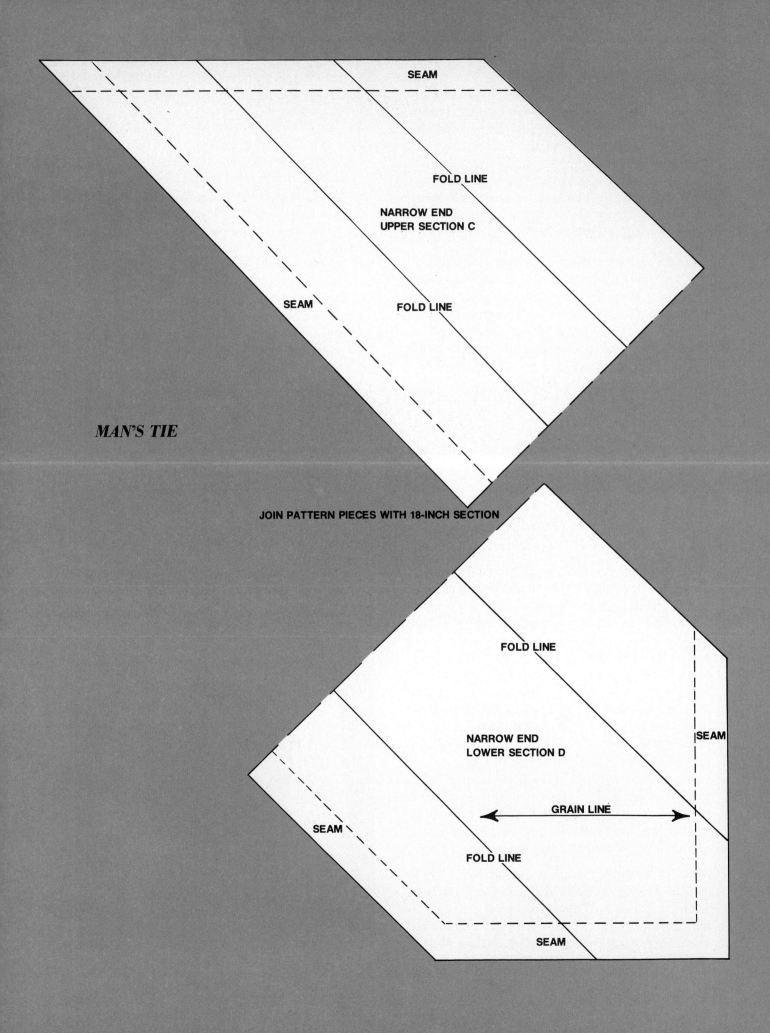

MAN'S TIE

SEAM

FOLD LINE

NARROW END
UPPER SECTION C

SEAM

FOLD LINE

JOIN PATTERN PIECES WITH 18-INCH SECTION

FOLD LINE

NARROW END
LOWER SECTION D

SEAM

GRAIN LINE

SEAM

FOLD LINE

SEAM

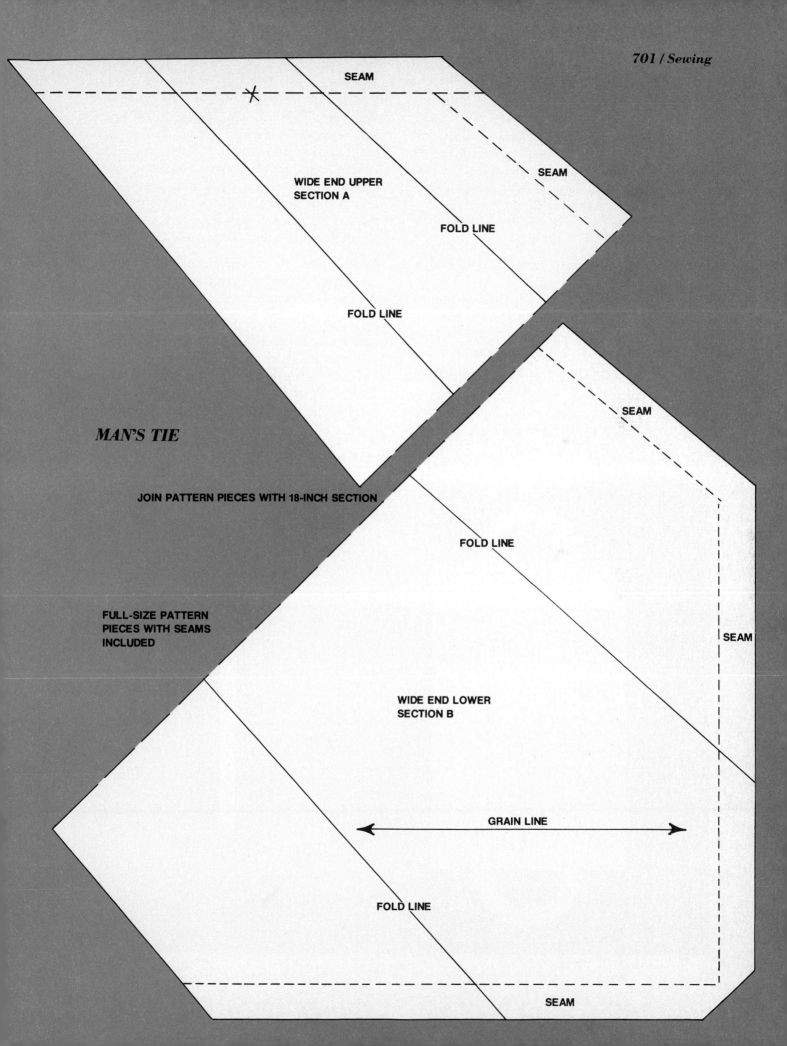

SEAM

SEAM

**WIDE END UPPER
SECTION A**

FOLD LINE

FOLD LINE

MAN'S TIE

JOIN PATTERN PIECES WITH 18-INCH SECTION

SEAM

FOLD LINE

SEAM

**FULL-SIZE PATTERN
PIECES WITH SEAMS
INCLUDED**

**WIDE END LOWER
SECTION B**

GRAIN LINE

FOLD LINE

SEAM

CANVAS LOG CARRIER AND TOTE BAG

Heavy, sail canvas makes marvelous bags and carryalls for anyone. It can be found in the fabric department of some department stores and in sail-makers' and farm supply stores. When sewing with sail canvas, remember to put a *heavy-duty needle* (size 16 or 18) in the machine. Use heavy-duty thread.

Log Carrier: Cut the log carrier 22 by 45 inches. Cut out a curve about 7 inches wide and 6 inches deep in the center of each end. Other necessary supplies include 3½ yards of wide **bias binding** to finish the edges and two 24-inch long wooden dowels about ¾ to 1 inch in diameter.

Bind the long sides and the curves with the binding. **Hem** the top ends 1½ to 2 inches deep by machine, reinforcing at the ends by backstitching. Machine appliqué square initials of the bias

binding on one side. Slip dowels into the hems.

Tote Bag: The tote bag is a generous grocery-size bag, but the same directions can be used to make it any size. Test for size with pieces of newspaper folded and taped. For the size shown, cut canvas 22 inches wide, plus seams and 38 inches long, plus hems. Stitch together the ends of a 3¼-yard piece of strong, woven cotton **braid** about 2 inches wide. Diagram A.

Center it on the canvas piece, as shown. Stitch along each edge of the braid to within 4 inches of each end of the fabric.

Fold the bag, right sides together, from side to side and seam each side. With the bag still wrong side out, stitch across the lower end of the seam, about 5 inches, as shown. Diagram B. Do not trim off the triangle of fabric. **Hem** the top edge by machine about 1¼ inches deep. Finish stitching the braid up over hem.

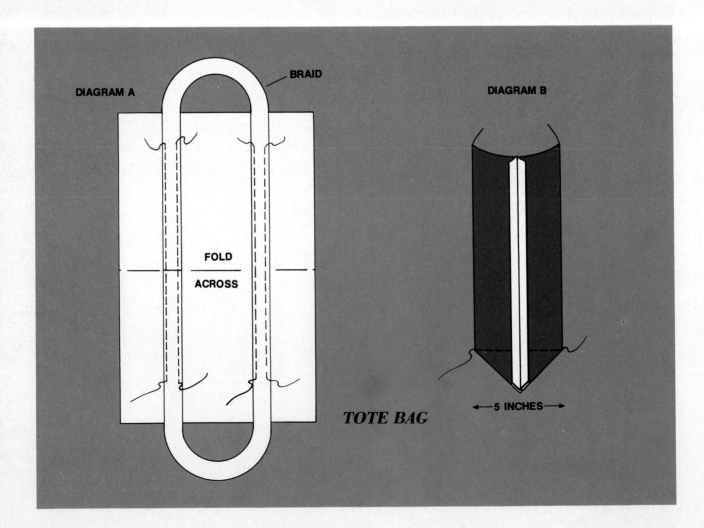

DIAGRAM A

BRAID

FOLD ACROSS

DIAGRAM B

TOTE BAG

←5 INCHES→

A long harvest table or picnic table can be attractively covered with this four-way design in unbalanced stripes.

CRAZY STRIPE TABLECLOTH

This cloth takes relatively little planning or pattern making and can be done with either balanced or unbalanced **stripes.** A medium-weight fabric is best; the one used here is pique.

These dimensions are for a 42- by 54-inch table, but the same principle works for any cloth. Add several inches to the table top dimensions for a graceful fall; nine inches were allowed here. Thus, the total dimensions for the finished cloth are 60 by 72 inches. Allow $4\frac{1}{8}$ yards of 45-inch fabric for the tablecloth. The yardage was determined by dividing the finished measurements (60 x 72 inches) by 4, making each piece 30 by 36 inches. Add 3 inches for seams and hems. (Each pattern piece measures 33 by 39 inches.) To achieve the desired effect, cut 2 pieces one way and 2 another or cut the fabric as shown in the diagram.

Seam the pieces together in the alternating pattern. Turn up a 2-inch hem and machine stitch. The corners may need to be mitered for a smooth look.

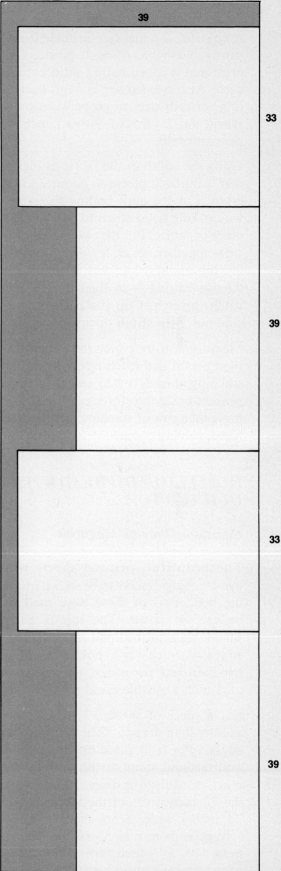

Layout of four pieces on fabric, single layer.

Piecing diagram for four striped pieces.

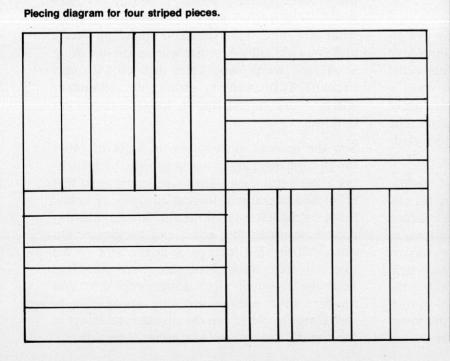

NURSERY SCHOOL NAP MAT

A colorful nap mat can be made from 2 pieces of sturdy, washable 45-inch fabric. Choose a gay print and a coordinating solid color, 3/4 yard of each. Also needed are enough dacron quilt batting, of crib size, to go between the 2 pieces of fabric and 2 yards of 1/2- to 1-inch wide cotton, peasant braid.

Using the width of the fabric as the length of the mat, trim both pieces to about 25 inches, on the grain. Cut the quilt batting the same size; baste with a long hand stitch to the wrong side of one piece of fabric. Pin the two pieces of fabric, right sides together; stitch a 1/2-inch seam all around, leaving about 12 inches open for turning. The dacron batting is so light that the machine will stitch through. Clip the corners and turn right side out. **Slip stitch** opening.

Measure at 6-to 7-inch intervals with chalk or a light pencil and stitch through all 3 layers, backstitching at each end to secure the layers. Cut the peasant braid into three equal pieces; center each piece on a row of stitching. Sew in place firmly by hand, leaving enough of the ends loose for tying.

RUFFLED BEDSPREAD WITH QUILTED TOP

Courtesy of Parents' Magazine

The beautiful, printed sheets which are so eye-catching deserve to be shown on the outside of the bed. Two of these were used to make the bedspread shown. The top is quilted onto a shrink-resistant bed pad which has elastic corner straps — a nice way to hold a spread in place. Use two twin bed, permanent press sheets and 9 yards of 2-inch washable braid trim.

Cut a piece of sheet, 37 by 73 inches, slightly smaller than the pad. (The trim will cover the raw edges.) Pin it in place on the pad and machine quilt around some of the flowers or designs, as much or as little as desired. Cut five strips across the 72-inch width of the sheet, having each strip 24 inches wide. Seam them together along the selvage ends to make a **ruffle.** Make a 1 1/2-inch **hem** with a 1/2-inch turn-under along the lower edge (machine blind hem is best). **Gather** the top edge to fit the sides and one end of the pad. Place the gathered edge, wrong side down, on the edge of the pad and pin or baste in place. Lay the **braid trim** over it and on around the top end, and stitch through all layers around the pad near the edge of the braid. Miter the braid corners; pin and stitch the other edge of the braid over the flat sheet that is quilted to the pad.

For the pillow sham, cut two pieces 22 by 26 inches plus two strips 9 by 72 inches for the ruffles, piecing as necessary. Seam the two large pieces together along the long edges to form tube (**French seams** are best). Hem and gather ruffles to fit the open ends of the tube. Seam them onto the ends with wrong sides together, and cover the raw seams with the trim.

BATH TOWEL CAFTAN

A perfect beach or bath caftan can be made from three average-size bath towels. Smaller towels can be used for a child's size. The ones used here were 24 by 48 inches after washing. If a towel without a self fringe is used, you can finish the edges with **ball fringe.**

Trim the fringe off the top ends of the two towels used for the skirt and zigzag the raw edges. Mark points 1 1/2 inches down from top edges and 1 inch in from side edges, as shown. Match and mark corresponding points on sides of other towel, 1/2 inch from edges. Cut **facing** by pattern from any thin, firm, washable matching fabric and sew right sides together with towel matching shoulders, as shown. Trim and clip around neckline. Turn facing to wrong side and **understitch.** Work thread **button loops** and sew on buttons.

Sew the ends of skirt towels to sides of other towel, from marking to marking only, backstitching at each end. Sew 1-inch side seams up to that point and backstitch, leaving an opening below the X on the left side for the slit. Sew 1/2-inch underarm seams to that point and backstitch. Do not catch the 1 1/2-inch piece at the tops of the towels in either seam. Press side seams open flat. Fold the 1 1/2-inch piece down onto skirt and machine stitch around for wide casing. Cut 1-inch elastic to the size of the rib cage and insert in the casing, then sew ends together. Hem side slit.

SHOULDER

⅛ Size Diagram

X

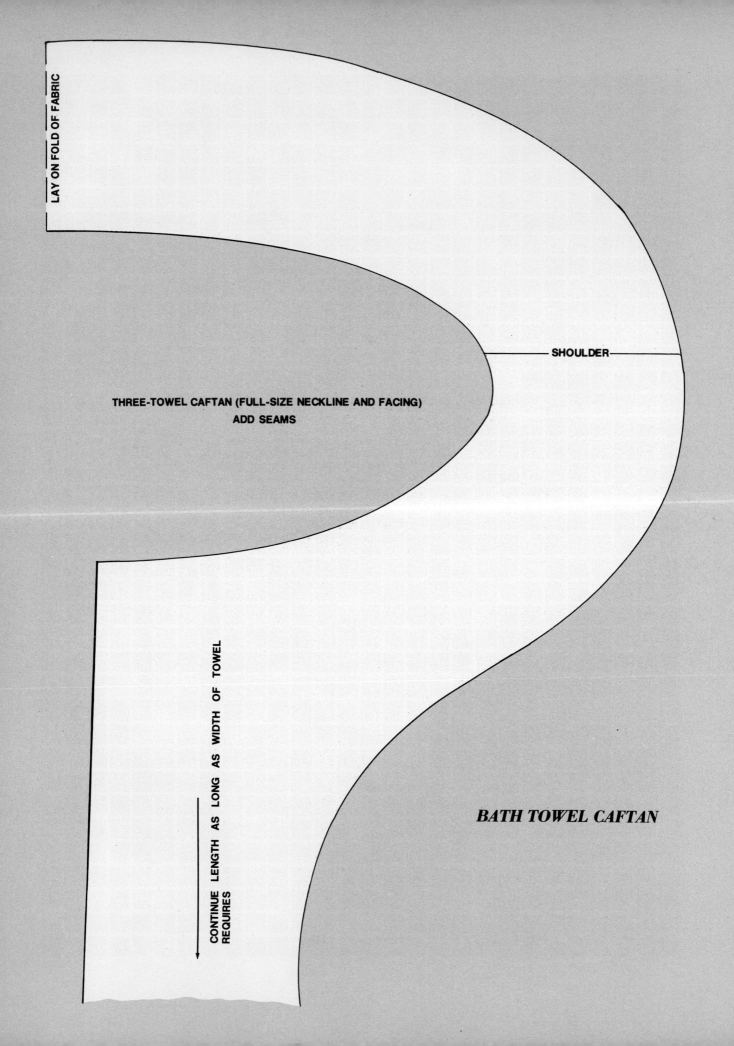

LAY ON FOLD OF FABRIC

SHOULDER

THREE-TOWEL CAFTAN (FULL-SIZE NECKLINE AND FACING)
ADD SEAMS

CONTINUE LENGTH AS LONG AS WIDTH OF TOWEL
REQUIRES

BATH TOWEL CAFTAN

POUF SCARF

This Pouf Scarf makes an attractive touch for an unbecoming neckline or a refreshing look to last year's suit. Use a bright-colored silk, synthetic or soft cotton fabric.

Fold ½ yard of 45-inch fabric cross grain, right sides together; seam the ends and open side with a ¼-inch seam, leaving a small opening for turning. Clip the corners; turn the right side out and press the edges.

Measure 10 inches from each side of the center and mark. Measure 5 inches from each end and mark. Bring the two markings together at each end, leaving a 20-inch space in the center. Run gathering thread through each set of lines, working through four layers of fabric; this is easier done by hand. Pull the gathering to about 4 inches and fasten off. There will be a bubble or pouf at each end of the scarf. When one end is pulled through and looped over the other around the neck, it will stay in place perfectly.

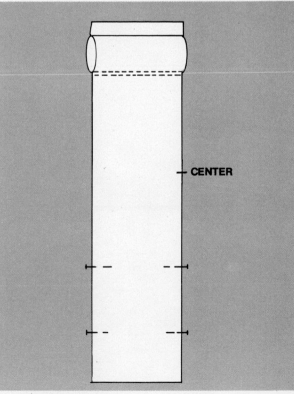

CENTER

At last, no-iron, stain resistant, inexpensive fabrics suitable for table mats are available. Many styles of mats can be made quickly by machine and are a welcome change from plastic. Rectangles and ovals are equally attractive and a variety of trims and finishes can be used on both.

MACHINE-MADE TABLE MATS

There are three simple mats shown and described here. The same sewing techniques can be used to make several interesting variations.

The basic finished mat sizes are 12 to 13 inches wide and 18 to 19 inches long. Napkins can be as small as 12 inches square or as large as 18 inches.

A set of six mats can be made from 1¼ to 1½ yards of 45-inch fabric. The yardage depends upon whether or not a hem allowance is needed. Six small napkins can be made from ¾ yard of 45-inch fabric. Allow a minimum of 1¾ yards of trim to edge either a square or oval mat. Since these mats will get many washings, all fabrics and trims should be **preshrunk.**

Mat 1: This fringed mat, with contrasting napkin, is made of a coarse-weave linen blend, which fringes easily. Trim the selvages from the fabric, mark the dimensions of the mats, then pull threads to make cutting lines easily visible. In this way the mats will be cut accurately on the grain. After the mats are cut, pull threads about ¾ inch from edges, stitch and **fringe.**

Mat 2: The child's mat is made of a cotton blend of sailcloth weight. There are marvelous nursery and children's prints available in both the dressmaker and home-decorating fabric departments. Allow for 1½-inch hems on all sides when

cutting. Turn back the hems and **miter** the corners. Turn under a scant ½ inch, leaving slightly more than one inch for the finished hem. Press or baste in place, using a ruler to keep hems even. Chalk or pencil a line lightly on the right side, a scant inch from the mat edge, making sure that it is just inside the hem edge. Using a bright colored thread and any one of the fancy zigzag stitches, stitch around the mat on the marked line. (The same mat can be finished by hand with simple embroidery stitches, such as the feather stitch.)

Mat 3: The toile print is a cotton blend, available in home-decorating departments. The trim is the jumbo width rickrack sold in packages. A lining fabric of a lightweight drip-dry cotton is needed for the back of each mat.

Make a full pattern from the diagram given here. Check the layout of the pattern on the fabric to be sure that it is placed attractively on the print of the fabric. When figuring yardage for a large print, buy extra fabric for easy placement of the pattern.

Trim the mat with the rickrack, used as an **edging,** neatly overlapping the ends. Finish by stitching the lining, right sides together, around all but about 4 inches of the mat for turning. Turn the mat right side out and slip stitch the opening. Pull the points of the rickrack as it is pressed to get a smoothly rounded edge.

One quarter pattern of oval mat, full size

ADD SEAMS

CUT PATTERN ON FOLD

CUT PATTERN ON FOLD

ASCOT (Man's or Woman's)

An ascot in soft silk, synthetic or cotton fabric is a perfect complement to a shirt. So quick and easy to make that they can be done in quantity as gifts.

For each ascot, buy ¹/₂ yard of 45-inch fabric; two can be cut from ⁷/₈ yard. Trim to 15 inches (the extra 3 inches are not needed) and fold in half lengthwise of the rectangle. Place the pointed pattern on the fold, as indicated. Cut the pointed shape at each end (along the selvage) leaving the other edge folded.

Fold the fabric, right sides together; stitch a seam around each point and along the cut edge, leaving an opening of about 4 inches in the center of the cut side for turning. Clip off seam corners and turn. Press out the edges and slip stitch the opening. In the center-back, make three ¹/₂-inch **tucks,** 12 inches long. Stitch these tucks; press in one direction. Stitch across the tucks at 4-inch intervals to finish shaping the ascot.

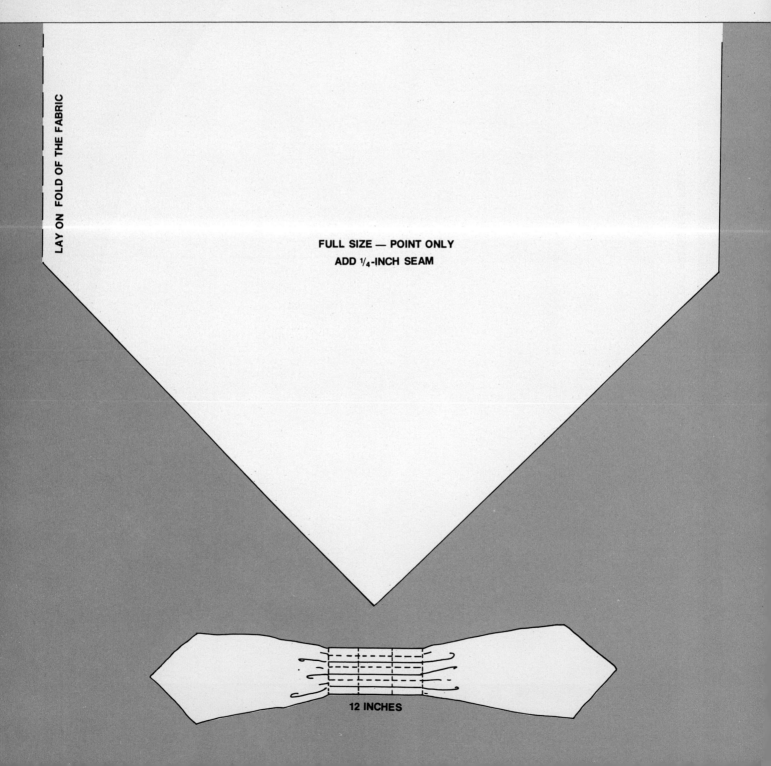

LAY ON FOLD OF THE FABRIC

FULL SIZE — POINT ONLY
ADD ¹/₄-INCH SEAM

12 INCHES

Stripes can form their own decoration, especially when bias edges are used to form a bright chevron pattern.

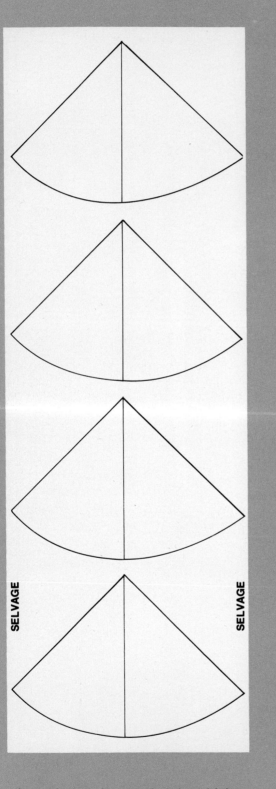

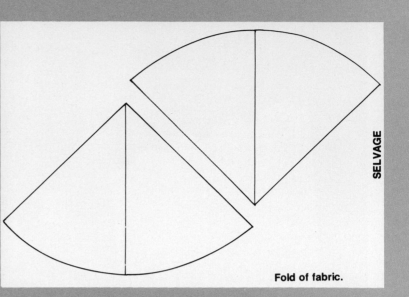

Fold of fabric.

Layout for two pieces on folded double-layer sheet.

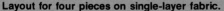

Layout for four pieces on single-layer fabric.

CHEVRON DESIGN ON ROUND TABLECLOTH

For this round cloth, the **stripes** must be even or balanced in order to create the chevron design. A light-to medium-weight, drip-dry cotton or even a drip-dry sheet can be used. A table as large as 48 inches in diameter can be covered with less than 4 yards of fabric using this design. Draw a pattern to fit your table, as described below, before purchasing the fabric.

The dimensions given here are for a table 48 inches in diameter. This is also the size of an extension top for card tables. The same principle works for any size round table. The total diameter, including a 7-inch overhang, will be $48 + 7 + 7 = 62$ inches; then add the seam allowance. To make the pattern, draw an arc from a given point with a 31-inch string, forming a 90° angle at the given point. Extend the arms of the angle to meet the arc as shown on the diagram. Fold the pattern evenly from the point to the edge of the arc; mark this line as the grain line. Place this pattern on the fabric as shown and cut out. Pin the pieces, right sides together, carefully matching the stripes before beginning to stitch. Press all seams open flat. Trim the edges with **ball fringe** (nearly 6 yards is required).

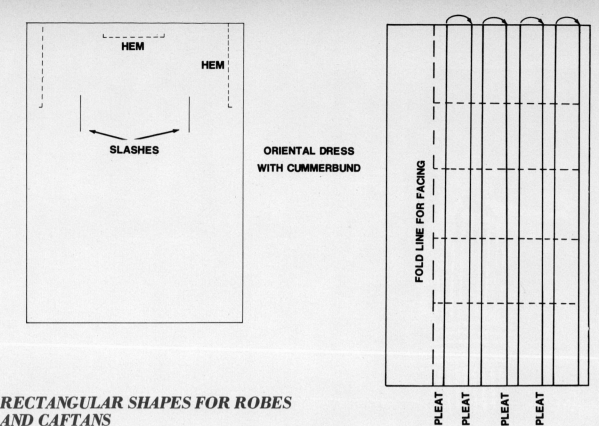

HEM

HEM

SLASHES

**ORIENTAL DRESS
WITH CUMMERBUND**

FOLD LINE FOR FACING

PLEAT **PLEAT** **PLEAT** **PLEAT**

RECTANGULAR SHAPES FOR ROBES AND CAFTANS

In many countries the rectangle is a basic shape for graceful comfortable clothing. When made of the right fabrics, these garments are decorative and even sexy; they move easily and feel weightless. Here is a collection for all the family, perfect for bath, beach or lounging.

An Oriental dress, pretty enough to wear anywhere, is made from two rectangles of fabric, 36 to 45 inches wide. This is an ideal way to use a beautiful panel print, or, as shown here, an elaborately embroidered linen. There were 3¼ yards of 39-inch fabric with an all-one-way embroidered design. If you have wider fabric, you will have slightly longer sleeves and wider "wings" on the sides. If you want to match patterns on the seams, you should buy 3½ yards.

Straighten the grain at the ends and cut the fabric across at the center, from selvage to selvage, so that you have two rectangles long enough to go from shoulder to floor, plus some hem allowance. Mark a 10-inch space across the top end at the center for the neckline. From that point out, sew shoulder seams 2 inches deep and then trim them to ⅝ inch, leaving the full 2 inches at the center for a hem along the neck edge. In the center back, from the finished neck edge down, sew a 22-inch **zipper** in with a **faced placket.**

Mark down 12 to 14 inches from the shoulder seam on each side for the armholes. From that point down, sew side seams 2 inches deep and then trim them to ⅝ inch, leaving the full 2 inches around the armholes for hem.

Allowing sufficient room at the waist to pull into soft folds with cummerbund, mark two 6-inch slashes which will run from somewhat above to slightly below the waist. Dimensions used in our medium-size dress are 18 inches across between slashes (making 36 inches around) and slashes running from 12 inches below the shoulder to 18 inches below the shoulder. Zigzag around the slash mark and split like a buttonhole, or straight stitch around, split and work buttonhole stitch by hand. Hem lower edge to desired length.

Cummerbund: Cut a straight strip of fabric 16 inches wide and 6 inches longer than your waist measurement, plus seams. Mark off 4 inches for self **facing** and back that piece with a fine firm **interfacing.** Make four ¾-inch **pleats** as shown in the other 12 inches. Press pleats in place and stitch across them at each end and in four other places, as shown. Fold facing over pleats, right sides together, seam open edge and one end. Turn right side out and finish with **hooks and eyes** to fit comfortably over dress.

TOP CORNER

Continue for 4½ inches

MAN'S APRON

Continue to side

MAN'S APRON

A chef needs an apron which really covers him and one which has enough pockets for all of his utensils. It should be made of a sturdy, washable, cheerful fabric. The one pictured is seersucker denim, but plain denim or ticking would also be suitable. Buy 1½ yards of 45-inch fabric.

Cut the body piece 35 by 28 inches which will in-*clude seam allowances.* Cut two 36 by 3 inch strips for waist ties; one 24 by 3 inch strip for neckband; and one piece 20 by 11 inches for the pocket. (Note: opposite grain for pocket.) *All of these dimensions include necessary seams and hems.* Fold body piece lengthwise along center. Place the curve on the top edge, 4½ inches from the center fold, leaving 9 inches across upper front. Cut along the curve from the top edge to the side area of the waist.

Narrowly hem the curved edge on the machine, clipping slightly if necessary. Machine stitch a 1-inch finished hem across the top and 1-inch finished hems on the sides and bottom, **mitering** lower corners. Machine stitch a 1½-inch finished hem along one long edge of the **patch pocket.** Press the other three edges under ½ inch and pin in place about 8 inches from lower edge of the apron and stitch. Make several rows of vertical stitching at intervals across the pocket, dividing the space for forks, spoons, hot mitts, etc.

Fold the ties and neckbands right sides together and stitch ½-inch seams, leaving an end open for turning.

Sew each tie in place at the lower end of curve, making an X pattern of stitching for reinforcement. Sew the neckband under one upper corner in same way. At other corner, sew a 1-inch piece of **Velcro**; adjust the length to suit the wearer and sew a matching piece of **Velcro** to the neckband.

HAT AND BAG

The blue and white ticking makes this a great casual outfit for summer and travel. However, tweed or plaid wool would be equally attractive for a winter version. The hat pattern is full size and should be traced and joined. The bag is based on a 13½ x 19½ inch rectangle, plus seams; the curved shape, which is cut out of the

top corners of the bag, is given full size. The pocket is 6 by 9 inches, plus hem and seams.

Cut two brim pieces on the fold. Cut one of non-woven interfacing using same brim pattern. Cut six crown pieces. Back one layer of the brim with interfacing and sew the center-back seams in both brim pieces. Sew the two brim pieces right sides together; turn, press and **top stitch** around, spacing ¼ inch between rows. Seam all six crown pieces together and top stitch ⅛ inch on each side of each seam. Seam the brim right sides together with crown edge and clip the seam all around. Sew ¾-inch grosgrain ribbon over the seam inside and press up into hat. Be sure to cut the ribbon to fit the head comfortably and use it to adjust the fit of the hat. Sew a large covered button on top.

Cut two pieces of fabric on the fold for the outside of bag and two pieces for lining. Hem the **patch pocket** and stitch it to the outside of one piece.

Make a pocket for the lining inside the bag and stitch it in place. Seam the two main pieces together across the short edge at the top of the handle and do the same with the lining. Press those seams open and lay the lining right sides together with the bag and seam around the two curved edges, stopping ⅝ inch from each side. Clip, turn right side out and press. It is now possible to seam the bag pieces, right sides together, and part of the lining pieces right sides together as they should go, as in the **alternate flip-lining** method. Leave a large opening in one side of the lining to work through. Finish that opening by hand. Trim with **appliqués** which can be purchased at notions counters.

HAT AND BAG

FULL-SIZE PATTERN

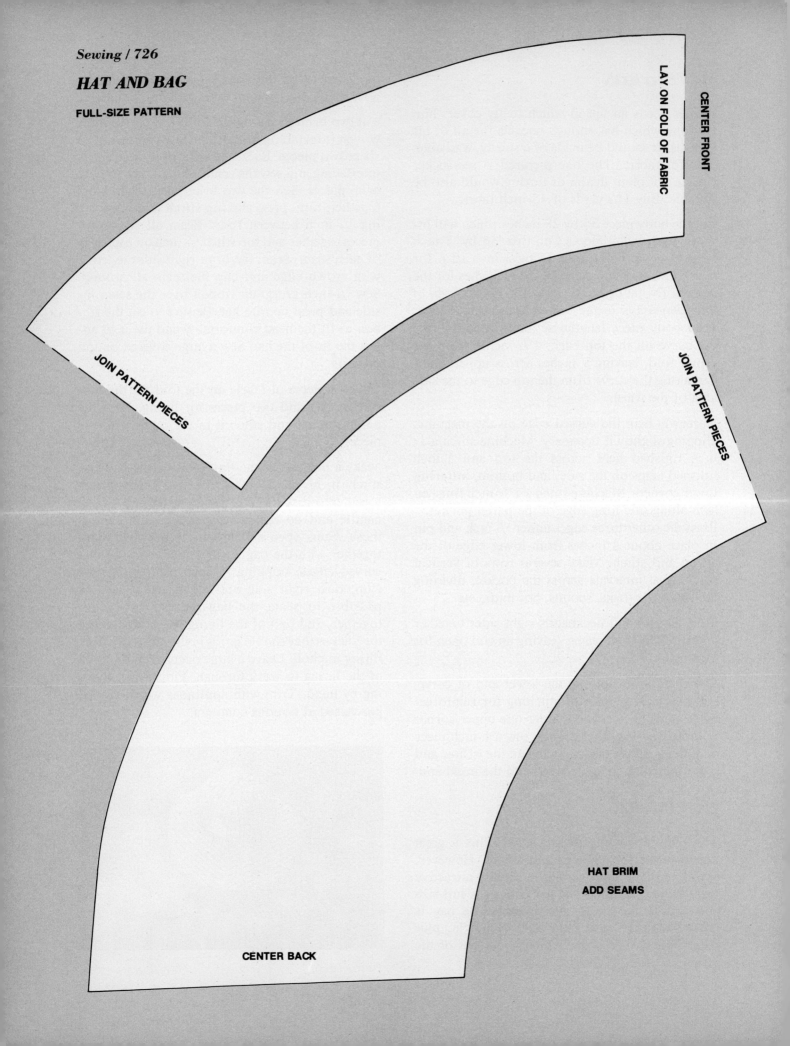

LAY ON FOLD OF FABRIC

CENTER FRONT

JOIN PATTERN PIECES

JOIN PATTERN PIECES

HAT BRIM

ADD SEAMS

CENTER BACK

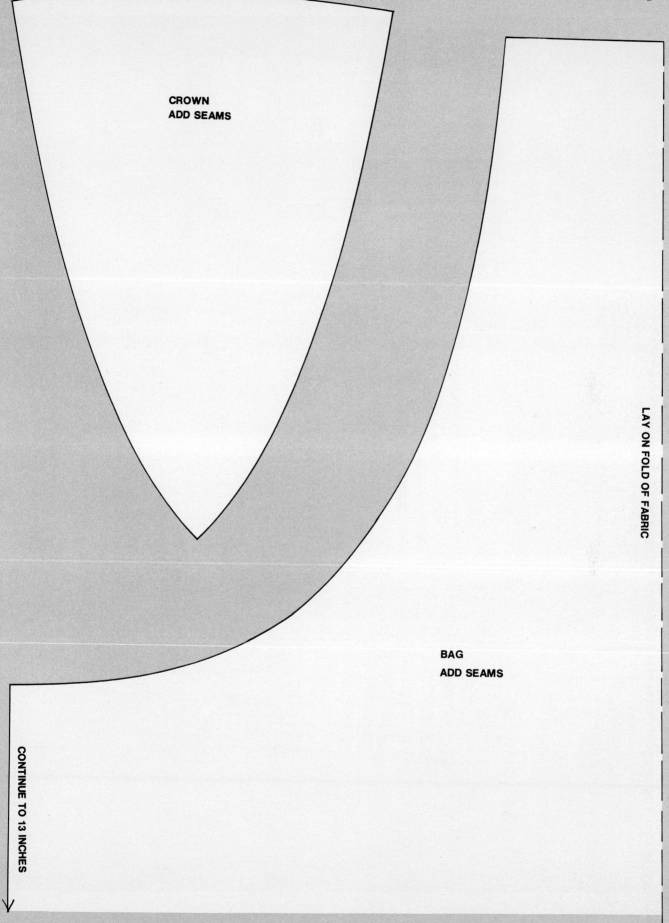

CROWN
ADD SEAMS

BAG
ADD SEAMS

LAY ON FOLD OF FABRIC

CONTINUE TO 13 INCHES

Patchwork

The American quilt is alive and well and living all over the country. Although this art flowered in the mid 19th century, it almost met its demise after the Civil War. With the coming of the Industrial Age, handwork and needlework began to decline. Some women seemed almost ashamed of it. Machines, they thought, could do the work better and cheaper. It didn't take long, however, to discover that machines could do neither. Manufactured objects were — and are — the direct opposites of the unique treasures produced by hand. Handwork is priceless because it is a personal expression of creativity. The resurrection and restoration of needlework to its rightful place is a very healthy sign.

Our pressures today are as relentless as those of two hundred years ago — perhaps more so, for they are more varied and widespread. Our own struggle for survival against deception, inflation, crime, and the false gods of money and power, need a pressure valve. Handwork restores balance and revives the spirit. Your handwork is a personal statement about YOU.

There is no such thing as an original design, but your interpretation or adaptation of any design makes it original. Needle arts are economical and accessible, beautiful and portable. Because our living patterns change constantly, we neither need nor want to return to our forefathers' style of life. However, we can adapt their good ideas to the present.

The word "Patchwork" is confusing, misused and misunderstood. Patchwork, literally, means to apply a patch of one fabric on a ground of another. However, in contemporary usage, it includes pieced work, patching with paper liners, Crazy Patch, as well as variations of both traditional and modern appliqué.

The American quilt is one of the few indigenous arts of this country. America can be compared to the youngest child of a large family — saddled with the hand-me-downs. Old world cultures were brought to our shores, just as were many different languages, social customs and religious practices. From these beginnings, coupled with the hardships endured by our pioneer ancestors, the American quilt emerged — bearing little resemblance to its European counterpart.

In the early years of our country, all energy was directed toward survival. Thus, the first bed coverings were drab, dark and strictly utilitarian. In time, however, life became a little easier. America began to raise its own raw materials for wool and cotton fabrics and soon learned to make its own dyes. Beauty became evident in the designs, color and form of this creative needlework — the only leisure-time outlet permitted the American woman. The creation of a beautiful quilt expressed her patience and dedication, her longing to fulfill herself. Many of the stunning quilts of this historic period were never meant to be used. They were to be admired, displayed and

Victorian Silk and Velvet Crazy Quilt from the collection in Knapp's Tavern (D.A.R. Headquarters) Greenwich, Connecticut.

handed down to the children and in turn to their children.

By the middle of the 19th century, quilt-making had come of age. Local exhibits and Grange fairs had a dynamic impact on the increased stature of the quilt. Women competed with each other to create outstanding examples. Piecing resulted in stunning graphic and geometric designs; the curved seam was conquered; appliqué work abounded — elaborate, elegant and intricate. Quilting itself was exquisite, with much of it an unbelievable example of time, patience and care — fourteen to sixteen tiny stitches per inch! Many of these breathtaking quilts are currently preserved in museums and private collections throughout the country.

Out of all this activity grew an integral part of the social history of our country. These times also produced a challenge which has been handed down to the modern woman.

PATCHWORK DESIGN

Design is the first essential. Color and fabric are part of it. The form comes basically from geometrics — squares, rectangles, triangles, diamonds, hexagons, circles or parts of circles. The design of a quilted project will be dictated partially by where and how it is used.

There are hundreds of old quilt patterns available today, and many of them take on an entirely different appearance when adapted to modern use and new fabrics. Original designs may be planned, using graph paper and colored pens or pencils; or, forms cut from colored construction paper can be moved around to form a pleasing arrangement. Above all, remember that a design does not have to be elaborate or difficult to be good; some of the simplest are the most commanding. Try new designs on a small scale for the overall effect.

Control the colors and pattern. Many beginners use too many colors which tend to break up the design causing loss of prominence. If you are lucky enough to have a scrap bag, work will be easier if you sort the fabrics into light and dark groupings.

For practice, start designing with a 4-inch square. This can be used as is or combined with other

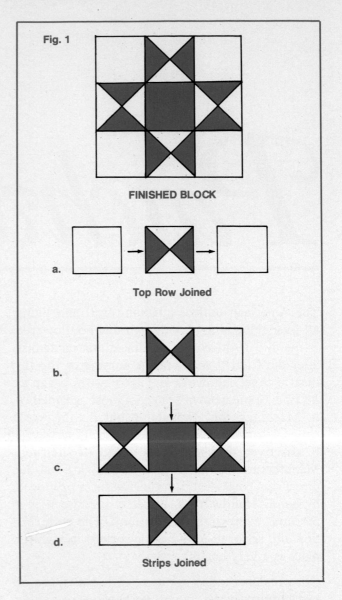

Fig. 1

FINISHED BLOCK

a. Top Row Joined

b.

c.

d. Strips Joined

squares of the same size. It can be divided into four 2-inch squares or divided diagonally into either two or four triangles. Practice joining these shapes together into strips; then, join the strips together to complete the design. Such practice will help you keep the corners and seams even. **Fig. 1.**

The Block

A block is a complete design. It can be any size — from a few inches to a full bed size as long as the design is complete within its boundaries. The block was invented by pioneer women who had neither time nor space to work on big projects. They divided the work into manageable units called "blocks." When these were finished, they were sewn together by various methods to make

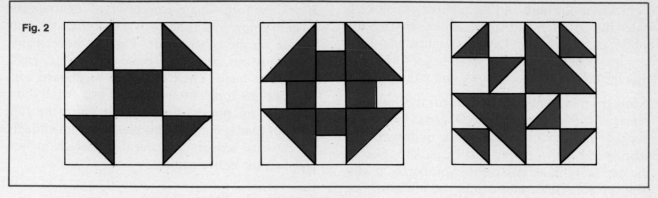

Fig. 2

Block Patterns

the quilt top. The pattern or design selected for the quilt top will help in determining the size of each block. Usually, a block is from 10 to 18 inches square. **Fig. 2.**

The Set

The set of a quilt is the way in which the blocks are joined together. This is also one of the important early decisions, since it governs the number of blocks used, whether patterned or plain. Consequently it governs the amount of fabric to buy. Most important, it also governs the final design or effect.

Some sets call for blocks to be sewed edge to edge or adjacent to each other to complete the design. This is called an all-over pattern. **Fig. 3a.** Another set calls for the patterned blocks to be alternated with plain ones. **Fig. 3b.** In still another set, blocks can be separated with strips or lattices, like framing pictures. **Fig. 3c.** A few blocks can be grouped together in a big center

medallion and finished in a series of borders. At this stage, any changes in the *set* of the quilt will have to be minor ones since all the fabric is purchased early and the blocks are probably completed.

FABRIC

Choice of fabric is also important in planning patchwork. If you plan to quilt the project — especially hand-quilt it — use dress-weight cottons, such as muslin, calico, gingham, percale or broadcloth. Cotton is increasingly expensive and is often blended with synthetics. However, finding and using cotton is worth the extra effort and expense. It looks better, is more traditional, and is easier to sew.

The amount of fabric needed will depend upon the project. If you want to make a full-size quilt, measure the surface of the mattress, the side, the end and the pillow over-hang. Plan the number

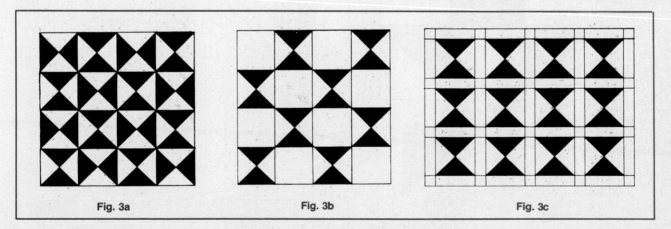

Fig. 3a   Fig. 3b   Fig. 3c

(a.) All-Over Pattern (b.) Patterned blocks alternated with plain blocks (c.) Blocks separated with lattices

of blocks in the quilt and the number of colors in each block; then multiply. When buying the fabric, it is wiser to have too much than not enough. Make use of your scrap bag too. Be sure that all fabrics are pre-shrunk and colorfast.

Aside from the amount of fabric for the quilt top, remember that you will need extra fabric for backing and binding. Binding the quilt with bias strips will require at least one extra yard. Get all the necessary materials before you begin. If you wait, a particular fabric may be sold out or available only in a different dye lot.

The Pattern

The pattern selection is also an important decision because care is required in scaling the pieces. First, make a small colored sketch of the design. You will often need this for reference. Next, cut cardboard or poster board to the size of the block. *Carefully* and accurately draw the units, using a ruler and a T-square. Cut the units apart with a sharp knife. These are pattern templates. For instance, in the "Shoo-Fly" pattern, only the triangle and the square are needed because the units are repeated. In using two colors in the

block, the following are necessary: four triangles of each color; four squares of one color; and, one square of the other color. **Fig. 4.** Since many pieces are cut from each pattern template, have several on hand. The edge of the cardboard will fray and get rough after repeated use. Small durable pattern pieces can be made from the flat sides of plastic bottles. This plastic is thin enough to cut with scissors and durable enough to last through the entire project.

Cutting The Fabric Pieces

Preshrink and press the fabric. Lay the pattern template on the *wrong* side of the fabric, keeping the grain consistent on all like pieces. A square, for instance, will be straight grain on all four sides; a triangle will have at least one bias side; and, a diamond will have two straight and two bias sides. **Fig. 5.**

The pattern template does not include seam allowance. Remember to allow at least an extra ¼ inch all the way around.

Trace around the pattern piece with a pencil. The penciled lines will be a true guide for sewing. Be accurate in cutting *and* sewing because crooked seams and sloppy corners can spoil the project.

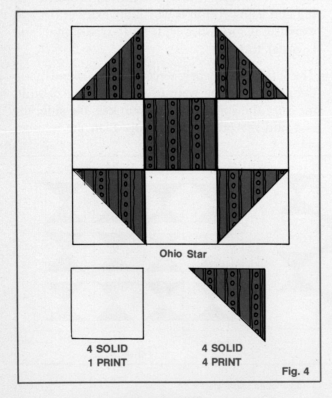

Ohio Star

4 SOLID
1 PRINT

4 SOLID
4 PRINT

Fig. 4

Two-Color Block

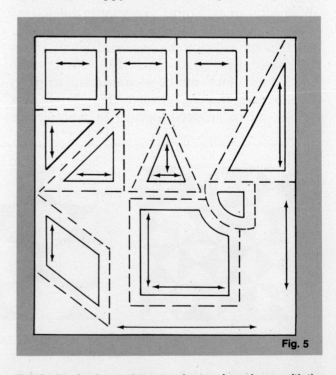

Fig. 5

Fabric showing how to lay out and cut various shapes with the grain

Put the fabric pieces for each block in separate plastic bags. This will keep them clean and will also make each block a portable unit; just add scissors, needle and thread.

PIECING

Piecing is the act of sewing pieces or patches of fabric together. Sew two pieces together to make a small unit; join small units to make a larger one and continue until the block is completed. The simplest method of piecing is in joining four-, five-, or nine-patch blocks.

The Ohio Star pattern, on page 732, is a nine-patch design. To piece this pattern, start with the top row. First, sew the triangles together to make a square: then sew the three squares together to make a strip. Finally, join the strips to make the block. **(See Figs. 1 and 4.)**

Use cotton or mercerized thread. Polyester thread tends to tangle in hand sewing. A short, fine needle works best and the use of a thimble makes work easier. Use a running stitch, with a backstitch at the ends. **Fig. 6.**

A backstitch seam is stronger; but small, even running stitches will make secure seams. You can also piece on the machine, following the penciled lines. Be sure the tensions are even and set the stitch length from 12 to 14. When joining strips, whether by hand or machine, press all seams in one direction. Do not try to open them. Press seams of alternating strips in the opposite direction to eliminate bulk at the seam intersections.

Curved seams are sometimes difficult for beginners, but it is worth the time and effort to master

them. "Wonder of the World" and "Fool's Puzzle" are two well-known designs with curved seams. **Fig. 9.** "Fool's Puzzle" is a two-patch design — two pieces of fabric joined for one unit. There are exciting and endless variations in this design among them, "Drunkard's Path," which usually have eight to sixteen units joined to make a block.

Curves are easier to sew by hand, especially if the pieces are small. To keep the work flat and without puckers, clip the *concave* or *inside* curve. Before you clip, it will help to stay stitch this curve on the seam line, or one thread outside. **Fig. 7.** A one-patch design means that one shape is repeated over and over. **Fig. 8.** Many old traditional designs were composed of geometric shapes. The

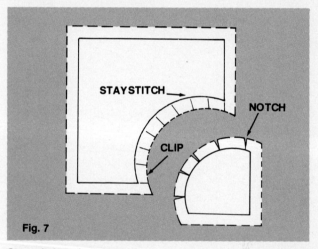

Fig. 7

Stay stitch and clip a curve to prevent puckering.

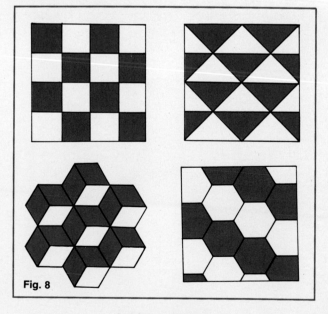

Fig. 8

One-Patch Designs

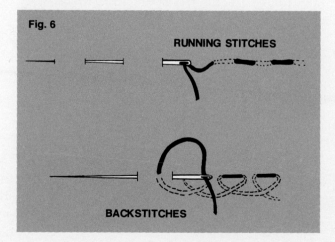

Fig. 6

RUNNING STITCHES

BACKSTITCHES

Fig. 9

Variations of a Two-Patch Design

Sawtooth and Zigzag. The *diamond* earned its reputation in the huge and stunning Star of Bethlehem, The Lone Star and other Star variations — all of which require great care and patience in cutting and piecing. The *diamond* was also used in optical illusion patterns, such as Baby Blocks or Tumbling Blocks. However, the favorite of traditional one-patch designs was the *hexagon*. Its origin remains a mystery, but its use has developed into a sophisticated art form. The hexagon is one of the easiest to join together. It can be used in any size and, of course, can be combined with squares, triangles and diamonds for dazzling effects.

Paper Liners: Paper liners are a great help in working with hexagons or diamonds. This method of backing and joining the pieces will prevent stretching the bias seams so as not to misshape the entire surface of the quilt. Using a master template, *which does not include seam allowances,* cut the required number of pieces from magazine-weight paper. **Fig. 10a.** Pin the paper shapes on the wrong side of the fabric. Paying close attention to the grain, cut the fabric pieces *with a seam allowance.* Now turn the fabric edges over the paper; fold the corners down sharply and baste all around the edge *through* the paper. **Fig. 10b.** It is best not to knot the basting thread. If the thread is knotted, begin to baste from the right side where the thread can easily be removed when the work is finished. When several of these patches have been basted to the paper liners, join them together. Place two patches right sides together, following the color plan. Whip stitch the folded edges together. **Fig. 10c.** Do not catch the paper. Continue joining in this manner, then lay the pieces out flat and press carefully. Next, remove the basting thread and gently remove the paper liners, which can be used again. **Fig. 10d.**

THE QUILT

A quilt is really a textile sandwich. The top layer is a quilt top, the middle layer is the filler or batting, and the bottom layer is the backing. You know all about the quilt top — it can be pieced, patched, appliquéd or embroidered. (There will be more details on this in later sections.) Whatever form the quilt top takes when com-

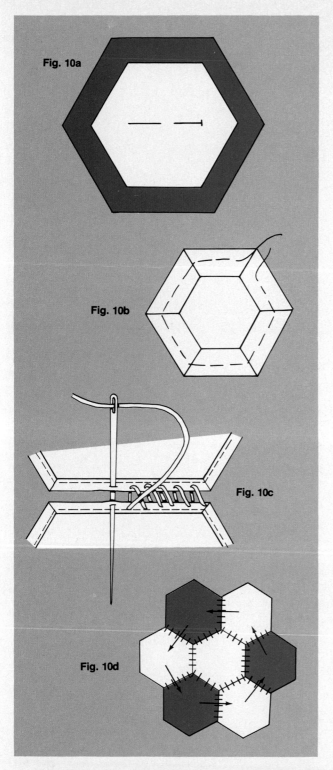

Fig. 10a
Fig. 10b
Fig. 10c
Fig. 10d

(a.) Place paper liner on wrong side of fabric. (b.) Baste around edges through folded down paper. (c.) Join folded edges with whip stitch. (d.) Continue joining in the same manner.

square was used on classic designs such as Postage Stamp, Hit and Miss, Grandmother's Dream and Trip Around the World. The *triangle* was used for a Thousand Pyramids, A Streak of Lightning,

pleted, it must be properly prepared for quilting. The filler can be a layer or two of cotton flannel, a fairly thin wool blanket or, either cotton or polyester batting made especially for this purpose. The cotton batting is thinner, but more difficult to work with. The polyester batting, though not authentic in tradition, will wash or dry clean equally well and does not have to be quilted as closely as cotton.

The *backing* or lining of the quilt may be unbleached, pre-shrunk muslin or it may be plain or printed cotton. Backing can be in one piece, as in wide muslin sheeting or it can be sewed together in strips or large squares. A purchased bed sheet can also be used for this. This decision must be made when the project is first started.

Preparing To Quilt

The three layers must be basted together. Spread the backing, *wrong side up,* on a flat surface (a table, if you have one large enough; otherwise, the floor). Square off the corners and smooth out any wrinkles. Now, unroll the batting and lay it carefully over the backing. Again smooth it out. Be especially careful when handling cotton batting, for it tears easily. Lay the quilt top *right side up* over the two other layers. Pin these layers together, starting at the center. The backing and batting both may be larger than the quilt top. When the quilting is finished, trim off the excess batting. The edges of the quilt can be finished by turning the backing over them. In this case, extra backing fabric will be needed.

During the pin-basting stage, you will probably have to crawl over the quilt top in order to reach all areas. Be careful that the layers don't shift. Keep the backing and top smooth and taut. After anchoring the quilt with pins, start to thread-baste from the center of the quilt. Since it is impossible to get your hand underneath, pin from the top side. Also, learn to baste from the top. From the center, baste diagonally to each corner; then baste lengthwise and crosswise. **Fig. 11a.** Continue basting in grid fashion, with the lines

Victorian Silk and Velvet Tumbling Blocks Quilt from the collection in Knapp's Tavern (D.A.R. Headquarters) Greenwich, Connecticut.

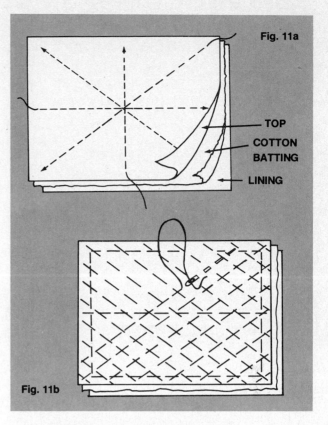

Fig. 11a
TOP
COTTON
BATTING
LINING

Fig. 11b

not more than 4 or 5 inches apart. Then baste around the sides. **Fig. 11b.** This is an important step in quilting, one which helps appreciably toward a good finished product. When the basting is finished, you are ready to quilt.

The *verb* "quilt" describes the act of sewing together the three layers of "the quilt," a *noun.* You will need quilting thread. It comes in both white and colors; is prewaxed and strong; and is easy to use. Use quilting needles. These are short and sharp, and are sometimes called "betweens." Size 7 or 8 is best. Be sure to use a thimble at this stage. White thread is most commonly used for quilting, but a colored quilting thread may be used if desired.

Keep in mind how the stitches will look on the back. Also, keep in mind that the color on top is not very important because you are dealing with the effect of light and shadows. It is the stitching itself, not the color, which creates the finished effect.

QUILTING DESIGN

The quilting design is the pattern used to sew the quilt layers together. You can wait until the quilt

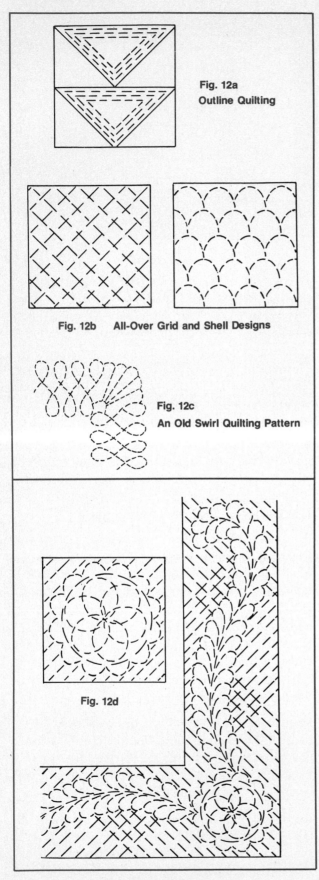

Fig. 12a
Outline Quilting

Fig. 12b   All-Over Grid and Shell Designs

Fig. 12c
An Old Swirl Quilting Pattern

Fig. 12d

Pattern Emphasis in Design

top is completed before deciding upon the quilting pattern. Usually on the patterned blocks, whether pieced or appliquéd, outline quilting is sufficient. Simply follow the seam lines with a parallel quilting line $1/4$ inch away. **Fig. 12a.** Plain blocks, areas or borders can be more elaborate. You could use an all-over design of grids or shells. **Fig. 12b.** For the grid, use a yardstick and a No. 3 pencil; for the shell pattern, use a master template and trace around it. Many of the old quilting patterns are still available — feathers, swirls, cornucopias, overlapping circles, lacy and geometric patterns. **Fig. 12c.** You might want to copy part of the design of the quilt top. For instance, if a rose is appliqued on a block, you can use this same pattern to quilt the plain block, thereby adding emphasis to the design. A good finishing touch would be a border quilted with vines and leaves, with a rose design quilted in each corner. **Fig. 12d.**

Transferring The Quilting Design: As noted above, use a yardstick and a No. 3 pencil to draw lines on the quilt top. For the remaining blocks, one way to transfer the design is to trace the pattern on thin cardboard or manila folders. Cut out around the pattern, then perforate the inside lines about every $1/4$ inch. We suggest using a push pin for this, although you can use the sewing machine. Use a size 16 needle, *without thread.* Very slowly feed it through the pattern, carefully following the marked lines. Center this perforated pattern on a plain block of the quilt top and with a *sharp* No. 3 pencil, mark a dot through each perforation. Repeat this procedure until all the plain blocks are marked.

Another way to transfer a quilting pattern is by means of a simply made light box. Use two stacks of books with a glass over them and a lighted bulb under the glass. Place the quilting pattern on top of the glass and the section of quilt top over this; trace carefully with pencil. A gum eraser will remove a heavy line or a mistake. Be sure that the entire quilt top is marked before proceeding to the next step.

The Quilting Stitch

The quilting stitch is a running stitch. **(See Fig. 6.)** Hold the needle at an acute angle, almost

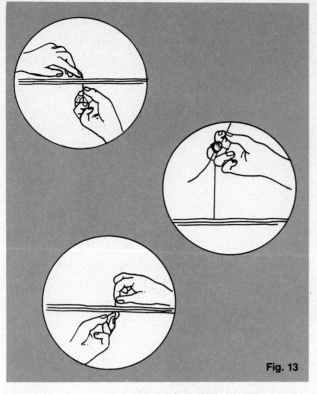

Fig. 13

Stab Stitch Technique

horizontal with the quilt, and push it through the three layers. Your left hand is an indispensible guide here, for each time the needle comes through you will feel it! Try to get two or three little stitches on the needle; with a little practice, you should be able to get eight to nine stitches an inch. This is very good. It is most important to keep the stitches uniform in size. This too, comes with practice. Some prize-winning quilters pride themselves on fourteen to sixteen stitches per inch, but this can only be done using a stab stitch. **Fig. 13.** For this, the needle is inserted straight down, pulled through underneath by the left hand, then inserted upward again right next to the previous stitch. These stitches are minute, so unless you are entering a contest, use the running stitch instead of the stab. Running stitches look fine, serve the purpose and take much less time. Practice is the keyword. After the first awkward stitches, you'll begin to establish a rhythm for quilting — and you'll find it very restful.

To finish off a line, tie a small knot in the thread before the last stitch or two. Pull it through the top so it does not show. Now, after the last stitch, work the needle into the batting for an inch or so. Do not go through the backing. Bring the needle up through the top, pull the thread taut and clip it. The end will sink back into the middle layer.

METHODS OF QUILTING

Quilting In A Frame

This is perhaps the oldest method of quilting. It has been handed down through many generations in both Europe and America. And, for many years, it was the only method used in quilting.

Today, frames can be purchased from mail order houses. These frames are fairly inexpensive and are made with hardwood stretchers and a top which tilts.

Making The Frame: Making a frame is relatively easy, and it is inexpensive. You will need four 1 x 2-inch pieces of lumber. The length of two boards should be equal to the width of the quilt plus an extra 12 inches at each end: these are the long stretchers. The two side pieces can be shorter — 4 feet is long enough. You will also need four C-clamps, and of course, chairs on which to rest the frame. Prepare the long stretchers as before, and baste the quilt to them. Roll one end *under* until only 1 or 2 feet of quilt is left exposed. Put the shorter side boards *under* the long ones, leaving a 12-inch extension at each long end. Place the C-clamp over the crossed boards and tighten it securely. **(See Figs. 14 and 15.)**

Using The Frame: Tack or staple a strip of heavy cotton or muslin to each of the long stretchers. Mark the centers of the stretchers and the center width of the quilt. Match these marks and baste the edge of the quilt to the strip. Use a double thread and work from the center to each side. Repeat for the other long stretcher.

With the quilt top *up,* begin rolling one end of the quilt *under,* keeping the roll as tight as possible and parallel to the opposite stretcher. **Fig. 14.** Secure the side bars with pegs, ratchets or C-clamps within a couple of feet from the end. Check to see that the quilt is taut. **Fig. 15a.** To keep tension even, pin a row of medium-sized safety pins along the exposed side edges. With bias or twilled tape, lace through the pins and around the side bars. **Fig. 15b.** This whole procedure is called "putting in" — you have *put* the quilt in a frame. Some frames come with legs or

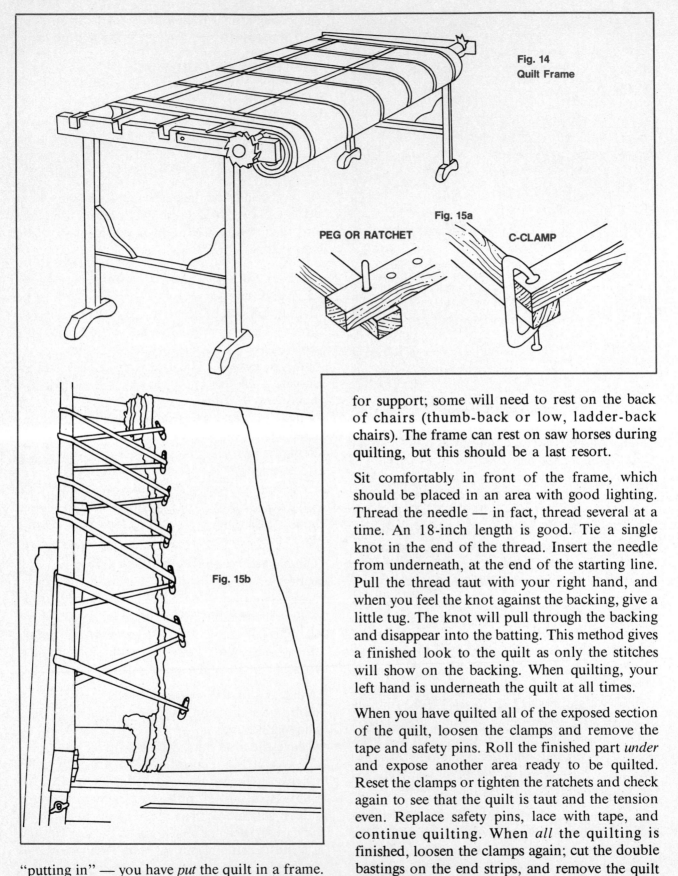

Fig. 14
Quilt Frame

Fig. 15a

PEG OR RATCHET

C-CLAMP

Fig. 15b

for support; some will need to rest on the back of chairs (thumb-back or low, ladder-back chairs). The frame can rest on saw horses during quilting, but this should be a last resort.

Sit comfortably in front of the frame, which should be placed in an area with good lighting. Thread the needle — in fact, thread several at a time. An 18-inch length is good. Tie a single knot in the end of the thread. Insert the needle from underneath, at the end of the starting line. Pull the thread taut with your right hand, and when you feel the knot against the backing, give a little tug. The knot will pull through the backing and disappear into the batting. This method gives a finished look to the quilt as only the stitches will show on the backing. When quilting, your left hand is underneath the quilt at all times.

When you have quilted all of the exposed section of the quilt, loosen the clamps and remove the tape and safety pins. Roll the finished part *under* and expose another area ready to be quilted. Reset the clamps or tighten the ratchets and check again to see that the quilt is taut and the tension even. Replace safety pins, lace with tape, and continue quilting. When *all* the quilting is finished, loosen the clamps again; cut the double bastings on the end strips, and remove the quilt from the frame.

"putting in" — you have *put* the quilt in a frame. Some frames come with legs or stretcher base;

Lap Quilting

Lap quilting is an easy method to use, but you must take extra precaution with the basting. It is very important to baste closely. Since there is no frame to keep the quilt tension even, you must be very careful to keep the three layers from shifting. On a frame, quilting can begin at one end. Without a frame, start quilting in the center, as in basting. To start on the sides or ends and work toward the middle will cause puckered areas which can never be smoothed.

You can lap quilt while sitting in a comfortable chair with the quilt spread around you — a good thing to remember in cold weather. You can spread it over a large table to be free of its weight. You can also roll up the basted quilt to the halfway point and rest the rolled part on a table or ironing board. Leave the rest of it hanging over the side, sit in front of it and begin to quilt. In using this method, it will also be easier to keep your left hand underneath while working. Several types of frames, especially for lap quilting, may be purchased commercially. Designed for quilting small areas at a time, these include round and oval frames with legs or on a stand; or, the large embroidery hoop variety. **Fig. 16.**

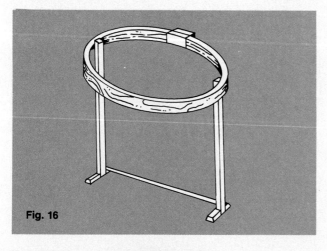

Fig. 16

Lap Quilting Frame

Block By Block Quilting

Quilting block by block is also an easy method. And, it has the added advantage of being portable — something to think of in these days of constant travel. Although this is not a new tech-

nique, it is not very widely known. In order to use this method, it will be necessary to make some changes in the early, basic procedures.

Finish piecing or appliquéing the blocks as before, but *do not join them together.* Cut the backing fabric into blocks the *same size* as the ones in the quilt top. Cut the batting in blocks 1/4 *inch smaller all the way around.* Remember — accuracy counts. Place the backing square, *wrong side up,* on table. Over this, center the batting square. Check to see that 1/4 inch of the backing is exposed on all four sides. Place the quilt top block on these pieces. Carefully line up corners and sides so that everything is true. Pin-baste first, then thread-baste. Quilt following the desired pattern, but quilt *only* to 1/2 inch from the edges of the block. To join two quilted blocks, place tops together face to face; line up corners and sides. Pin the block *tops* together and fold the backing out of the way. With a running stitch or a backstitch, seam the two top pieces together at 1/4 *inch.* Turn blocks face down on table, opened out and with backing side up. The batting squares, which were cut 1/4 inch smaller, should now meet and butt together evenly. Smooth one raw edge of backing over the batting; fold under the 1/4-inch seam allowance along the edge of the adjacent block. Blind or slip stitch the folded edge over the smooth edge. Continue joining other blocks to the first two until a strip is completed; then join strips. When all are sewed together, you are ready to bind the edges of the quilt.

Tying A Quilt

There may be times when you will have neither the time nor the inclination to quilt your masterpiece. When this happens, use a well-known and quite satisfactory shortcut — "tie" it. Such a technique of course, is not true quilting. The bedcover will actually be a "comforter" and not a quilt. When using this method, a double layer of batting or a thicker type of batt will make the comforter fluffier.

Baste the filler or batting securely to the wrong side of the *backing.* Now put the right side of the quilt top against the right side of the backing and line up the corners and edges; the backing will be in the middle of the three layers. Stitch around three sides and part of the fourth by hand or

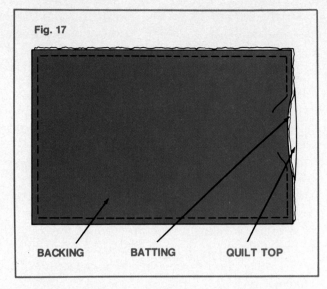

Fig. 17

BACKING   BATTING   QUILT TOP

or 3 inches of yarn on the top side, enough to tie. From the back, push needle through to the top side, keeping the second stitch very close to the first. Then tie the yarn in a double or square knot. Pull it tightly so that the knot will lie against the comforter and hold it securely. Cut the ends to make a little tuft. Continue in this manner until the entire cover is tied.

BINDING THE QUILT

One of the easiest ways to finish off the edges of the quilt is to incorporate the binding in the backing. For instance, the backing can be cut 1 inch larger all around. When the quilting is finished, bring the extra width of backing over the raw edges. Turn under a narrow seam allowance and pin in place along the four sides of the quilt. Whip this binding in place by hand with

machine, leaving an opening large enough for turning. **Fig. 17.** Reach inside this big fabric envelope and turn it right side out. With your fingers, work along the seams until they lie perfectly smooth along the edges. Pin to hold it in place. Slip stitch the opening closed on the fourth side. Then, run a line of stitching (by hand or machine) around the edges close to the seam to hold it together. When this is done, you are ready to tie. **Fig. 18.** Use a sharp-pointed yarn needle and double the worsted, orlon, or nylon yarn. Mark locations every 3 or 4 inches for the tying or where pattern indicates. Insert needle straight down from the top through the three layers. As you pull the needle through to the back, leave 2

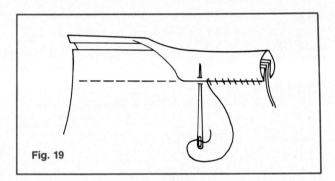

Fig. 19

Binding Blind Stitched In Place

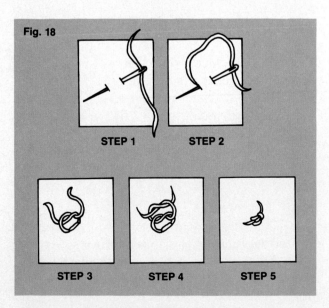

Fig. 18

STEP 1   STEP 2

STEP 3   STEP 4   STEP 5

Five Steps for Tying a Knot

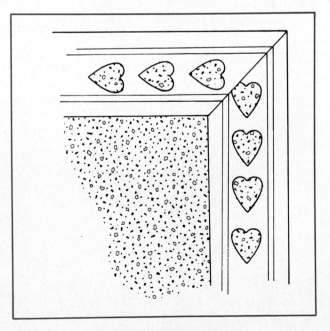

Border with Mitered Corners

small secure stitches. **Fig. 19.** This will give a finished binding of about ¹/₂ inch or slightly less. For a wider binding, cut the backing larger — also remember to cut the batting larger. For example: for a finished binding or border strip 1 inch wide, the backing must be 2¹/₄ to 2¹/₂ inches larger. The batting must be 1 inch larger. Fold the backing over the batting; fold under the seam allowance of the backing and pin in place ¹/₄ inch along the quilt top. This will keep the pattern intact.

Another way to finish the edges is with a bias strip. Purchase commercial bias binding 1 inch wide. Called "quilt binding," this comes in a wide selection of colors. You can also cut bias strips to match a particular color or print. Remember to add enough for seam allowances. If it is necessary to piece the bias ends together to make long strips, remember to seam the pieces on the straight of the grain. **Fig. 20.** Place the right side of the bias strip against the right side of *backing,* lining up the raw edges evenly. Stitch completely around the quilt sides, ¹/₄ inch from the edge. This can be done quickly on the machine. Bring bias up over the edge of the quilt with seam allowance folded under and hand whip into place. The hand-finishing of the binding on the face or top side of the quilt gives an extra mark of quality.

If the quilt is to be used frequently, a French bias binding on the edges will give extra protection. Cut the bias strips six times wider than the desired finished width. (For example, a 3-inch wide strip will give a finished width of ¹/₂ inch.) Fold the strip in the center lengthwise and press

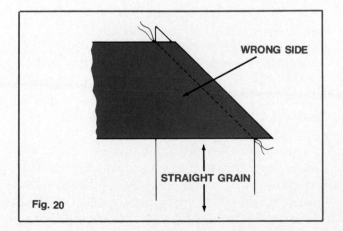

WRONG SIDE

STRAIGHT GRAIN

Fig. 20

carefully. Do not slide the iron as this may stretch the bias strip. Place the two raw edges of the bias against the edges of the quilt on the backing side as before, and stitch using a third of the doubled bias strip as seam allowance. Turn bias over the quilt edges and whip securely through the folded edge of the bias and the quilt top. Bias finishes do not need to be mitered at the corners.

TRAPUNTO OR ITALIAN QUILTING

This method of quilting comes to us from Italy, where from the Middle Ages on, it had reached perfection in technique. It gives the design a raised effect and can be used alone or with padded or stuffed quilting. It is most effective on solid colors or white fabric of silk, lightweight wool or cotton. Unlike other quilting, trapunto is not reversible and must be lined if the back will ever be seen.

The scope of trapunto designs runs from very easy patterns to difficult interwoven and interlocking linear patterns.

It is easier to begin with a large simple design. Trace this design on backing or lining material, lightweight muslin or cotton. Then, baste this backing, design side up, to the wrong side of the chosen fabric. Your project can be a collar and cuff set, a belt, an eyeglass case; it can be a purse or a pillow; and when you become more ambitious, upholstery for a chair. Trapunto can also be used effectively on skirts, vests or jackets.

After basting two pieces of fabric together, you are ready to begin. Either by hand or machine, depending upon the desired design and the effect, run a line of stitching ¹/₈ inch on either side of the line of the traced design. This will make a channel of parallel lines ¹/₄ inch apart. Thread a tapestry (blunt end) needle with one or two strands of bulky yarn. Start at one corner or one end and do not knot the yarn; leave a couple of inches. Always working from the back, be careful that the needle does not pierce the surface fabric. Work the needle carefully through the channel; bring the needle out through the backing at the bottom of a curve or at an angle and leave a tiny loop of yarn here; then, reinsert the needle in the same hole if possible and continue until every channel

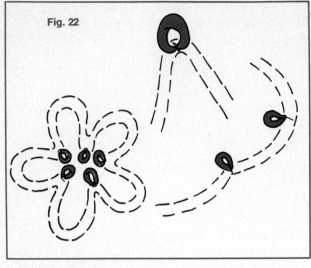

Trapunto showing loops of yarn at curves and angles

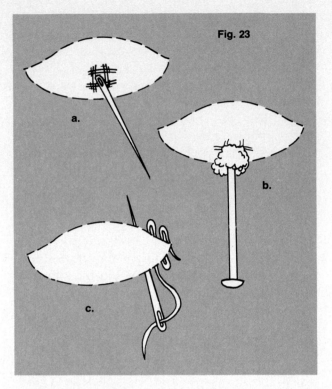

(a.) Work threads apart (b.) Push padding in (c.) Trapunto method can be used

is filled. This small loop will provide enough easing in case of shrinkage to keep the design from puckering. **Fig. 22.** If the article is to be dry-cleaned, any of the above yarns can be used. If it is to be washed, it is safer to use the synthetic yarns.

PADDED QUILTING

Padded quilting is similar to trapunto in giving a raised effect to the work. But, it is usually used in areas larger than the ¹/₄-inch channels. The famous all-white quilts of years ago were masterpieces of this type of work; the entire design was dependent alone on the quilting. It was often combined with trapunto and required great care and patience. For instance, a vase or basket of flowers, or a variation of this, was a fairly standard design. The outlines of the vase, some of the flowers and the stems would be done with trapunto quilting. The petals, leaves, etc., would be padded or stuffed.

As with trapunto, work is from the back when padding. Make a very small hole in the center of the area to be padded; carefully work the *eye* of the needle into the backing, moving it around in a circular motion to make a small hole. Do not break any threads. When the opening is large enough, use a knitting needle to poke small amounts of yarn or cotton through the hole until the space is filled. **Fig. 23.** It is also possible to use the trapunto method here. With a tapestry

needle, thread the yarn back and forth, close together, to fill fairly large areas.

THE CRAZY QUILT

The crazy quilt of Victorian fame was not a true quilt, since it was not actually quilted. It does fall in the patchwork category, however. It is a bed cover or throw, made of pieces of cloth of various fabrics cut in various shapes. These pieces are patched or sewed directly to a backing which is either cut in blocks to be joined later or cut to the full size of the finished article. Seams are often embellished with embroidery stitches. Many times, plain patches can also be embroidered with a bouquet of flowers, an animal, a butterfly, a name or a monogram. Like its cousin, the comforter, crazy quilts can be tied. More often, they are simply lined. Early ones were lined with woolens, dark cottons, or velvet, and often bordered in velvet. The crazy quilt reached the peak of its popularity at the end of the 19th century and continued in vogue for about forty years. There was scarcely a parlor which did not boast a crazy quilt thrown over a piano, a table, love seat or chair. Most of them were very elaborate and also quite dark. Made of velvets, silks, brocades, bits of ribbon and memorabilia sewed to a muslin backing, they were also impractical. They could not be washed and often, the more delicate silk fabric wore out long before the sturdier velvets. Yet, in their way, these needlework creations deserved attention and admiration.

Crazy quilts today cover the spectrum of colors and fabrics, and there is no limit as to what can be used. Cottons and lightweight woolens work as well or better than silks and velvets. Light shade against dark gives an interesting tonal quality not present in the originals. However, the same technique prevails in hand-sewing crazy quilts.

As with other types of quilts, it is easier to work with blocks. Cut the backing squares the desired size, from 12 to 18 inches. Choose a lightweight cotton or cotton mixture for this. In spite of its "hit and miss" effect, crazy patchwork needs to be planned as carefully as any other type. **Fig. 24a.** Harmony and balance can be achieved through repetition of a color or through the placement of patches. Be careful of the play of light against dark. Move the fabric pieces around on a table top to get an idea of how they look together. One interesting feature of this kind of work is that changes in fabrics or arrangement can be made after the project is started. Do not hesitate to cut them if the shape can be improved. Of course, in crazy patchwork, there is no specified shape. But, since straight seams are

easier to sew, try to come up with as many straight sides as possible without spoiling the effect. A curve here and there will give a dramatic impact.

Start patching in a corner. Use a piece of fabric with a right angle and fit it in place on top of the backing square; then, baste around the edges. Each succeeding piece is overlapped or underlapped about 1/2 inch and basted in place. After basting the block, sew each piece on securely with a tiny whipping stitch or blind stitch. Turn under the raw edges with the needle as you go. You will be sewing through three layers here — this will keep the patches from shifting. When this is done, any or all of these seams can be covered or decorated with embroidery stitches.

Another method of sewing crazy patches is called the "pressed" technique. Start with the corner patch and baste it into place. The next piece is laid edge to edge with the first, right sides together, and stitched through the three thicknesses with a 1/4-inch seam. The second piece is then pressed open, and a third piece stitched to it, and so on. **Fig. 24b.** Obviously, this is successful only where straight edges or seams are available. It becomes too difficult to try this with curves. You can do part of a block this way, then applique the curved piece in place, covering the edges of the preceding blocks. After you make

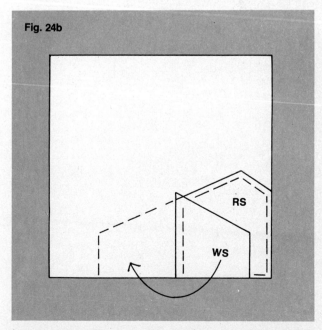

First patch basted to foundation block in corner. Second patch seamed to it, ready to turn over. Note arrow.

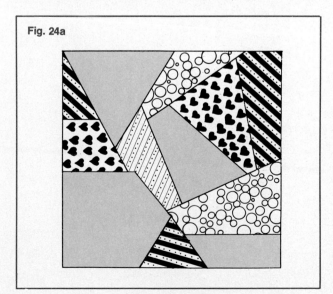

Crazy Patch Block

a block or two, you will easily work out your own system.

You might like to try combining unusual or unconventional fabrics in crazy patchwork. This is especially effective for pillow covers. Use real or fake suede or leather; real or fake fur; felt and vinyl. It is not necessary to turn any of the edges under. Merely sew them in place on the backing. Be careful in fitting and cutting so that the background block will not show through. An ordinary needle will handle most of this, although special needles are available for sewing leathers and furs. When sewing the fur patches, whether real or make-believe, take a pin and pull the hairs out of the stitches afterward so they will stand up.

Machine-Stitching Crazy Patchwork: To machine-stitch crazy patchwork, use a close zigzag or satin stitch or use one of the decorative stitches. Thread can match or contrast. The sewing machine can be a great short-cut here; and, the stitching will be strong and very effective. Plan the crazy quilt blocks as for hand-stitching, but leave the raw edges overlapping; do not turn the seam allowance under. Experiment with the width and variety of the machine stitches and experiment with contrasting threads. Often, with either or both, you will get an unexpected and pleasant result. When all the patches on the block

have been machine stitched, join the blocks with traditional seaming or zigzag them together. **Fig. 24c.**

Embroidery On Crazy Patchwork: Embroidery used in this way should be a definite part of the design. Finish the blocks as outlined above, with raw edges turned under and patches whipped or blind-stitched by hand. With six-strand embroidery floss or crochet cotton, work the stitches. (See Embroidery Chapter) Depending on the fabric and design, only two or three strands of the embroidery floss or fine quality crochet cotton may be used. Try a few sample stitches on a scrap before beginning. The most popular stitches for this are outline or stem, single or double feather, herringbone and buttonhole. This can be simple or very fancy. **Fig. 24d.**

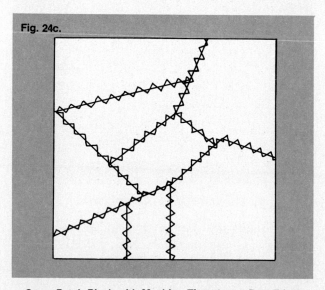

Fig. 24c.

Crazy Patch Block with Machine Zigzag over Raw Edges

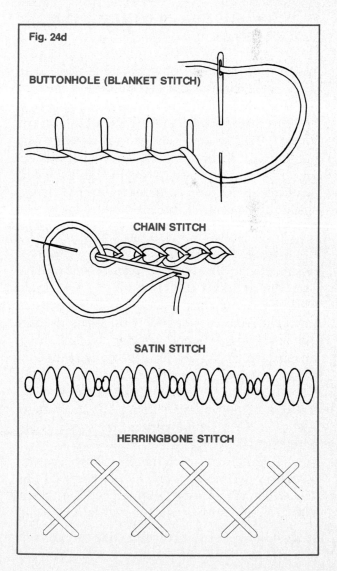

Fig. 24d

BUTTONHOLE (BLANKET STITCH)

CHAIN STITCH

SATIN STITCH

HERRINGBONE STITCH

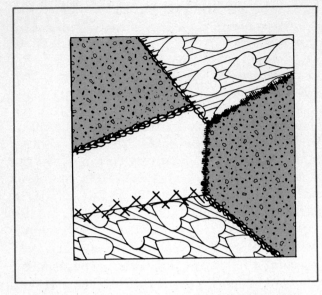

Hand Embroidery Covering and Embellishing Seams

PATCHWORK FOR CLOTHING AND ACCESSORIES

Patchwork, in pieced or appliqué designs or in crazy patchwork, is just as creative and interesting in clothing and home accessories as it is in bed coverings and quilts. Any and all fabrics can be used. But, remember the general rule — if you plan to quilt the project, use lightweight easy-to-sew fabrics. You can machine-quilt slightly heavier fabrics, but sometimes even a trusty machine balks at such thickness under the presser foot.

In clothing, consider skirts, short or long; vests of any length; robes, jackets, pants. Some of these articles are suitable for men or women. Children's clothes are also easy to do. The easiest way to use pieced work for clothing is to make the fabric first. Simple piecing is best, using squares, rectangles or an easy combination of squares and triangles. Plan the general color scheme and stitch all the pieces together to make a length of fabric large enough for the pattern. Also, choose a simple pattern, one with as few darts and seams as possible. Following the commercial pattern instructions, lay out the pattern pieces on the pieced work fabric, and cut. **Fig. 25a.** When the garment is all seamed together, it should be lined for a professional look.

If a whole skirt or jacket seems like too great an undertaking, consider patchwork trim. You can

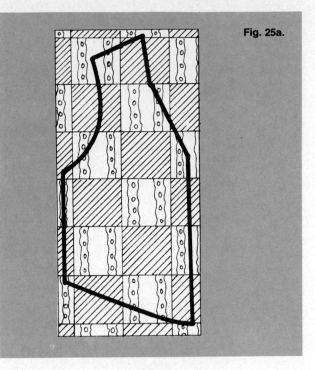

Fig. 25a.

Laying Out The Pattern

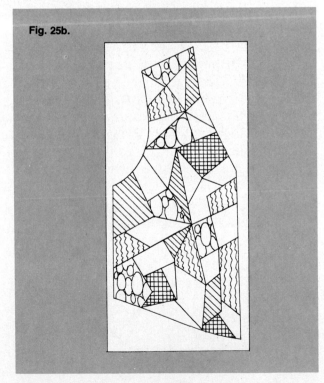

Fig. 25b.

Arranging Patches on Backing Pattern

make collars and cuffs, belts, pockets, a tote or evening bag. Borders are most effective when used to accent clothing. For instance, you could appliqué a hexagon or clamshell border (using paper liners) on a skirt or jacket; flowers or but-

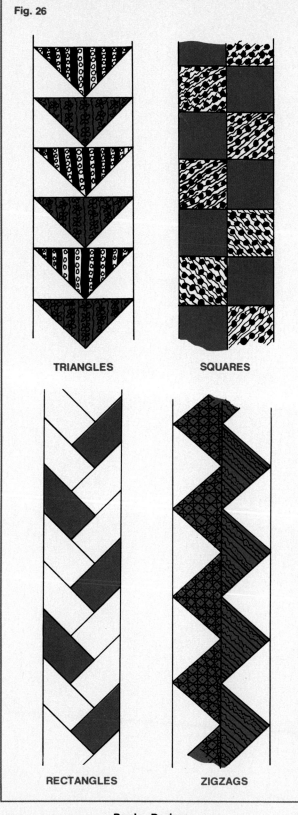

Fig. 26

TRIANGLES SQUARES

RECTANGLES ZIGZAGS

Border Designs

many young people wear all the time! An eight-pointed star made of silks and metallic brocades would be stunning appliquéd to an evening skirt. Once you begin to think along these lines, new ideas will open up for you.

When using crazy patchwork for clothing, instead of sewing pieces into fabric lengths first, cut out lining or backing pieces from the pattern sections. Then arrange the crazy patches on the backing pattern as described earlier. When each section is finished, seam the main pattern pieces together and finish with lining. **Fig. 25b.**

We've mentioned combining off-beat fabrics, such as suedes, leather, fur, felt and vinyl. A man's vest in any of these will be a conversation piece. This type of patchwork will be easier if pieced. First, cut backing pieces of muslin or cotton from the front pattern pieces of the vest. Use 4-inch squares and arrange them on the backing, then sew by hand or use a machine zigzag. Wool or even velveteen patches can be combined with these fabrics. Remember to cut wool and velveteen squares slightly larger than 4 inches to allow for turning under the raw edges or underlapping them with other patches.

The field of home accessories is limitless. First, consider wall hangings. Many hangings or banners can well be classified as art. Pillows are easy and exciting to do. They are small enough to try complicated, difficult patterns and striking enough to accent any room. Pillows can be pieced, appliquéd, crazy-patched and quilted. Table runners and place mats — round, square, or oblong — are also possibilities. Use borders on curtains or draperies too. **Fig. 26.**

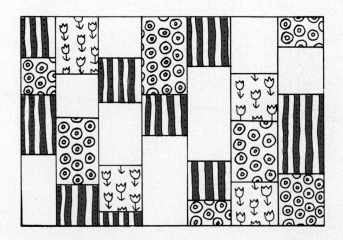

terflies are attractive on almost any piece of clothing. Remember all the patched jeans so

PATCHWORK PROJECTS

CHILDREN'S PATCHWORK TOYS

GENERAL DIRECTIONS FOR TOYS: The bodies of the toys are made like patchwork pillows, in rectangles according to the measurements shown. Add ¹/₂-inch seam allowances when cutting these pieces. Enlarge all other pattern pieces, each ¹/₂-inch square equals 2 inches, and add ¹/₂-inch seams.

Make up enough patchwork in squares or stripes or both to accomodate all the pieces to be cut for that toy. The legs and arms may be made of solid pieces of fabric, mixed as you like. The heads are solid color. If you wish to keep the entire toy washable, make the facial features, boots, hands, buttons, etc. of woven washable fabric instead of felt as shown. To prevent raveling, use the zigzag on the machine or blanket stitch by hand to apply facial features made of woven fabric.

Cut two of each body piece and the number noted of each of the other pieces. Sew two each of the pieces right sides together on the machine, leaving openings for turning and stuffing. After stuffing with foam chips or polyester batt, sew up the body opening by hand. Turn under the seam allowances on the open ends of each of the other pieces and overcast the pieces in place on the body with a double thread. On all toys, except the Hound Dog, squeeze the legs together at the knee and elbow joints and stitch across.

The facial features must be sewn on one side of the head piece before assembly. Place a piece of non-woven interfacing on the wrong side of one ear piece for each ear. Do not stuff ears.

Doll

Cut and assemble according to general directions. Embroider nose with chain stitch in crewel yarn or six-strand embroidery thread.

Make hair of knitting worsted or rug yarn as follows. Lay 36-inch pieces of yarn in a closely packed row across a 7-inch piece of paper. Machine stitch through the center of the yarn and the paper. Tear the paper away and hand sew the stitched line down the back of the head. Braid the ends and hand tack the hair in place along the sides of the head. For bangs wrap yarn closely around a 4-inch wide piece of paper for 6 or 7 inches. Machine stitch through one edge of paper

and yarn, cut yarn at other edge, tear paper away. Hand sew stitched edge across forehead as bangs. Trim if necessary.

Cat

Cut and assemble according to general directions. Embroider nose with outline stitch in crewel yarn or six-strand embroidery thread.

Hound Dog

Cut and assemble according to general directions. Embroider eyelashes with outline stitch, mouth with two rows of chain stitch, in crewel yarn or six-strand embroidery thread.

To make ears perkier, top stitch ¹/₄ inch from edge all around and also top stitch a circle 3 inches in diameter in center. If you wish, add a smaller appliquéd circle of another fabric in the center of that circle.

Horse

Cut and assemble according to general directions. Embroider eyelashes with outline stitch and mouth with two rows of chain stitch, in crewel yarn or six-strand embroidery thread.

Mane is made of six 14-inch hanks of knitting worsted or rug yarn, tied in the middle and hand tacked along the neck. The tail is made of a 28-inch long hank of same yarn tied in the middle and hand tacked firmly in place.

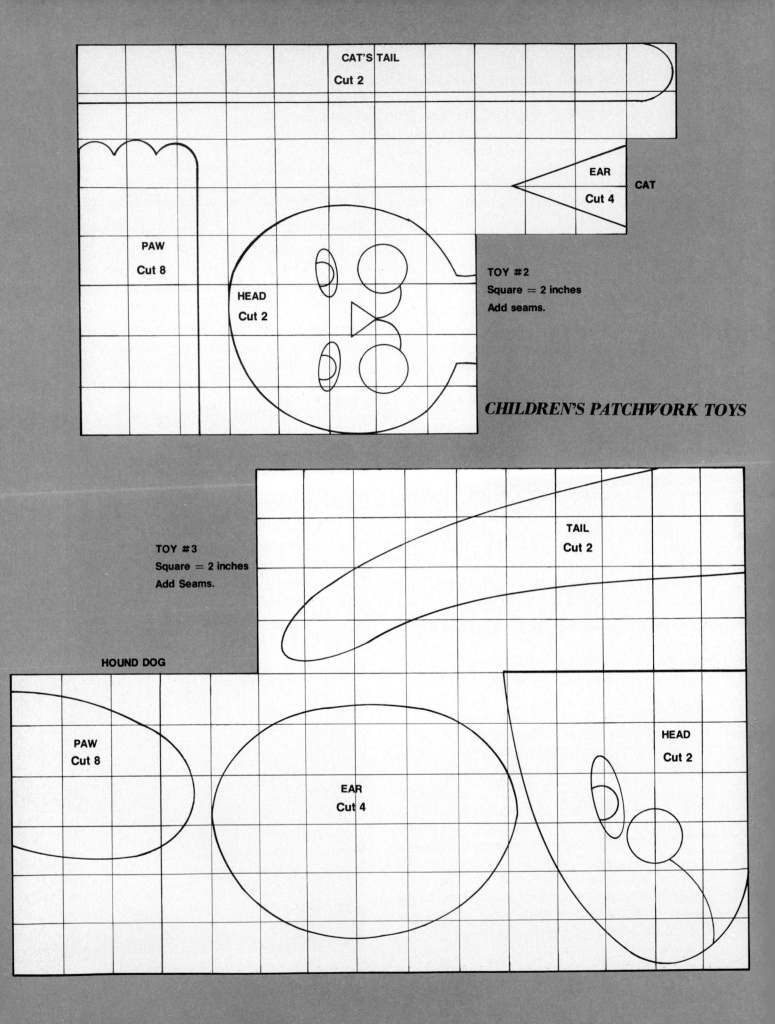

CAT'S TAIL
Cut 2

EAR
Cut 4

CAT

PAW
Cut 8

HEAD
Cut 2

TOY #2
Square = 2 inches
Add seams.

CHILDREN'S PATCHWORK TOYS

TOY #3
Square = 2 inches
Add Seams.

TAIL
Cut 2

HOUND DOG

PAW
Cut 8

EAR
Cut 4

HEAD
Cut 2

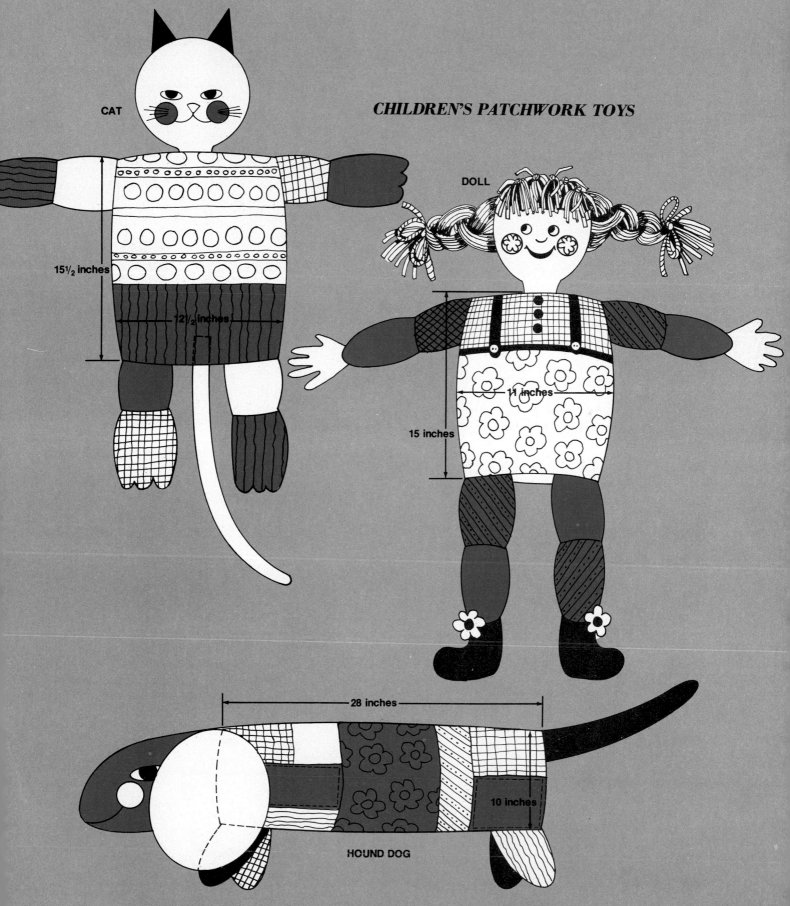

CAT

CHILDREN'S PATCHWORK TOYS

DOLL

15½ inches

12½ inches

11 inches

15 inches

28 inches

10 inches

HOUND DOG

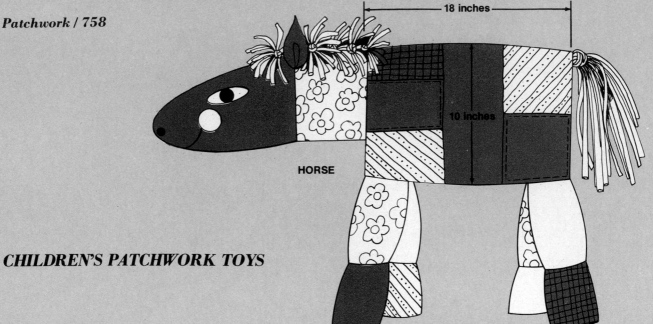

HORSE

CHILDREN'S PATCHWORK TOYS

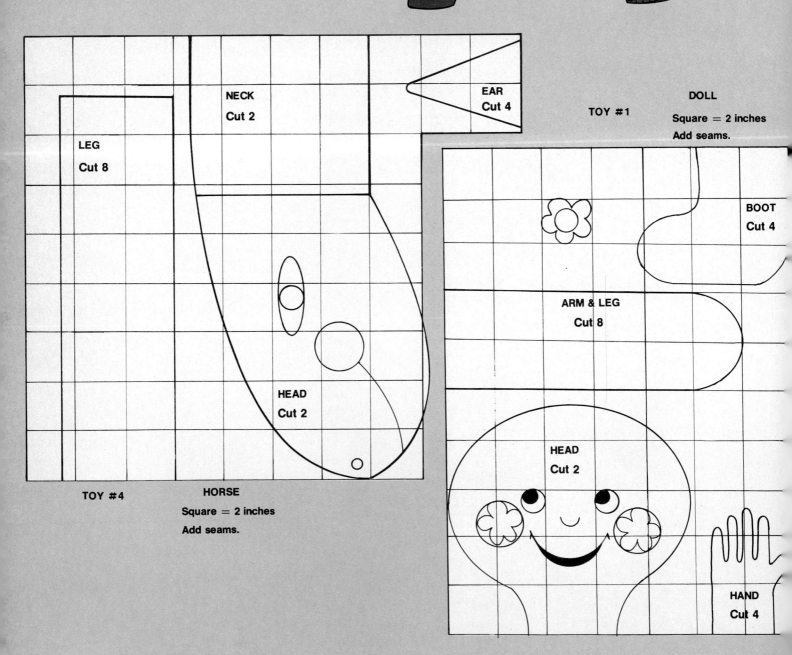

LEG
Cut 8

NECK
Cut 2

EAR
Cut 4

HEAD
Cut 2

TOY #4

HORSE

Square = 2 inches

Add seams.

TOY #1

DOLL

Square = 2 inches

Add seams.

BOOT
Cut 4

ARM & LEG
Cut 8

HEAD
Cut 2

HAND
Cut 4

RAINBOW ROUND THE WORLD PIECED QUILT

From the collection of Jinny Avery (made by her mother)

Even a one patch pattern can create a design of great intricacy when the colors are properly arranged. Here three main colors, burnt orange, melon and yellow, combine with many calico prints and plain white to produce a stunning effect.

Cut stacks of 2-inch squares in each color and white. The white can be simplified by cutting one 10-inch square for the center of each white diamond. Piece in graduated strips according to the diagram. Finish with plain borders of desired width in the three main colors.

JOB'S TROUBLES

Courtesy of Smithsonian Institute

Use all the scrap bag pieces to make this wonderful easy traditional design. The edge-to-edge piecing creates an effect of motion from the two-patch pattern.

If this is to be pieced in squares that are to be put together, cut the No. 2 piece in two down the dotted line, remembering to add seam, of course. Then each design will be centered in a 6-inch square.

The quilt pictured is pieced continuously. The finished size is approximately 78 by 90 inches. It is finished with a dark binding. It might be even more attractive to omit some rows of the design and finish with a 6-inch print border.

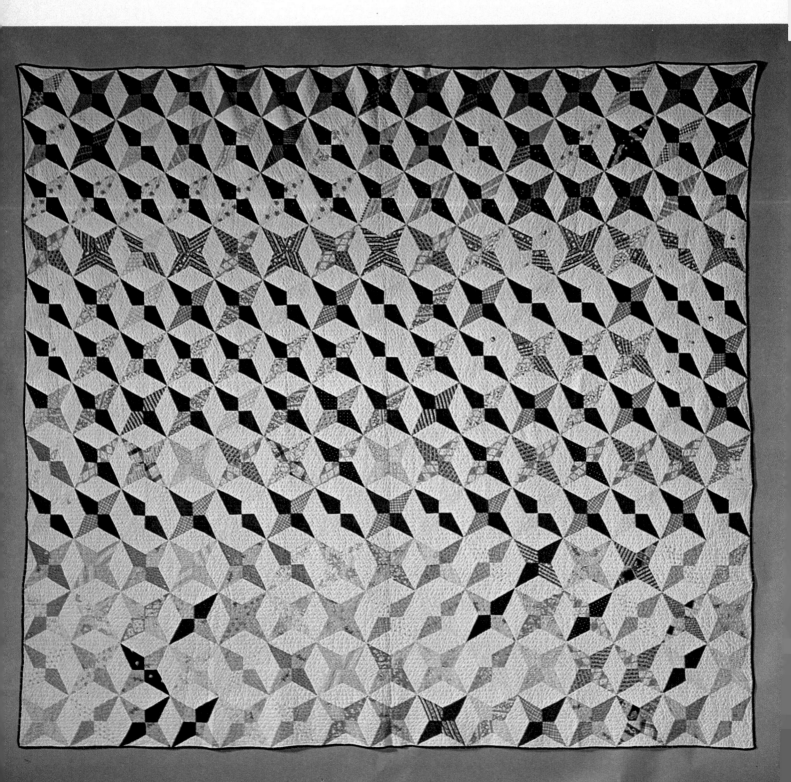

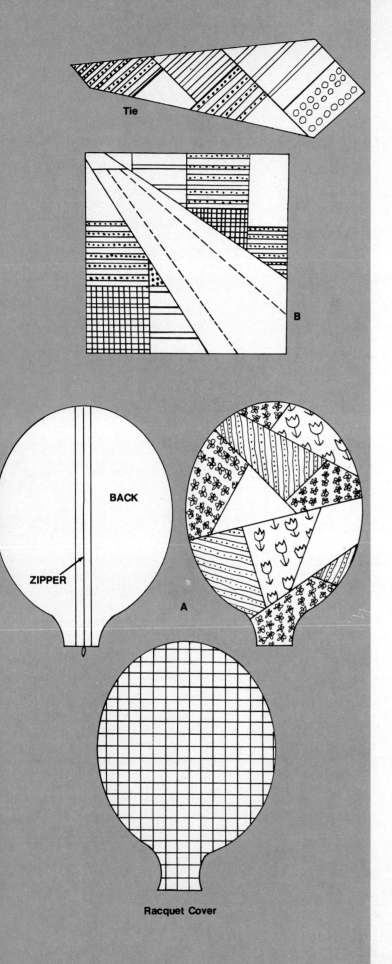

Tie

B

BACK

ZIPPER

A

Racquet Cover

TENNIS RACQUET COVERS

Designed and created by Jinny Avery

Two different types of patchwork are used for the two covers pictured — seamed squares and crazy patch. Both can be made on the machine, though the seamed squares shown here are quilted by hand.

On brown paper draw a pattern around a tennis racquet, leaving a little extra room for the thickness of the frame so that it is easy to zip the finished cover. Allow seams, being sure to allow seams along the center line of the back piece for zipper. Both sides can be patched or the back can be of a solid sturdy fabric such as denim or canvas. Make corded piping to match or contrast, using $1/8$ to $1/4$-inch cable cord.

Piece an area of fabric large enough to accommodate the pattern. The squares may be seamed together on the machine, then laid on Pellon® fleece or heavy non-woven interfacing and quilted by hand or machine. The crazy patches are worked directly onto the fleece backing with zigzag machine stitch as described in Crazy Quilts. A third layer of very fine cotton under the fleece makes the cover wear better.

Apply the zipper in the center of the back piece, join front to back with corded piping between. Stitch seam binding around lower edge, turn up and hem in place.

TIES

Designed and created by Jinny Avery

Use any tie pattern. Piece enough squares and rectangles by machine to accommodate the pattern for the wide tie piece, remembering that it must be laid bias, as shown. The narrow back piece of the tie may be cut from any of the fabrics used in the front. Lightweight fabrics work best, cottons, wools, silks or synthetics, but they must be crease resistant. The squares should be about $1 1/2$ inches in size.

RAINBOW ROUND THE WORLD
PIECED QUILT

X Burnt Orange

O Melon

I Yellow

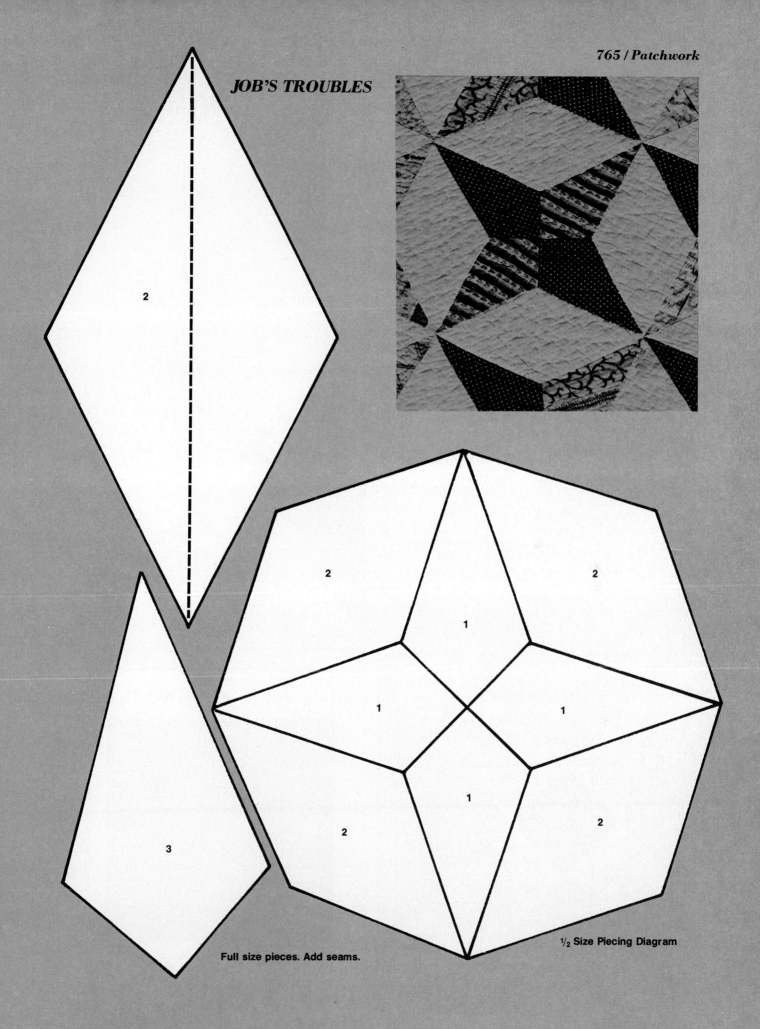

JOB'S TROUBLES

2

2

2

2

1

1

1

1

1

2

2

3

Full size pieces. Add seams.

½ Size Piecing Diagram

ODDFELLOW'S CROSS

Full size pieces. Add seams.
1/4 Size Piecing Diagram

2

CHECKERBOARD
PIECE FOR
BORDER

6

5

4

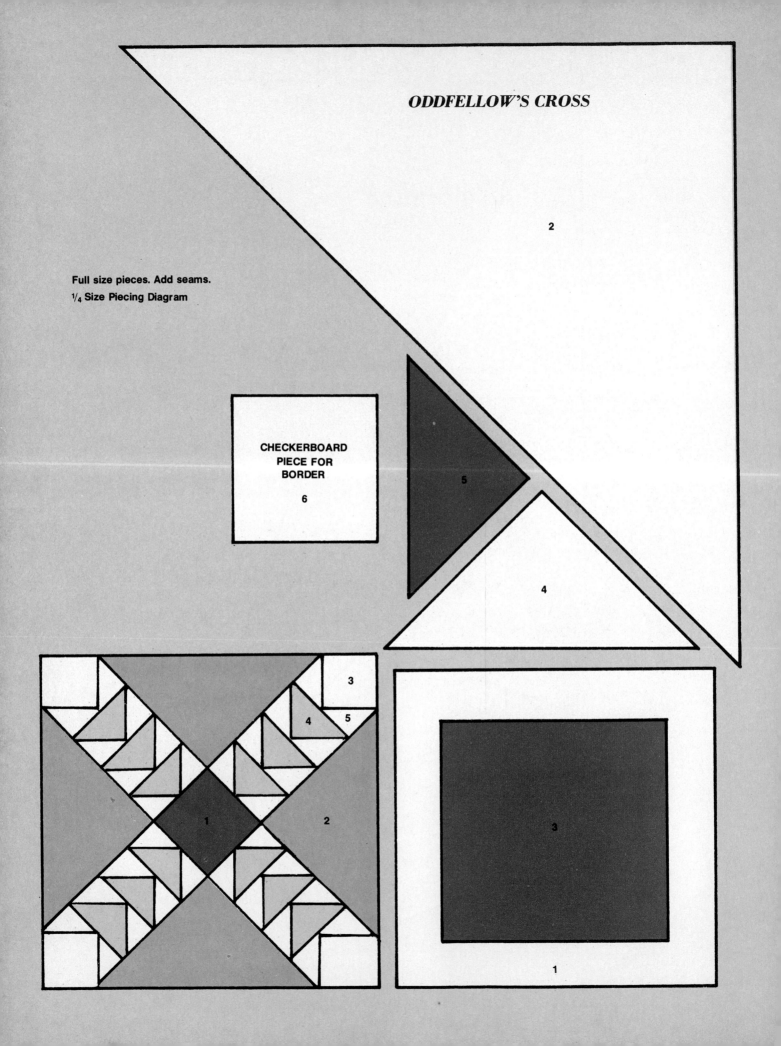

3

4   5

1   2

3

1

ODDFELLOW'S CROSS

Courtesy of Smithsonian Institute

Anything goes, in terms of colors and prints, so Oddfellow's Cross is the ideal scrap bag quilt. Each finished square is about 13+ inches and each set or border about 4½ inches so this quilt is close to 90 inches each way. One more row on the length would make it a perfect double bed quilt for modern beds.

For each square–cut one of No. 1, four of No. 2, four of No. 3, twelve of No. 4, all in print scraps.

Cut thirty-two of No. 5 in white. For the borders–cut strips 4½ inches wide to match the length of the pieced squares and five solid color and four white No. 6 pieces for the checkerboard block in each corner.

Quilting is stitched around the shapes of the pieces. The edge can be finished with a narrow bias binding of the solid color used in the checkerboard.

This design is also a suitable size for a pillow and can be extended to 16 inches with a border.

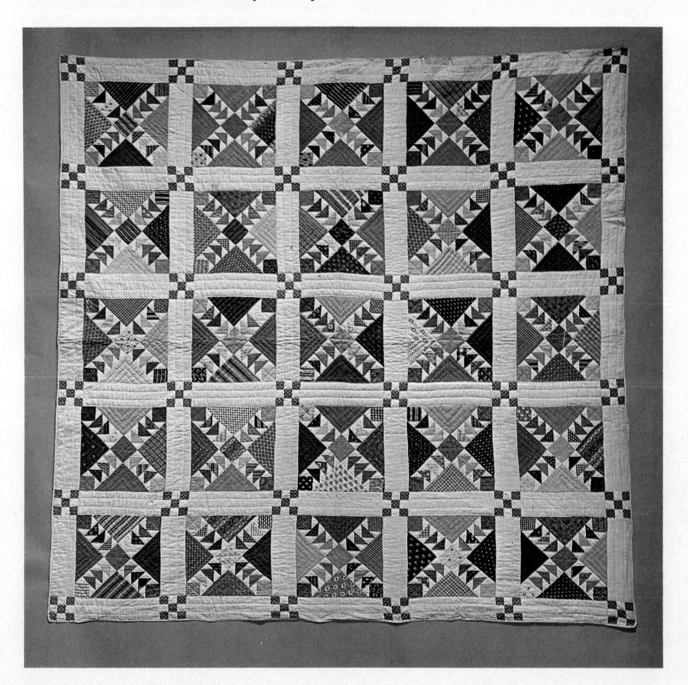

CHIPS AND WHETSTONES

Optical illusion plays a large part in this elaborate pieced or pieced and appliquéd quilt design! It is made in the same way as Mariner's Compass and Sunburst designs but the use of white spaces produces an entirely different effect.

For use as shown, piece only the four points and appliqué them on a solid white background, appliqué the center on, then quilt the circle around or, cutting pieces 5 and 6 in white, piece the entire circle. If working in the first way, four No. 1 in a dark shade, eight No. 2 in a contrast, sixteen No. 3 in a medium shade and one center in a print will be needed. If working in the second way, four No. 5 and thirty-two No. 6 in white will also be needed. The flowers for the corners are made in the contrast shade of No. 2.

The quilt, as shown, with 5-inch print borders, is approximately 80 by 100 inches, a good double bed size. It will also make a marvelous top for a round pillow.

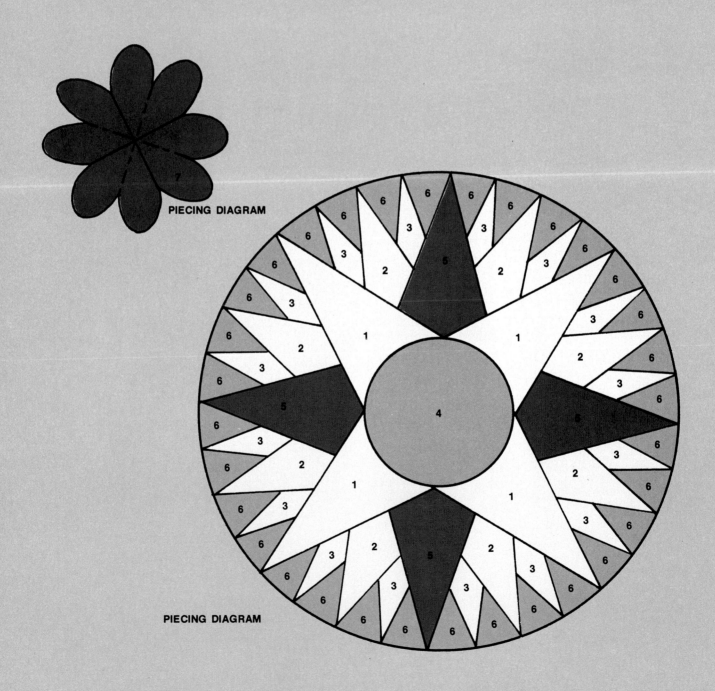

PIECING DIAGRAM

PIECING DIAGRAM

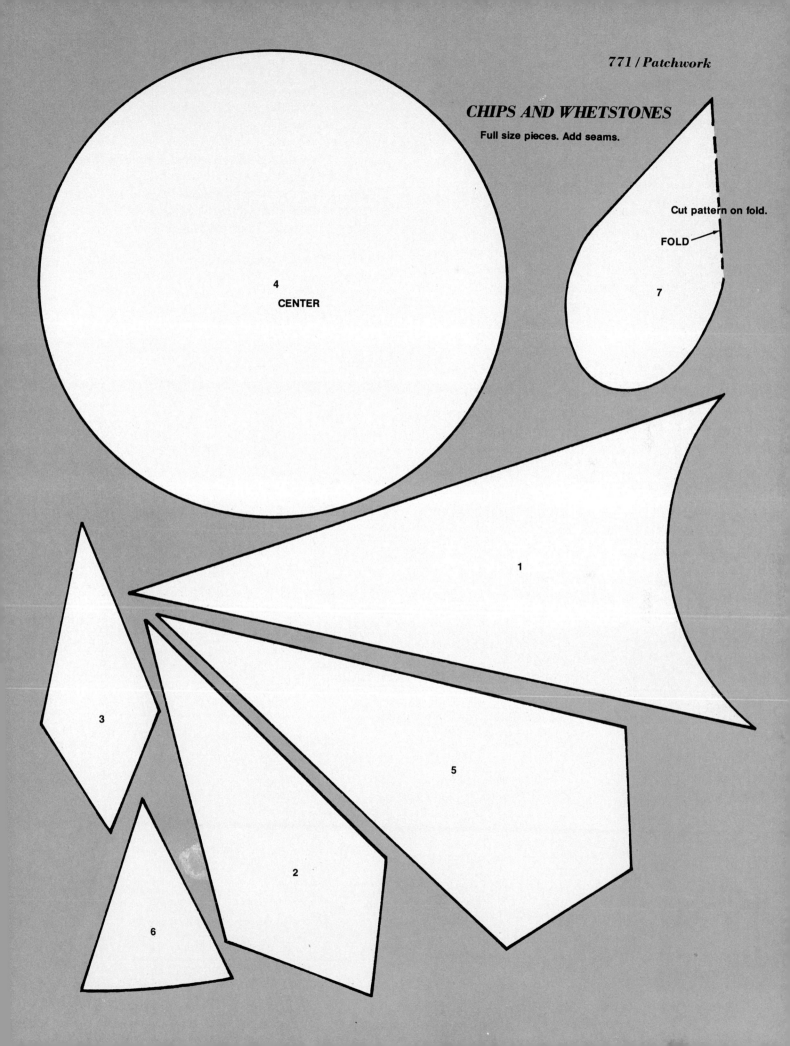

CHIPS AND WHETSTONES

Full size pieces. Add seams.

Cut pattern on fold.

FOLD

7

4
CENTER

1

3

5

2

6

FREE FORM MODERN PILLOWS

Designed and created by Carter Houck

The diagrams given are really suggestions to use as a point of departure for individual designs. Draw designs on a small scale, using ruler, dressmaker's curved ruler and compass. After selecting a design, draw it on brown paper the size of the pillow being used. Especially with the velveteen, which is difficult to press smoothly, it is good to have the cover ½ inch smaller than the pillow form so that the fabric is tightly stretched.

Cut the brown paper pattern apart on the lines that have been drawn and *add ½-inch seam all around each piece.* Do this as with any quilt pattern, drawing around pattern pieces on the back of the fabric and cutting ½ inch away from the lines. This will give a marked stitching line. Stitch the pieces together by machine, assembling them in whatever order makes for the least number of continuous seams. Assemble the pillows with a solid color back and an invisible zipper.

Five colors were used; three will do but the more the merrier. One-half yard each of three to five colors will make three to five 14-inch or 16-inch knife-edged pillows.

PIECING DIAGRAM

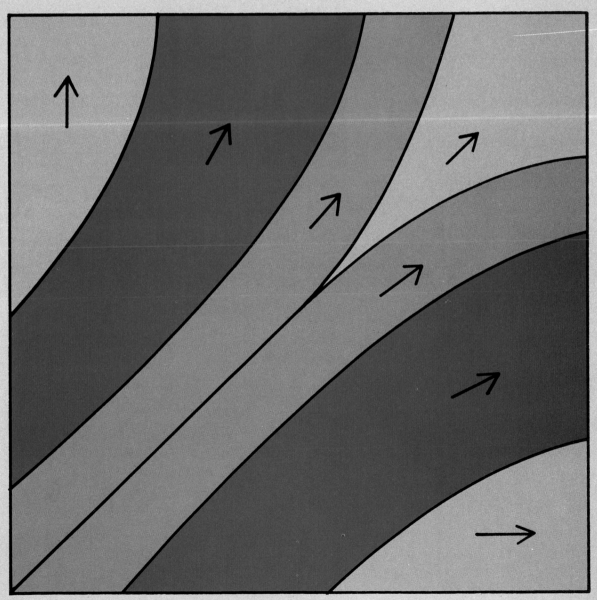

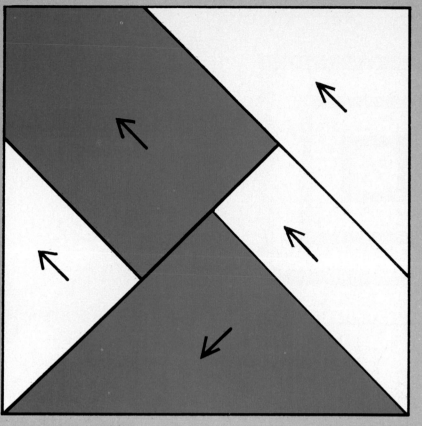

PIECING DIAGRAM

FREE FORM MODERN PILLOWS

PIECING DIAGRAM

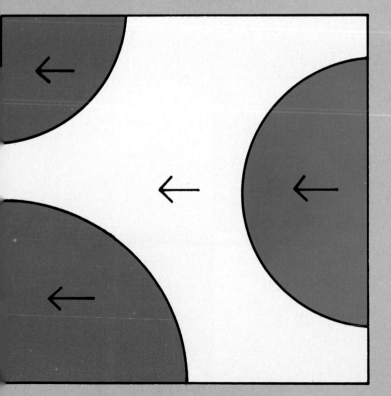

STRIPED FOUR-PATCH PILLOWS

Designed and created by Carter Houck

The designs for these pillows are old standard four-patch designs, made by folding a square of paper the size of the pillow either diagonally or straight into four sections. The sections are then divided into various smaller elements and the stripes played against each other to enhance the effect. Cotton, silk or wool are effective; the fabric pictured is Mexican hand-woven cotton. India cotton bedspread fabric gives much the same effect. It is wise to preshrink fabrics of this type first.

The patches can all be joined by machine and then machine seamed to a solid color back. Use an invisible zipper in one edge. It is necessary to pin crosswise along each seam carefully to keep the stripes lined up or alternated as desired.

One-half yard each of two striped designs and 2½ yards of the solid color, 39 inches wide, was used for four pillows. It is best to make a layout and check yardage when buying fabric in other widths. Remnants are perfect for projects like this. (See next page for diagrams.)

STRIPED FOUR-PATCH PILLOWS

POT HOLDER PATCHES

Designed and created by Carter Houck

The pot holders and apron pockets shown are about 7 inches each when made from the four traditional quilt patterns. The same patterns can be used for quilt patches or, if a quilt that looks boldly modern is desired, double the size of the blocks.

Piece the square or hexagon for one side of each pot holder and cut a solid piece the same size for the other side. Machine quilt each side to a piece of Pellon® Fleece or a layer of quilt batt. Seam around edges, leaving one side open about 4 inches for turning, including a small fabric or cord loop in one corner of the seam. Trim interfacing nearly to stitching, cut off corners and turn. Slip stitch opening. The pocket is also lined to the edge but no interfacing is included.

MAN'S PATCHWORK VEST

For the ultimate in wacky wonderful vests, make a patchwork of fur, suede, leather, vinyl and fake fur. Use any relatively plain pattern and leave out any front darts; the side seam can be nipped a little tighter to make up for it. We chose one that met at the front with a zipper but even eliminated the closing altogether. If a man preferred the vest to close, a conventional type could be used and velcro put under the edge instead of buttons and buttonholes which could present a problem.

Cut the vest fronts of a firm interfacing fabric. Make a happy arrangement of patches on the backing so that the edges meet closely. If the fakes and the fabrics are put along the edges, it may make seaming easier but a good heavy-duty machine and a special leather needle should make all things possible. Zigzag or hand-sew the patches to the backing like a crazy quilt, using heavy-duty thread. If hand sewing, choose a decorative stitch such as chain. Leave the long-haired fur pieces until last and sew only the top and side edges so that the fur will hang down freely.

Make the back of wool knit or flannel and the lining front and back of any firm fabric. Sew the vest together leaving either sides or shoulders open for a flip lining and sew the lining exactly the same way. Sew the two together around the edges and armholes and turn right side out. Finish side seams or shoulders which were left open.

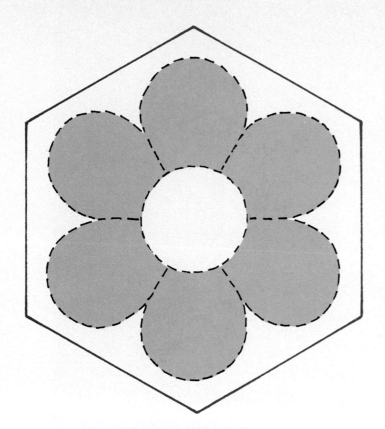

GIANT HEXAGON MOSAIC QUILT

Courtesy of Smithsonian Institute

An old pattern, the same one used in much smaller scale for Grandmother's Flower Garden, is shown here in colors that a child would love. This one is a single bed size.

When all the pieces have been cut, start seaming them together from the center out. One very clever with a sewing machine may be able to machine join the whole quilt. Unless very soft fabric is being used, the paper liners suggested for this design in smaller sizes probably will not have to be used.

The borders can be any of the happy colors in the quilt in bands. The little floral quilting designs may be used on all or alternating hexagons. The other hexagons can be quilted in shadow form following the outline of the pieces themselves.

Quilting Suggestion

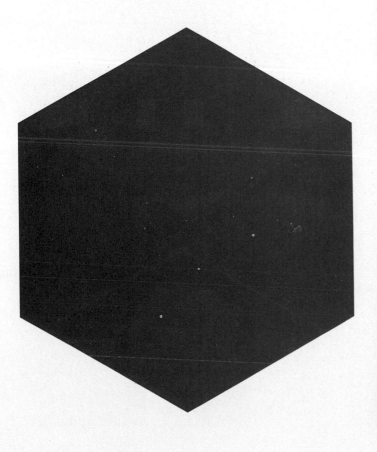

POTHOLDER PATCHES

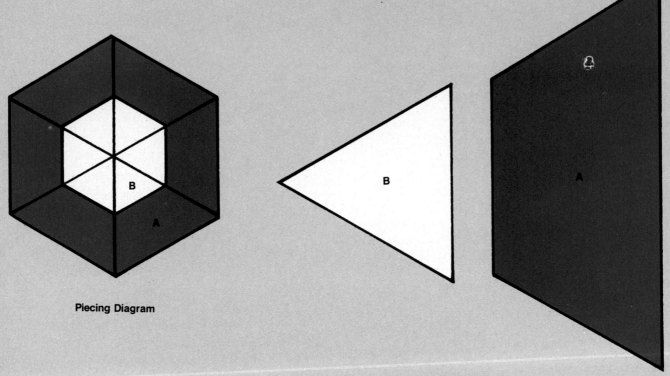

Piecing Diagram

Full Size Pattern Pieces
Add seams.

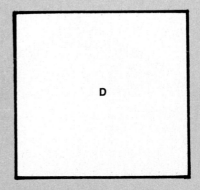

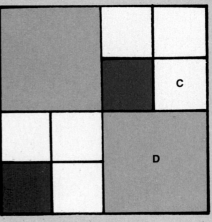

PIECING DIAGRAM

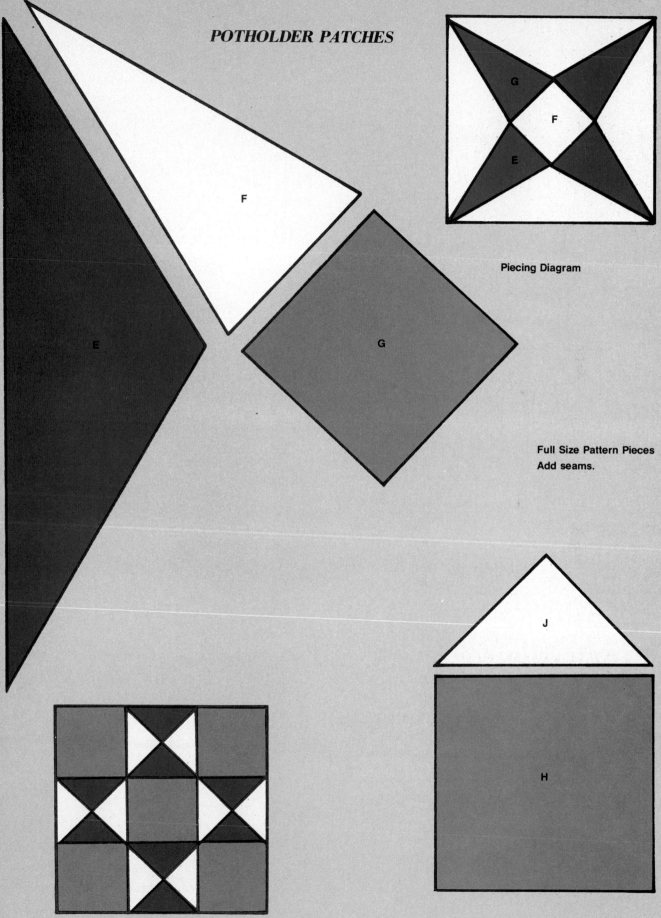

POTHOLDER PATCHES

F

E

G

Piecing Diagram

Full Size Pattern Pieces
Add seams.

G

F

E

J

H

Piecing Diagram

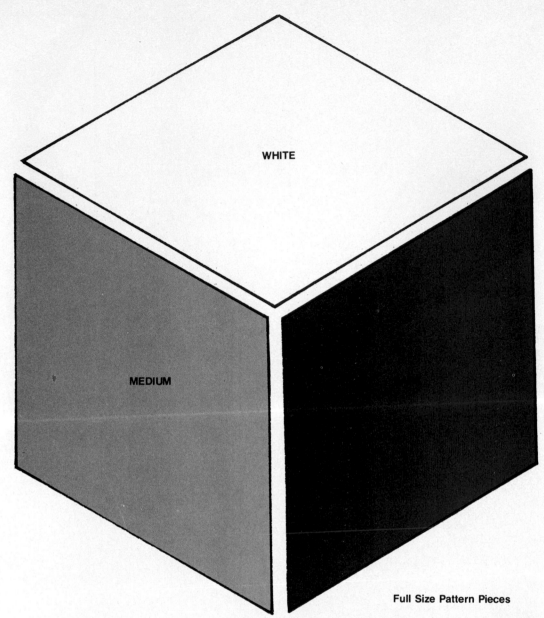

WHITE

MEDIUM

Full Size Pattern Pieces

GIANT TUMBLING BLOCKS

Courtesy of the Smithsonian Institute

What child could resist the big bright tumbling blocks of this crib quilt?! The trick is one light, one medium and one dark piece in each block, always in the same order.

Someone handy with the sewing machine may be able to piece this quilt that way. Piece one block at a time and then start putting them all together.

Any simple quilting design will work as there are nice large spaces to work in. Finish with a border of your choice.

BEAR'S PAW OR DUCK'S FOOT IN THE MUD

Courtesy of Smithsonian Institute

The early quilt designs acquired some marvelous names and this one is a prizewinner! It is an especially interesting star variation and a great scrap bag design.

For each block cut a 2½-inch (plus seams) center square and four of No. 2 in the same color or tone. Cut four rectangles 5 x 2½ inches (plus seams), four of No. 1 and eight of No. 3 in white. Cut sixteen of No. 4 in assorted scraps. Piece the corner blocks and then put them together with the four rectangles and the center square.

The borders are similar to the borders on Odd-fellow's Cross, with a checkboard pattern of four solid color and four white squares. The alternating striped rectangles in between add more color interest but solid pieces could be used. Quilting is all done in straight line designs.

INDIANA PUZZLE (Crib Quilt)

Pieced by Jinny Avery

Not only is this design a puzzle but a never ending source of amazement. Such a wonderful whirling pinwheel is created with three triangles and one square, placed exactly so!

For each square cut two red and two white in each of the four shapes. Piece four squares as shown in the diagram and put them together back to back so that the four red large triangles meet in the center to form a red square from which the arms whirl out as shown in the picture. The small squares first pieced measure 10 inches each, the large four-square pattern measures 20 inches. Twelve large blocks with appropriate border will make a full-size quilt.

Jacket With Simple Lines: Designed and created by Jinny Avery from a Crazy Quilt. A super evening jacket can be made by piecing the fabric from scraps or from an unfinished Victorian quilt found in an attic.

Bag With Mosaic: Designed and created by Carter Houck from unfinished quilt pieces. Someone started a mosaic quilt but never got very far. However, there was enough for the appliquéd decoration and lining for a giant sail cloth shopping bag.

BEAR'S PAW OR DUCK'S FOOT
IN THE MUD

1

2

3

4

Full Size
Pattern Pieces–
Add Seams

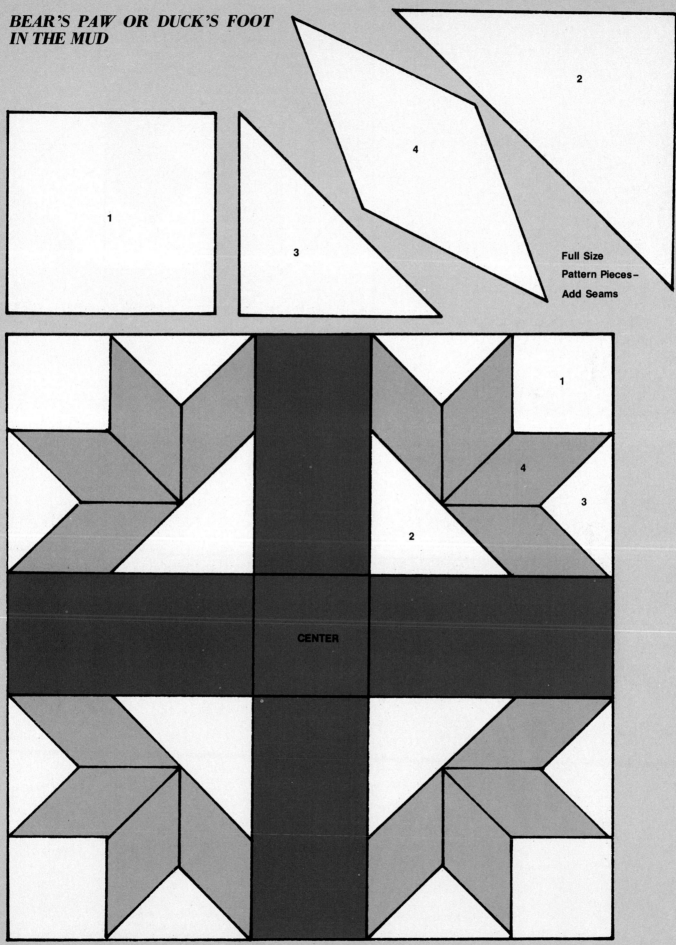

1

4

3

2

CENTER

PIECING DIAGRAM

INDIANA PUZZLE

PIECING DIAGRAM

Throw Made From Ten Silk Pieced Squares Found At A Sale: Designed by Carter Houck and created by Martha Ann Crowe. These Victorian silk crazy quilt squares, 14 inches each, made a perfect afghan stretched with 4-inch bands and 8-inch borders of black velveteen. The extra square fit a pillow to match.

PATCHWORK POTPOURRI

Here are a number of project ideas that can be made from 4-inch squares or 1½-inch strips.

Originality in design is the key to attractive patchwork. Use your favorite combination of colors in fabrics — solids, prints, checks, stripes and polka dots.

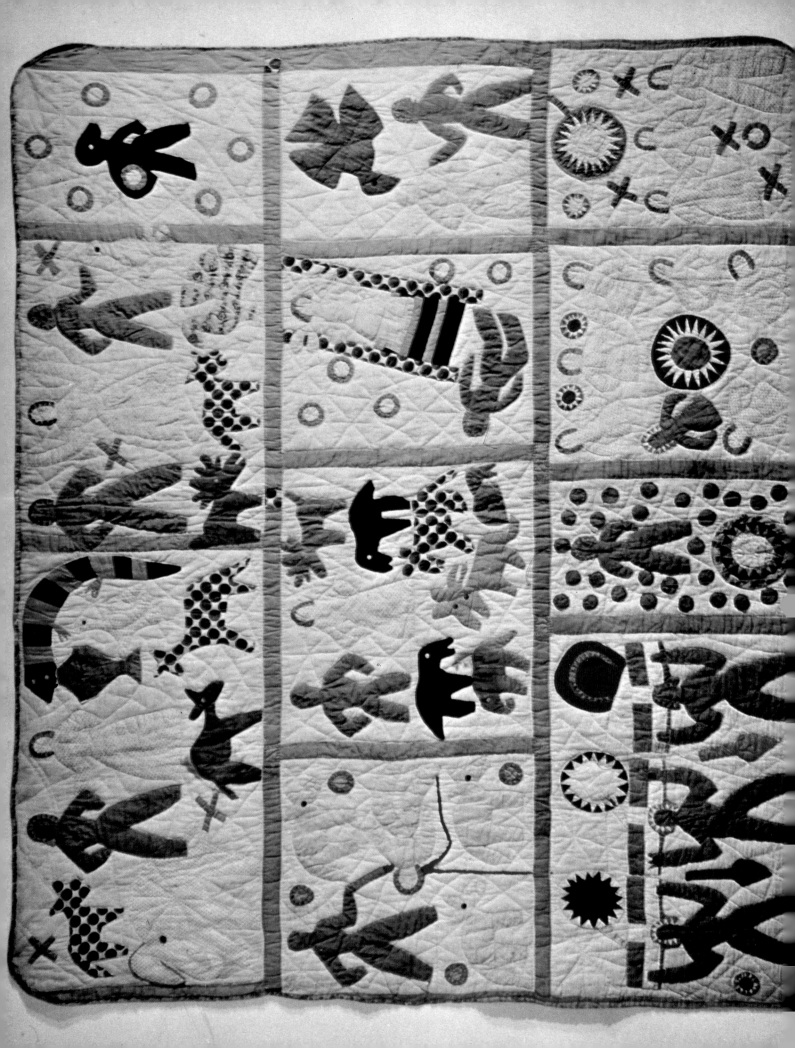

Appliqué

The word "Appliqué" is a French word which literally means, "laid on." A design is cut from one fabric; appliquéd, or laid on, to another; then sewed into place. Appliqué, like embroidery, dates back for centuries, its history lost in ancient, uncertain origins. Robes and hangings with lavish surface decorations are mentioned throughout the Bible; a Cairo museum has an appliquéd funeral tent about 3000 years old. During the Middle Ages, appliqué was used in heraldic and domestic work as well as ecclesiastical designs — Crusaders carried appliquéd banners and flags. Because the Church was all important through the 16th century, there are a number of fine examples of ecclesiastical needlework in museums throughout the world. In Europe particularly, Church robes and hangings were lavished with appliqué and embroidery; the use of gold and silver, silk and velvet was quite common.

Early American forms of appliqué were designs cut from the *palampores* brought back by New England sea captains from their long voyages.

These were hand-blocked fabrics from India, vibrant with color. Women cut out the birds of paradise, the flowers and the intertwining trees and arranged them in a pleasing pattern on a homespun sheet, then carefully sewed them into place with tiny stitches. However, since these Indian fabrics were scarce and expensive, women gradually began to plan their own designs and cut patterns from available materials. It was challenging and exciting work; it permitted a change from the straight seams of geometric pieced work and was not confined to rigid mathematical design. Such appliqué work was gradually refined into an art form.

From these beginnings emerged the appliquéd quilt, which reached its peak of perfection in America in the 19th century. It was during this era that quilt makers discovered the curved seam and the flowing elaborate designs of appliqué. Many of the quilts made during this period were called "Masterpiece" quilts — and indeed, they were. These quilts were never intended for actual use. They were the personal statements of the women who made them, and often it took years to complete a large quilt with an intricate design. Such quilts were made to exhibit, to admire, and eventually, to hand down to children and the children's children. Many patterns, both traditional and new, were passed from family to family, and from village to village. Each quilt

Harriet Power's "Bible Quilt, 1886" Courtesy of Smithsonian Institute.

maker used them, but often changed details of the design or chose a new color scheme.

Appliqué designs, of course, changed constantly, and were adapted to different uses in different countries. A piece of colored fabric sewed to a background was an inexpensive but challenging substitute for solid embroidery. Thus this idea grew and enlarged old ideas of needlework.

Many of the appliquéd designs used on clothing today reach back into the past, but have been changed and modified for current styles. Tapestries, bedcovers and wall hangings were changed and modified too. Today there are virtually no limits or rules to appliqué — but certain techniques and directions are helpful as a guide for the beginner.

DESIGN

Design, like ancient Gaul, is divided into three parts — color, form, and pattern — and all are equally important. Nature will probably be the most abundant source for ideas — trees and leaves; flowers and their petals and seedpods; butterflies and insects; birds; the sun and moon; the star patterns of the sky, etc. Add to these, pictures in magazines and newspapers; photographs; the pattern on china or wallpaper, shapes of bottles and kitchen utensils, and the simple lines of

children's drawings and toys. The list is endless. It is important to jot down original ideas in a notebook, along with the clippings. Look at other examples of appliqué work, from early to modern, simple to elaborate. Don't copy — remember personal interpretation and adaptation are the most important elements in creative needlework. A beginner should start with something simple — geometric shapes, an illustration from a child's coloring book, an original drawing. In planning the design, cut or tear shapes from colored paper. Move them around on a piece of fabric until the arrangement is satisfactory. Often, these shapes, spontaneous as they are, can suggest new ideas as the arrangement progresses.

FABRICS AND FOUND OBJECTS

Fabrics are, of course, an integral part of the design, both in color and texture. Sometimes an idea for a project will lead the craftsman to search for a particular fabric to best express this idea. Other times, the fabric itself will suggest an idea from which to build a project.

In appliquéing quilts, dress-weight cottons, such as those used in pieced work will be used most frequently in the appliquéd design. However, almost any fabric or combination that achieves the

desired effect is permissable. Loosely woven fabrics, such as burlap or tweed, give interesting effects when the edges are frayed. For clear, sharp outlines use firm fabrics with turned under edges. For delicate, misty and muted effects use nets, laces and organza. Often appliqué work can be embellished further with bits of leather, yarns, shells, beads and feathers. Background fabrics should be firm, preferably plain or with a subdued pattern. Good choices are felt, denim, various weights of linen, lightweight wools and flannels, and lightweight upholstery fabrics.

TRANSFERRING THE DESIGN

Once the pattern or design is drawn on paper it is necessary to transfer it to the fabric. In starting, choose a firm, neutral fabric for background. Cut the background fabric 1½ to 2 inches larger than the proposed project. Outline the exact measurements of the finished project with a thread-baste line. This will help to keep the design in balance. Mark the center of each side on this line with crossed pins; mark the intersection of these imaginary lines in the middle of the background fabric. This will make it easy to center the design.

Depending upon the design and background fabric, there are several ways to transfer the design. *First,* use dressmaker's carbon paper and a tracing wheel, orangewood stick or the end of a knitting needle. This works well with plain smooth fabrics. A *second* method is hot iron transfer. Transfer pencils are obtainable from needlework shops and mail order houses. Place tracing paper over the design and copy it with the transfer pencil. Place the tracing paper, transfer side down, against the right side of the background fabric. Pin it in place. Then, use a hot iron (not steam) on the paper. Use a lifting motion so the design will not smudge. The heat of the iron transfers the design to the fabric. Remember, however, this will produce a mirror or reverse image. A *third* method is to draw the design on tissue paper. This is an especially good method to use if the background fabric is nubby or loosely woven so lines are difficult to see. Baste the tissue paper in place on the fabric; then work each design area over this, tearing the tissue away as each section is finished.

If, instead of drawing the design on paper, the design is planned with cut or torn paper shapes, these are pinned to the background fabric. Trace around each shape carefully with a pencil; if pencil lines are indistinguishable, use needle and thread to outline the shape with a running stitch. Then, carefully remove one paper shape at a time to use as a liner or template for the fabric pieces. Chalk can also be used to transfer the design. But since it has a way of disappearing, it should be replaced with thread basting or pencil. Sharpen the chalk with a single edge razor blade or use a sharpened chalk pencil.

Another method of transferring design on sheer or transparent fabric is to outline the design on paper with black ink. Place this drawing *under* the fabric and copy the design lines with a hard lead pencil. If the fabric is too opaque to see the design clearly, use a light box for this. (See pg. 740). Tracing or transferring key points instead of copying the complete pattern may often be sufficient to use as a guide.

Of course, in some instances it is not necessary to transfer the design. The shapes may be cut directly from the fabric itself.

PATTERN PIECES

Once the design is transferred to the ground fabric and the color has been decided, it is time to duplicate the shapes of the design for use in creating pattern pieces for the appliqué fabrics. An easy method for making these patterns is to trace the design shapes on cardboard. Remember, these shapes are the *finished* size of the appliqué — they *do not* include seam allowances.

For fabrics that require a turned under edge, trace around the cardboard pattern on the *right* side of the fabric. In cutting, allow an extra ¼ inch for turning. Remember too, inside or concave curves must be clipped at frequent intervals; convex curves must be notched to eliminate bulk. Stay stitching with a small machine stitch around the outline of design or shape is often quite helpful. It makes for a neat turning and aids in controlling the fabric. It is easier to stay stitch *after* the design is drawn, *before* it is cut.

Because felts, vinyls, leathers and suedes have a finished edge, they can be cut out on the finished

line. Burlap and tweed are too coarse and heavy to turn under on the raw edge; some sheer, delicate fabrics have a prettier, cleaner look if a seam allowance is not turned under. To keep such fabrics from fraying, before cutting out the appliqué pieces, spread a thin layer of white glue over the design outline. When it dries, it will be transparent; the edges will be smooth and the threads held in place.

For an opposite effect, deliberately rough up or fray the edges of the cut shape. This gives an uneven and softened outline that may add to, rather than detract from a particular design. Don't be afraid to experiment.

Some fabrics must be lined or interfaced for easier handling. Unbleached muslin or Pellon® held in place with a tiny spot of white glue works well. Often an iron-on interfacing is useful. The lining can be attached to the fabric with one of the fusible webs. First test these on samples to see that the character of the fabric is not altered. Such linings are cut *only* to the finished outline; the raw edge or seam allowance of the fabric is folded over them and basted in place.

HAND APPLIQUÉ STITCHES

The stitches of appliqué can be as varied as the fabrics. For traditional appliqué, a blind stitch — an almost invisible stitch — is the most commonly accepted procedure. From the wrong side, bring needle up just barely inside the design line on the ground fabric; catch a thread or two of the folded edge of appliqué shape; then, insert the needle into ground fabric directly underneath

NOTCH ¼-INCH

CLIP

STAYSTITCH

GLUE

this little stitch. To continue, bring needle again up through the ground, about $1/4$ inch from the first stitch; repeat all the way around.

In positioning the shapes for the design, it is important to remember that the edges of some shapes will overlap — thus, it will not be necessary to turn under the edge of the bottom shape. The folded edge of the overlapping piece will cover the raw edges of the bottom shape.

Many times the design will be complemented or completed by the use of embroidery stitches. A simple buttonhole or blanket stitch is often used. Crazy patch appliqué offers variety — (See Patchwork, pg. 749). Modern appliqué projects are often made more interesting and exciting with the use of different yarns and threads. A heavy yarn will give a bold, definite outline; silk thread will produce a sheen; and, stranded embroidery floss gives a matte look. Try straight stitches, or long and short stitches to hold down the appliqué design; the running stitch is also excellent for this. However, since any embroidery stitch will become part of the design, select one that will enhance the overall appearance of the project.

Puckering: Puckering is the greatest threat to successful appliqué work. Once puckering begins, it is very difficult to remedy so try to prevent it. When basting the fabric shapes into place on the ground fabric, baste through the centers. In basting only around the edges, the middle will sometimes puff instead of laying flat. Another way to prevent puckering is to use a frame or hoops for at least part of the work. In working on a block, a pillow top or a picture, it is possible to use a picture frame slightly larger than the project. With

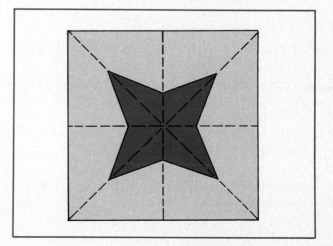

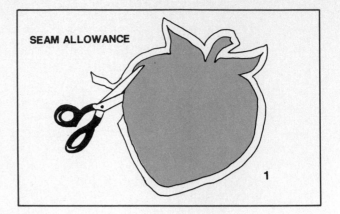

heavy button or carpet thread, lace the edges of the work around the sides of the frame; simply clip the thread when finished. As you experiment and progress in appliqué work, as in other types of needle art, you will develop and master your own techniques.

MACHINE APPLIQUÉ

Machine appliqué gives an entirely different, yet quite desirable, effect from that of hand appliqué. Machine appliqué is practical, particularly for articles that will get hard everyday wear and frequent laundering. It is also a fast, easy way to create a decorative design.

The more the beginner practices using the machine for this type of work, the more control she will gain. Pin or baste fabric shapes to the background material. The weight of the two fabrics should be sufficient to feed evenly through the machine. If this is difficult, waxed paper or tissue paper placed *underneath* the work and against the machine bed will keep the project from slipping. It can be removed later. The following are for machine appliqué.

Method 1: Leave the seam allowances on the appliqué shapes but do not turn them under. Baste shape in place. Machine stitch on the design outline with short straight stitches. Some machines are equipped with a quilting foot, which should be used. This is a short, open foot which makes it possible to see lines and curves with ease and to follow them accurately. If a quilting foot is not available, the regular foot will suffice, but stitching must be done more slowly. After the outline is stitched, use sharp scissors to trim seam allowance as close to the stitching line as possible.

Method 2: Set the machine for a close zigzag or satin stitch (a more decorative stitch may be used). Stitch around the shape completely enclosing the raw edges.

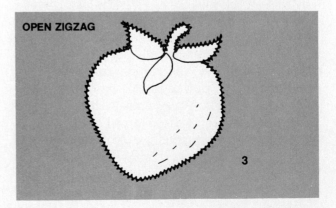

Method 3: Turn under the raw edges of the shapes. With a wide, open zigzag stitch catch the edge of the shape to the ground fabric. This is attractive in a thread of a contrasting color.

Method 4: Stitch around the shape several times with irregular lines. Use a short straight stitch, as in Method 1, but overlap the stitching lines and let them extend freely onto the background fabric.

Very large pieces of appliqué are sometimes difficult to handle in a machine and need a chair or an extra table to support the weight. Also, if the piece is long, roll the ends up as work progresses. Sometimes a large appliqué project can be worked in strips or sections. In attempting this, always sew as much of the appliqué work as possible before the sections are joined together.

PADDED APPLIQUÉ

Appliqué designs take on a new dimension when sections are raised or padded. The effect of light

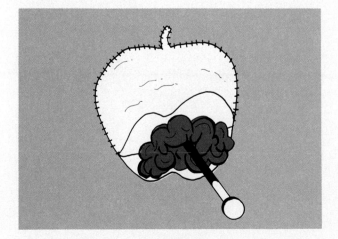

and shadow on the work makes the difference by causing the padded areas or shapes to stand out. The easiest way to pad or stuff a design is to sew three quarters of the way around the shape; then, with a knitting needle or orangewood stick, stuff bits of cotton, foam, polyester or old nylon stockings into the area. After it has been raised to the desired height, finish sewing around the edge. This technique is very attractive for flower petals, birds' wings and clusters of berries or grapes. For designs of the human figure, padding can be used on the bosom, hips, hair, hands and feet.

Another way to pad appliqué is with one or more layers of felt — remember, this is not washable. Before applying the appliqué shape, put a small piece of felt on the ground fabric in the center of the design; tack it down with a stitch or two. Cover this small felt piece with another slightly larger piece of felt; and, tack it down. Cover the second layer (if more height is desired) with a third, also slightly larger; tack it down. Now cover the felt layers with the appliqué shape; sew in place firmly all the way around. The applique shape should be cut slightly larger than the pattern so that it will completely cover the felt layers.

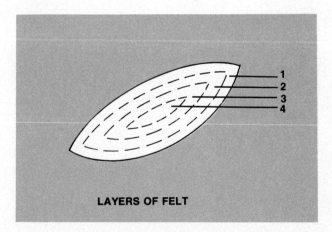

LAYERS OF FELT

Quilting The Design: This technique will also give appliqué a three-dimensional look. It is a subtle way to continue an idea. For example: with matching thread, quilt rain or rays from the sun with a slanting line from the sky; waves in the ocean with stitching lines that rise and fall; or clouds with stitching in loose curving lines. Use either hand or machine quilting, whichever suits your purpose. (See Patchwork, page 736.)

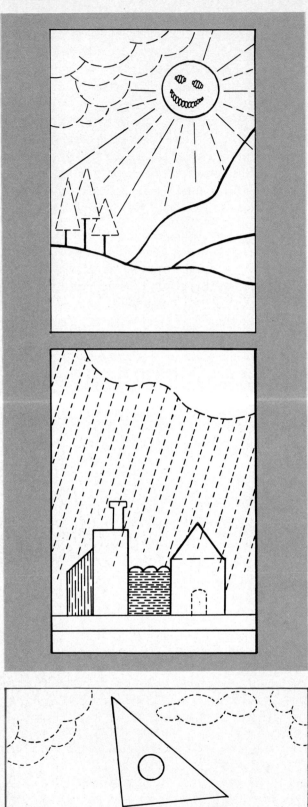

DETACHED APPLIQUÉ

Detached shapes must be cut double because both the back and the front will be seen. Motifs or designs can be cut from printed fabrics or the shape can be an original design. Flower clusters and leaves work well as detached appliqués — they are particularly attractive when used around the neck, sleeves, or hem of a dress or sweater. A variety of prints may be used for the flowers and a plain green for the leaves. For the flowers, cut out two shapes with seam allowance included. With right sides together, by hand or machine, stitch *all* the way around. Make a small slit in the center back, just large enough to get a finger or two inside to turn the appliqué right side out. Work the seam into place around the edge with fingers; press lightly if necessary. Now, attach the flower to the garment with a few small French knots (See Embroidery, pg. 302) in the center; the slit in back will be protected and covered.

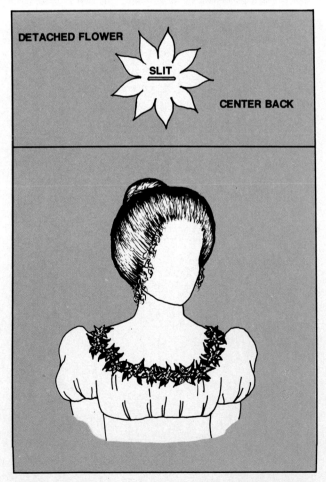

Saint Francis Feeding the Birds, worked by Jinny Avery from a design of the London Embroiderer's Guild.

When making the leaves, do not stitch all the way around; leave an opening along the edge for turning. After turning, close the opening with several tiny blind stitches. Fasten leaves slightly under flowers. Such appliqués are more effective if clustered.

Detached appliqué can be used on place mats too. A butterfly with gaily printed cotton for the wings is very attractive. Double the fabric and cut the butterfly in one piece; use the slit method on the back for turning. Pin the butterfly in place on the upper left-hand corner. Use a chain stitch or an outline stitch (See Embroidery, pg. 296) with black floss to attach the butterfly in the center; this will make its body and also protect and conceal the slit.

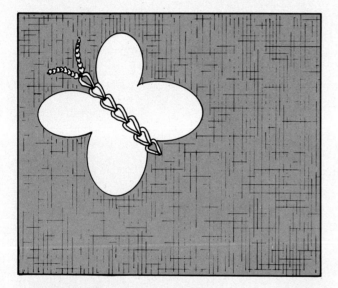

In appliquéing a simple animal shape, the ears and tail can be detached. On a Christmas tree panel, the ornaments — a few if not all — could be detached for unusual effect. There are endless ways to use creative detached appliqué — and, original ideas are always the most fun.

APPLIQUÉ QUILTS

Appliqué quilts, as mentioned earlier, were synonomous with the Golden Age of quilting at the end of the 19th century. The most popular design for American quilts was the rose. There are more

Quilt Sampler, Patchwork and Appliqué designed and created by Jinny Avery.

than 100 variations, but the Biblical Rose of Sharon is best known. Some other patterns are Rose Tree, Rose Wreath, Rambling Rose, Wild Rose, Rose Cross, Mexican Rose, Indiana Rose and Missouri Rose.

Rose of Sharon

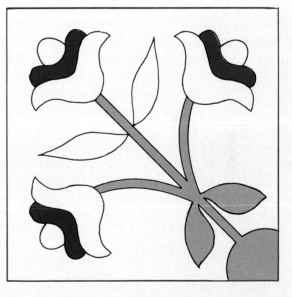

Rare Old Tulip

Tulip patterns were also popular and the appliquéd heart was a special favorite used lavishly on bridal and friendship quilts. The Eagle, either fierce or peace loving, was a popular political and patriotic symbol.

In the way of designs, little escaped the quilt maker's eyes. Many quilts of that period combined piece work with appliqué — a pieced basket filled with appliquéd flowers; a pieced Dresden plate pattern appliquéd to a plain block; an appliquéd Prince's Feather with a pieced star in the center where the feathers meet.

There were many women — then as now — who preferred to design and plan their own quilts. Some told stories or related family histories or events. Some were gay and warm and simple; others were sad. Many of these have emerged as fine examples of true folk art. The Shelburne Museum in Vermont is the proud owner of the Civil War quilt, a stunning reminder of that tragic event, and recorded in appliqué by a foot soldier who was hospitalized with injuries. The Smithsonian Institute in Washington owns the appliquéd Biblical treasure made by Hariett Powers.

Consider starting a family quilt by appliquéing simple versions of places or events that have special significance. Another personal project might be to make a small quilt for a child, picturing favorite toys, pets and games. Creative designs such as these will be cherished possessions.

Group quilt making, like the old-time quilting bees, is once again becoming popular. Aside from the social aspect, many groups make a significant contribution to their communities on a local level. One group made an appliqué quilt to draw attention to the need for conservation and restoration of a river and its environs. A group of churchwomen appliquéd a quilt as a gift to their minister; each block portrayed a different type of cross. Such quilts can be made for exhibit purposes or used for fund-raising through auctions.

DESIGN AND FABRICS

Proper techniques for making a quilt are discussed in detail in the Patchwork chapter, pages 737-745. Before planning an original quilt project, refer to this chapter.

In appliqué, as in pieced work, the first decision is the design or pattern. It is easier to work by the block method, and the size and "set" of the blocks will determine the number needed. The size of the block should accommodate the design without crowding, and there should be some space around it.

Also as mentioned earlier, all-cotton fabrics are best to use, and worth the search and the price. Some cotton blends are suitable, but select them with care. Add to a personal fabric collection constantly. Consider articles of clothing before discarding — a child's cotton dress, an apron, a man's shirt or a gay set of curtains. Any of these may contain sections of fabric worth using; discard any worn areas. Ask friends that sew to save scraps; check remnant counters.

Select the colors and fabrics for the quilting project. Cut or tear the background blocks true to the grain; preshrink and press *all* fabrics. The design should be correctly aligned on each block. First, make a sample block; fold it in half lengthwise and run a basting thread along the fold. Do this on the crosswise fold also; note the center — where the thread lines cross. Now, fold the rest of the background blocks in half lengthwise; press gently. Fold in half again; then crosswise. Press

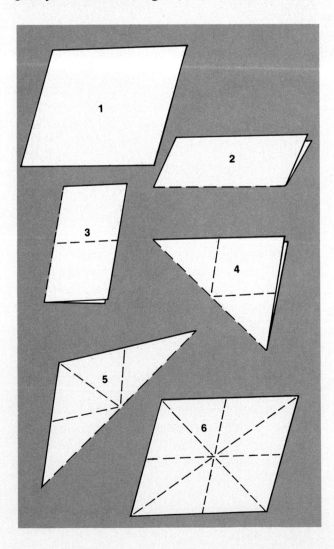

again. Compare these "quartered" blocks with the sample. The position in which the design must be placed can readily be seen. Trace the design lightly; the marks will later be covered.

After the blocks are prepared, appliqué shapes can be applied. If necessary make pattern pieces or templates for the design; trace it in entirety on cardboard; then, carefully cut each section apart. Make notes on each shape as to how many are needed for each block; note the color also. Cutting is tiresome but must be done one at a time for accuracy. Rather than cut the shapes ahead of time for the entire quilt, it is easier to cut enough for three or four complete blocks; put the makings of each block into separate envelopes.

Place the cardboard or plastic template on the *right side* of the fabric; draw around it with a pencil. These templates, as in pieced work, *do not include seam allowances.* Be sure to include a 1/4-inch allowance when cutting. Curves can be clipped after cutting or it is possible to wait until time to sew. Clipping is necessary so the work will lie flat.

Pin the appliqué shapes on the background block, matching up the pattern; then, baste in place. As noted earlier, the blind stitch is most acceptable for traditional appliqué. (See pg. 744.) It gives a soft, rounded effect to the appliqué and seems to raise it slightly from the surface. Pressing with an iron on these edges will take away this soft look; thus, finger pressing is sufficient. Appliqué can also be attached with a whipping stitch. It is stronger, but shows more and is not as pretty. In using a whipping stitch, try to keep the stitches as tiny as possible. This stitch is necessary in deep angles or at points.

Stems and other curving parts are easy to make with commercial bias tape, which comes with edges already pressed under. Since it is bias, the tape shapes easily to follow the curves of the design. It is available in two widths, the 1/2-inch standard width and the 1-inch "quilt binding" width. Either are helpful and convenient to use and come in a wide range of colors.

When all of the appliquéd blocks are finished and ready to join, proceed with the set and quilting in the same manner as a pieced top. (See Patchwork, pg. 733.)

HAWAIIAN QUILTS

Hawaiian quilts are appliquéd quilts, but quite different from other American counterparts. They present a unique form of design and a marvelous use of color and balance — often, only two colors are used in the Hawaiian quilt. The art of quilt making was carried to the Hawaiian Islands by missionaries. It met with almost instant success, but not in the way anticipated. In sharp contrast to New England colonists and Midwestern pioneers, the people of the Pacific Islands had never known poverty. Living in a warm, tropical climate, with little need for clothes, they were surrounded by lush vegetation, exotic flowers and fruits. Trade ships which stopped at the Islands left bolts of colorful cotton fabrics. Native women did not cut it up into hundreds of small pieces then sew them all back together again as did the Americans. For their designs, the Hawaiians looked to the bounty of nature surrounding them; they imitated and stylized flowers, fruit, trees and shrubs. The designs were big and bold, and the use of two colors further dramatized the effect.

Many old patterns have been cherished and passed down through families just as on the mainland. The Pineapple, an old favorite, is a symbol of hospitality. Others such as Silver Sword of Haleakalia; the Queen's Vase; Kahili, a fan-shaped pattern; and Ti-Leaves, Breadfruit and Ohelo Berries have all been worked into stylized and intricate patterns.

These natives usually cut patterns from folded paper, in the same manner a child makes snowflakes. This is an easy technique from which to devise original patterns.

Fold a square in half to make a rectangle, then fold again to make a square. Bring the folded edges together to make a triangle, then cut out the pattern through all the folds. Four 36-inch blocks of one of these patterns could easily be the basis for a quilt top.

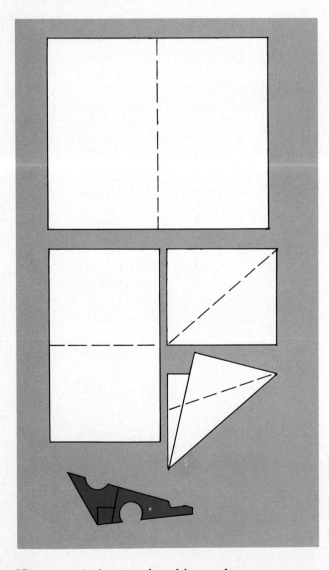

However, before undertaking a larger venture, try Hawaiian-type design on a pillow top. Cut several designs from paper, then choose the best. Fold the fabric in the same way as the paper; then align the folded paper on top of it, matching up the sides; pin firmly. Scissors must be very sharp to cut through these layers. If the layers are too thick to manage this, just lay the complete paper pattern on the single layer of fabric; pin securely; then cut. Be sure to center the design on the background block and to clip the curved edges. The raw edges can be tucked under with the needle during sewing. Check frequently to see that the work is not puckering.

Island women not only changed and developed their own designs, but they initiated a different type of quilting too. Their quilting lines follow the design both inside the appliqué and outside on the background fabric. The quilting lines are close together; they swell from the center outward like echoes or ripples on a pond, and somehow create an illusion of the seas that surround the Islands. Hawaiian women do not use quilting frames; they prefer to sit on the floor or ground with the basted quilt spread around them. They take great care and just pride in their careful stitching. The "wave" quilting they execute so beautifully is called *luma-lau*.

POPULAR STYLES OF MODERN APPLIQUÉ

INSTANT APPLIQUÉ

This is a speedy application of very simple geometric shapes. These simple shapes are suitable for children's clothes, curtains and pillows,

bedspreads or towels, and pillowcases. Several of them, used as repeats, could be used as blocks for a quilt.

Think of a circle. A circle can be a balloon, an orange, a sun or a lollypop. A half circle can be a turtle with a small circle for a head and four straight lines for feet. Two circles overlapping on top of a triangle can be an ice cream cone. Three triangles are a sailboat; two triangles are a butterfly — and so are four triangles. A diamond is a kite; two triangles make a basket filled with flowers of circles. These simple forms and designs can be used on jeans and jackets, skirts, anything at all. The sewing goes quickly with machine appliqué; and, of course, it is strong and durable and withstands a great deal of laundering.

CONTEMPORARY APPLIQUÉ

Contemporary appliqué is simply appliqué that has taken on new dimensions designed or adapted to modern ways of living. There is little discipline involved — new techniques and forms are part of a constant experiment. Banners and flags date back to Crusade times, but after that their appeal faded. Now there is a great resurgence of interest in banners, flags and all types of wall hangings. These are similar, except that a flag or banner is never stretched on a frame. A wall hanging can be mounted or it can hang free.

Appliqué has assumed an important place as wall decoration and often takes the place of familiar paintings. Folding screens, panels, room dividers, window shades and headboard hangings now enjoy common usage in homes. Significantly, industry has also embraced appliqué. Theatres, restaurants, airlines and office buildings constantly find new uses for needle arts. And, many churches are veering from the old traditional patterns of appliqué toward new freedoms of design in vestments and altar cloths.

Embroidery often enriches these articles — using all types of threads (including metallic) and yarns. Read about these in the Embroidery section, pg. 309.

For a contemporary look, fabrics are frayed, stuffed, padded, pulled apart, or overlaid with nets or organza. Some fabrics are mounted over shadow boxes; then sections are cut away to reveal further design underneath. This is new perspective on old forms, and it has great appeal for many people.

LINERS AND INTERFACINGS

By now you are familiar with the use of paper liners for quilt making; liners other than paper may help a great deal in other types of appliqué work. This is especially true for larger pieces — wall hangings and banners, pictures, etc. Velvets and metallics are among the fabrics that are enhanced most from such treatment.

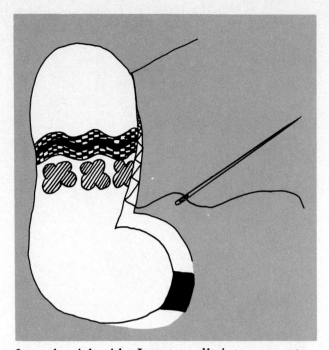

from the right side. Insert needle into one or two threads of the folded edge of one piece, then into the folded edge of the adjoining piece. Continue in this manner, gently but firmly pulling the stitches together. They will be almost invisible.

Letters or numbers are easy to handle on applique when treated this way. Instead of using glue, try a heat-fusible web, such as Stitch-Witchery, to hold the Pellon® to the fabric. But, first try it on a

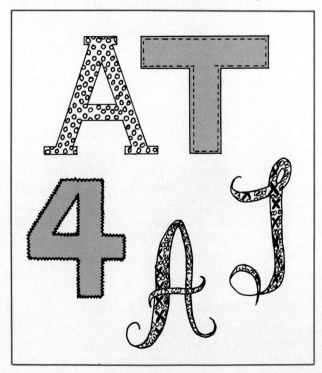

Regular or medium-weight Pellon® used in this manner will add body and ease in working; Pellon® fleece is heavier and will give a slight raised effect to the work. Cut either weight or Pellon® along the finished outlines of the design shape; place on wrong side of fabric, and pull the fabric seam allowances smoothly over the Pellon®. Hold in place with a small amount of white glue. If several of these shapes fit together on the applique (like a jigsaw puzzle), they can be held together with a ladder stitch. For this, work sample. Because the style and size of both letters and numbers can be easily changed, they offer many possibilities for unusual design. Try them with different fabrics, or combinations of fabrics; add a few embroidery stitches for emphasis. It is easier to do the embroidery before the appliqué is cut out and mounted.

REVERSE APPLIQUÉ

Reverse applique is just that — the reverse of regular appliqué. Instead of applying a fabric design *on top of* a background, the ground fabric is cut away to reveal several layers of different colors. The best known examples of reverse appliqué are done by the Cuna Indians of the San Blas Islands of Panama. Long ago, these women perfected the technique for use on their "molas," or blouses. Collectors prize such work highly, and use them for wall decorations or pillows. These designs are highly stylized, brightly colored and very intricately worked. The tiny slits give almost a carved or quilted effect to the surface.

This type of work is also called inlay work, as regular appliqué is called onlay. Reverse appliqué is also called cut-through work. It is more difficult to do than regular appliqué, but it is very exciting and challenging.

Dress-weight cottons are by far the easiest fabrics for this work, since there will be several layers. Percale, broadcloth, unbleached muslin and calico are all suitable. One layer of fabric for each main color of the design is necessary; four layers are quite enough to use at the beginning. Stack the layers one on top of the other, and secure the stack with basting stitches.

Draw the design on paper first, and color it; this will act as a guide. Draw the design on the top layer of fabric with a pencil. With sharp-pointed scissors, cut the shape out of the *top layer only.* While cutting out the shape from the top layer, the color of the second layer is revealed. In regular appliqué, the shape is *larger* than the design to allow for turning under the raw edges. In reverse appliqué, the shape will be smaller. However, as the curves and sharp angles are clipped and the raw edges turned under, the design shape will assume its proper size.

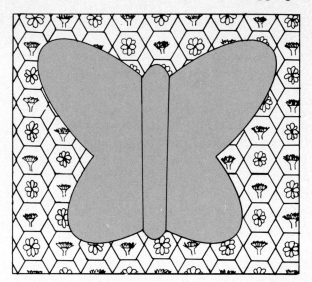

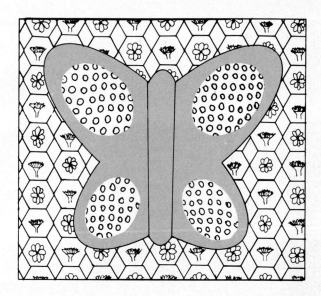

Turn under the raw edge with the needle or with the edge of a seam ripper; use a blind stitch to sew the folded edge down. Sew through all layers. Obviously, the cut out shapes of the top layer should be fairly large so that the succeeding layers will show through to reveal different colors: each shape will be correspondingly smaller. It is not necessary to sew in sequence from the top to bottom layer. A layer or two in one section of the overall design can be skipped. Simply cut through the two or three layers to reveal the one on the bottom. Trim out an extra seam allowance on the *skipped* layers to eliminate bulk — the turned under edges of the top layer will cover these raw edges. The bottom layer of these fabric stacks is never cut; it serves not only as color accent, as the background, lining or base fabric.

In addition to the colors in the design, spot colors can also be introduced. Cut a small piece of fabric slightly larger than the opening; slip the colored cloth into place underneath; sew the top layer down as described above. This is also a good way to correct a mistake. If the wrong color is accidentally revealed, just cover it with another scrap and sew it in place.

Many techniques can be combined. Use a little regular appliqué with this type of work, if desired; or add a few embroidery stitches to complete the design plan. Reverse appliqué is easily adapted to modern decor — it is not necessary to follow the minute detailed forms of the Cuna Indians. The technique is just as effective — and easier — with larger projects.

APPLIQUÉ PROJECTS

GOOD MORNING ROOSTER

RED
YELLOW
GREEN
BROWN

YELLOW

ORANGE

RED
GREEN
BROWN
RED

GREEN

ORANGE

GREEN
RED

Each ½-inch square = 1 inch
Add ¼-inch seams

APPLIQUÉ MATS (ALPHABET)

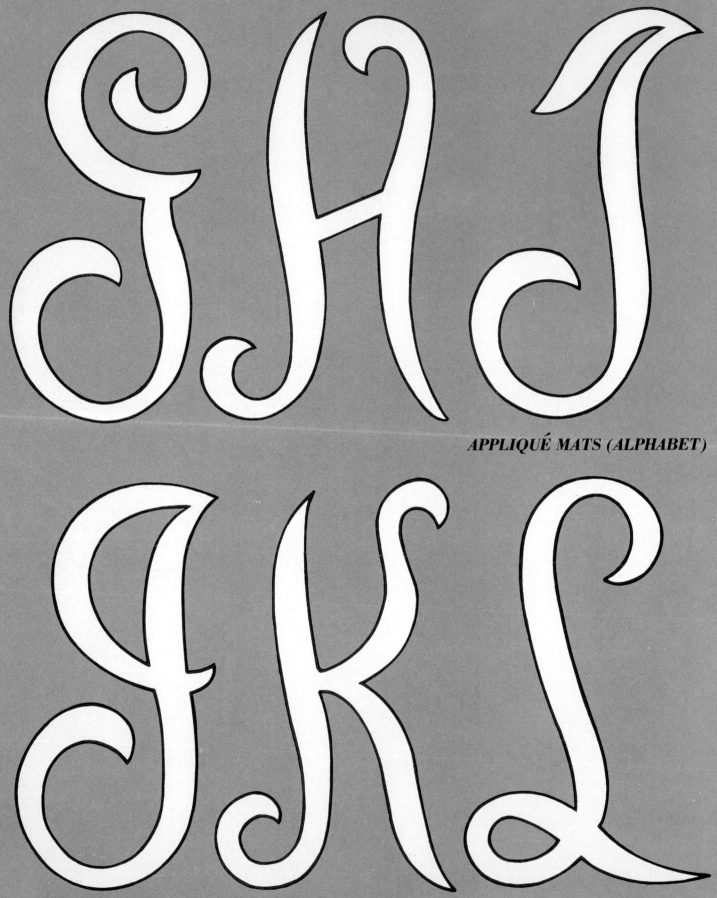

APPLIQUÉ MATS (ALPHABET)

GOOD MORNING, ROOSTER

Designed and created by Carter Houck

The smooth outlines of this design make it especially easy for appliqué and machine appliqué. For use on the man's caftan, double the size. Trace all the pieces and add seams, then proceed as described for machine or hand appliqué. Five colors are used in this design.

APPLIQUÉ MATS (ALPHABET)

APPLIQUÉ MATS (ALPHABET)

APPLIQUÉ MATS (ALPHABET)

APPLIQUÉ MATS

The designs used here for mats are equally beautiful for any other household items. The photo shows three different treatments for appliqué — machine appliqué for the initials, padded appliqué for the grapes and detached appliqué for the daisy. Linen-type fabrics are best for the two fringed mats. Sheer permanent press fabrics, such as voile or organdy, are best for the daisy.

Special instructions for daisy mat: The petals, leaves and stem are all stitched on the machine. The center of the daisy is padded slightly with nonwoven interfacing and hand appliquéd after the petals are sewn in place onto a single layer of fabric. The mat is cut double with 1-inch seams all around. After one layer is embroidered, both pieces are seamed together. Leave a 4-inch opening for turning and cut off the corners of the seams. After mats are turned and pressed, top stitching is used at the edge of the seam where it shows through the sheer fabric. This gives a shadow effect.

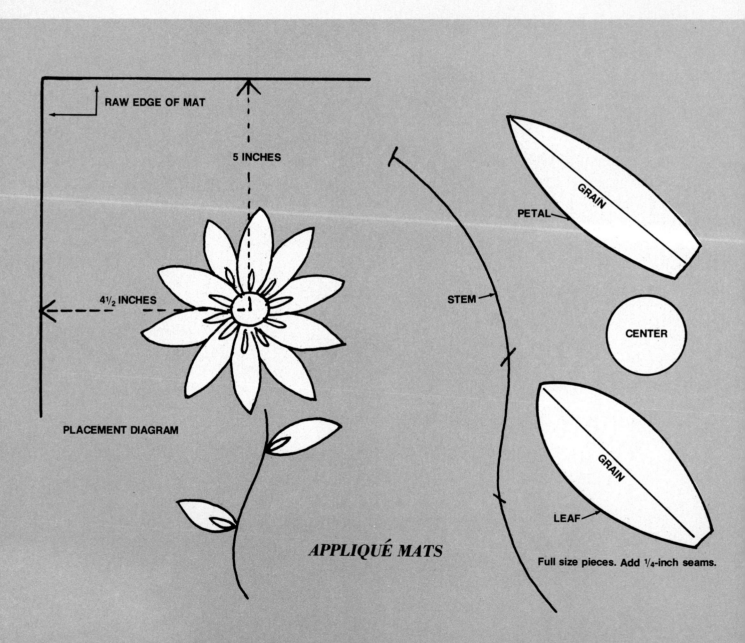

RAW EDGE OF MAT

5 INCHES

4½ INCHES

PLACEMENT DIAGRAM

PETAL

GRAIN

STEM

CENTER

LEAF

GRAIN

APPLIQUÉ MATS

Full size pieces. Add ¼-inch seams.

Full Size Pattern
Add Seams

821 / Appliqué

STEM STITCH

2 ROWS CHAIN STITCH

APPLIQUÉ MATS

NEW IDEAS FROM OLD

Planned and created by Courtney Bede from a quilt at the Smithsonian Institute.

Quilts of this type were made as money raisers for bazaars and church fairs. Anyone could pay to sign their name or have it signed, then the finished product was raffled. This white on red cotton pinwheel was ideal for that purpose. However, we saw it as a wonderfully modern design for velveteen and ribbons on a pillow.

The center circle is 4 inches in diameter plus seams, and the cut-out in the middle is 1 inch in diameter finished. The squares on the quilt are 12 inches; each spoke is slightly less than 4 inches long and 1 inch wide.

Our ribbons were cut about 4½ inches long to fit a 14-inch pillow. We used eight different patterns of 1-inch wide ribbon, so we needed ⅜ yard of each color for the sixteen spokes. Three-fourths yard of black velveteen is needed for the front and back of the pillow and for the corded piping.

"GENESIS" WALL HANGING

Designed and created by Jinny Avery

This project measures 33 x 22 inches and can be hung with dowel or rod slipped through loops at

the top. The fabrics needed are light blue cotton and navy cotton, approximately 22 x 15 inches. Strips of green, purple, lavender, browns, prints or solids are needed to overlap through the middle section representing the earth. The light blue is the day and the navy blue bottom piece is the night.

Cut a large sun from scraps of yellow or orange cotton, and pin in place in upper right-hand corner. Cut freehand, pieces from various prints and pin in place throughout middle section. These pieces represent forms of life — trees, flowers, growth, etc. Cut a quarter moon and several stars from yellow cotton and pin them on the navy section. Cut the letters *Genesis* from various fabrics and pin them in a line along the bottom edge of the project. Cut a piece of backing fabric the same size as the wall hanging, using any cotton fabric available. Cut a layer of polyester batting and place on top of backing. Secure the three layers together.

Set machine for satin stitch or close zigzag. Beginning with the sun, stitch around all parts of the middle section. Put extra stuffing in some of the shapes by stitching about three quarters of the way around; fill with bits of nylon stocking or cotton, then complete the stitching. Run straight lines of stitching from the sun to represent the rays. Complete the rest of the project in the same manner.

It will not be necessary to quilt the middle section because most of the shapes are small. Machine quilt the night section with random curving lines to hold the batting in place. With contrasting thread, machine stitch two or three stars using a straight stitch.

Cut four 6-inch squares for loops. Fold the squares lengthwise with right sides together and stitch the long side. Turn and press, folding crosswise. Baste raw ends of loops to right side of hanging, lining up the raw edges of loops with raw edge of the hanging. Cut and pin the backing to the hanging, pinning right sides together securely. Stitch up one side, across top, down the other side; leave the bottom open for turning. When turned, slip stitch bottom opening closed. Baste around edges, keeping seam on the edge. Top stitch through all thicknesses about $3/8$ inch from edge.

MOLA WITH TWO CATS

From the collection of Jinny Avery

This reverse appliqué design or mola from Panama is a good first project in reverse appliqué because it uses only three base colors, red, orange and black. The five bright colors are appliquéd on top. A few simple embroidery stitches are used to complete the design. The piece is just the right size for a small pillow, footstool or handbag.

Decide on the total dimensions for the project; the border of black can be larger than shown here if required by the proposed project. Cut one piece each of red, orange and black cotton fabric in desired size. Trace the outermost outline in white carbon or chalk pencil on the black or top layer. Baste the three layers together, black on top, then orange, then red. Baste around all outlines about 1/4 inch from the lines drawn. Cut away the black, leaving a tiny seam allowance (about 1/8 inch) *inside* the lines. Clip to corners and proceed with reverse applique as described on page 809.

Full Size Diagram

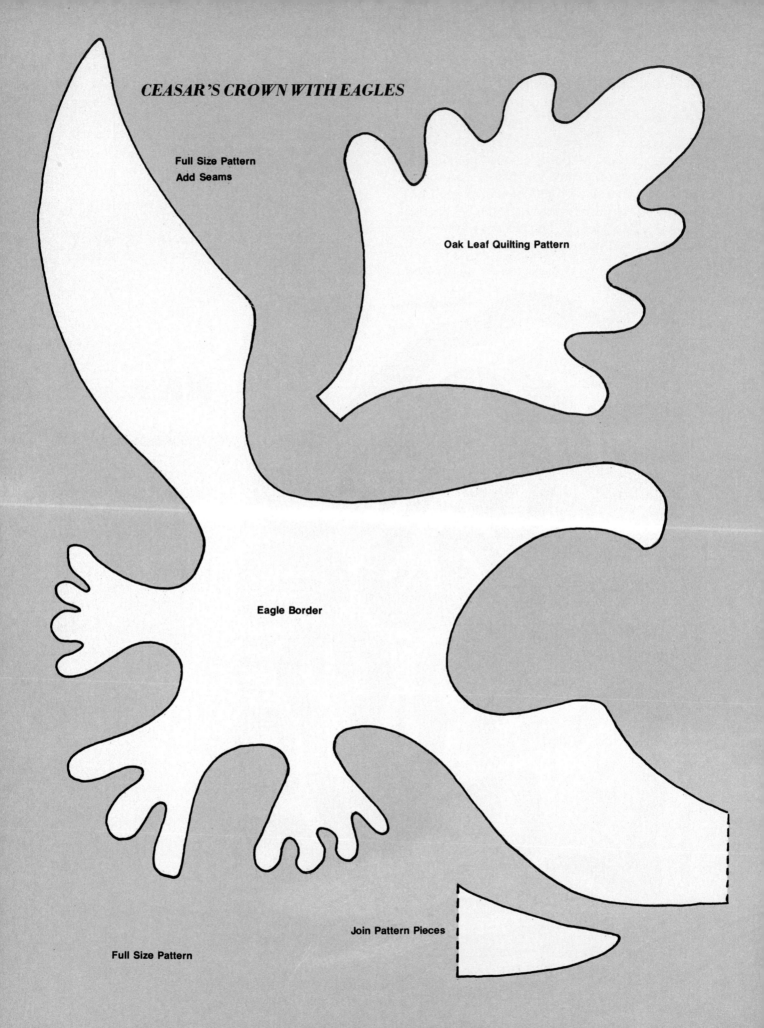

CEASAR'S CROWN WITH EAGLES

Full Size Pattern
Add Seams

Oak Leaf Quilting Pattern

Eagle Border

Full Size Pattern

Join Pattern Pieces

TOP

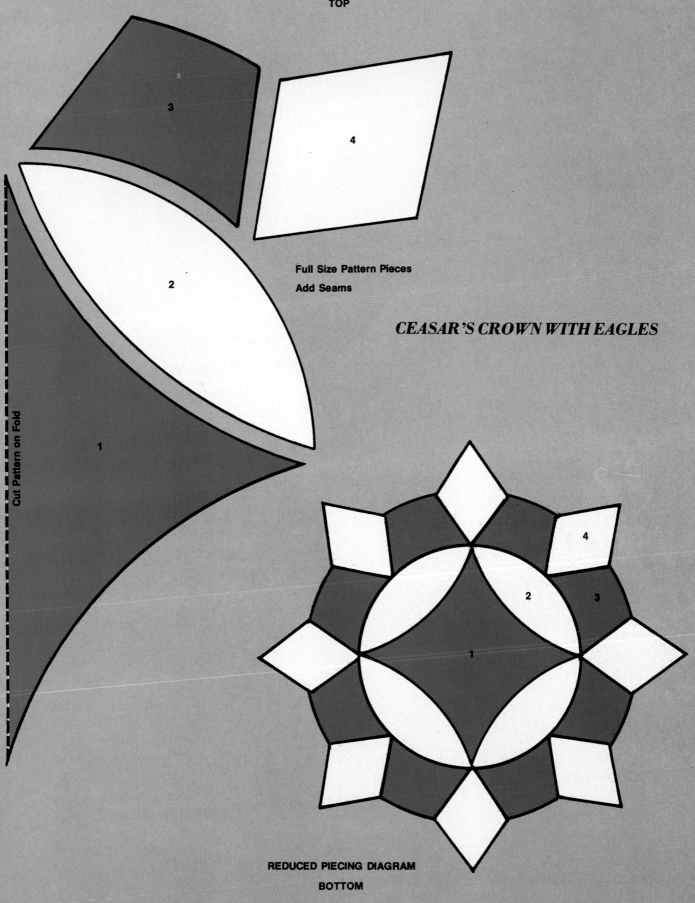

3

4

Full Size Pattern Pieces

Add Seams

CEASAR'S CROWN WITH EAGLES

2

Cut Pattern on Fold

1

4

2

3

1

REDUCED PIECING DIAGRAM

BOTTOM

LONG DOG PILLOW

Join Pattern Pieces

Full Size Pattern
Add Seams

LONG DOG PILLOW

Designed and created by Jinny Avery

An amusing design for a long pillow is only one way to use Long Dog. He is worked in simple appliqué and detached appliqué (for ears and tail) with touches of embroidery. The design is worked on a 6 x 20-inch piece and two 1-inch bands are added. The entire piece is hand quilted to a batt or Pellon® fleece, and finished with corded piping. Cover a pillow made-to-size and stuffed with polyester.

Join Pattern Pieces

CAESAR'S CROWN WITH EAGLES

From the collection of Jinny Avery

This old standard design is in navy pin-dot and rose print on muslin. It is partly pieced and partly appliquéd. For each crown, cut one of No. 1, four of No. 2 and eight each of Nos. 3 and 4. Piece according to the diagram given. Appliqué onto a 15-inch muslin square. The squares are then joined edge to edge. There are twenty-five in all.

The border is 7½ inches wide with six eagles in alternating colors along each edge and four on each end. The appliquéd initials in the border add a personal touch.

The quilting is done mostly in outline and echo. There is also an oak leaf design worked into the larger muslin spaces on both quilt and border.

HAWAIIAN PILLOW

Designed and created by Jinny Avery

This pillow is made exactly like a Hawaiian quilt, see page 805. Place the pattern on the fold, as suggested on the diagram, thus cutting four layers of fabric.

The pillow is 18 inches square finished. Cut two 19-inch square pieces of green fabric and one 19-inch square piece of navy fabric. The green ones are for the back and front of the pillow and the navy is cut into the design. Remember to add ⅛-inch seams on all the curved edges inside the design, for appliquéing.

Appliqué the design onto one green square, then quilt the entire top onto Pellon® fleece, or batting and a thin washable lining fabric. If the loose batting does not have a lining, it may disintegrate but the Pellon® can be used without lining. Continue to follow the echo quilting lines indicated on the diagram. Join the green squares together for the finished pillow.

MOON OVER THE MOUNTAIN

Designed and created by Judy Avery

This may be the ultimate beginner's appliqué quilt block! The lines are simple and the effect is gained entirely by choosing exciting fabrics. The mountain should be the darkest shade denoting Earth, the sky should be a medium blue and the sun a bright shade.

Cut blocks of the medium blue shade, 10 1/2 inches square plus seams. Cut circles by pattern for moon, and triangles by extended pattern for mountain. With a simple border the block will make a fine 14-inch pillow, or as many as desired can be joined for a whole quilt. The quilting patterns depend somewhat on the prints of the fabric, though the sun rays used here in the sky are most appropriate.

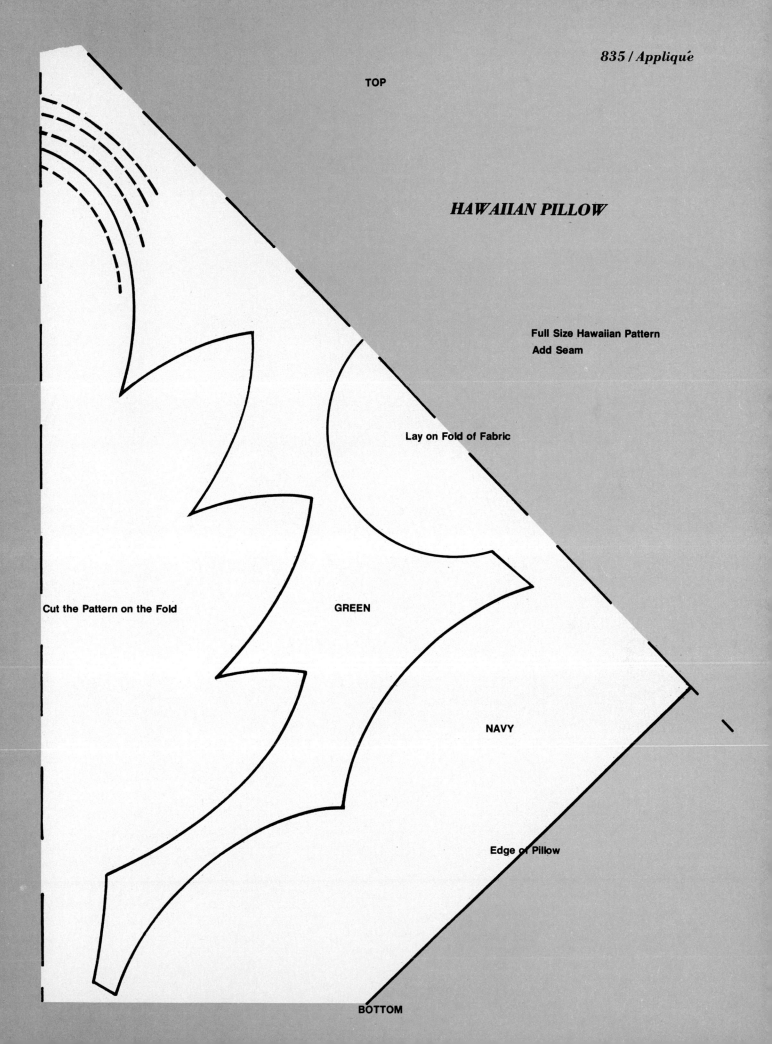

TOP

HAWAIIAN PILLOW

Full Size Hawaiian Pattern
Add Seam

Lay on Fold of Fabric

Cut the Pattern on the Fold

GREEN

NAVY

Edge of Pillow

BOTTOM

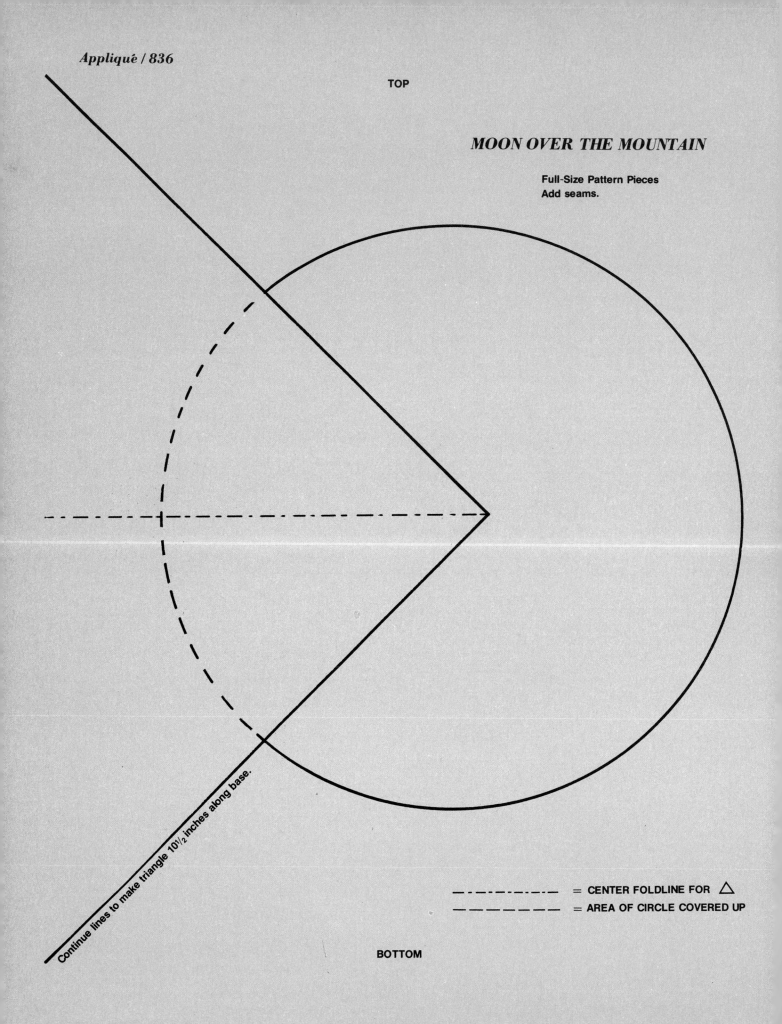

Appliqué / 836

TOP

MOON OVER THE MOUNTAIN

Full-Size Pattern Pieces
Add seams.

Continue lines to make triangle 10½ inches along base.

— · — · — · — · — = CENTER FOLDLINE FOR △
— — — — — — — = AREA OF CIRCLE COVERED UP

BOTTOM

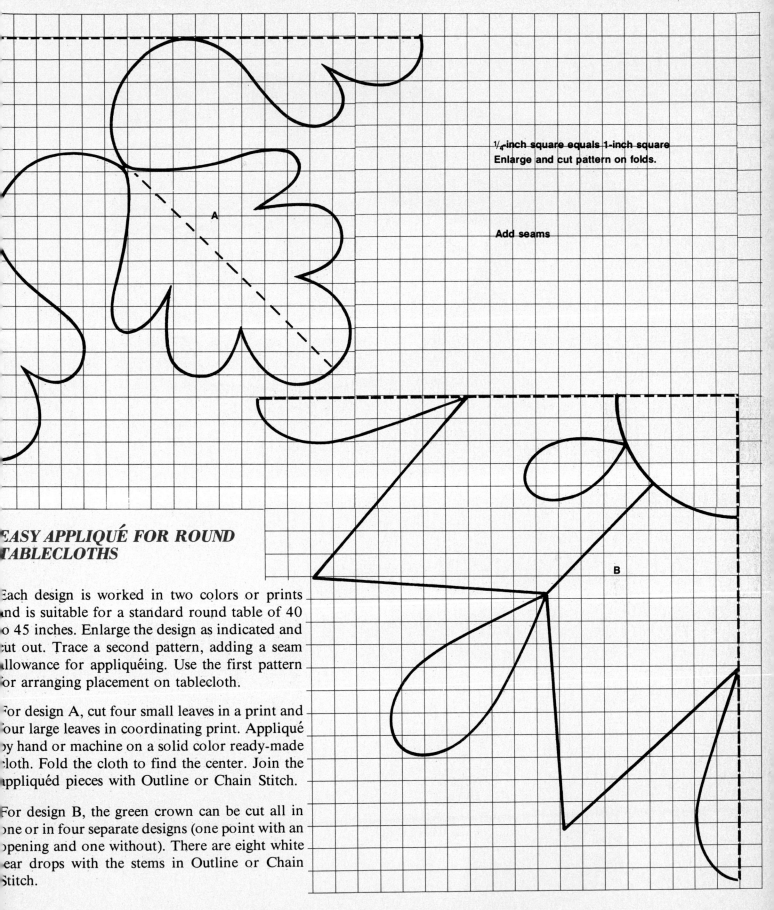

¼-inch square equals 1-inch square
Enlarge and cut pattern on folds.

Add seams

A

B

EASY APPLIQUÉ FOR ROUND TABLECLOTHS

Each design is worked in two colors or prints and is suitable for a standard round table of 40 to 45 inches. Enlarge the design as indicated and cut out. Trace a second pattern, adding a seam allowance for appliquéing. Use the first pattern for arranging placement on tablecloth.

For design A, cut four small leaves in a print and four large leaves in coordinating print. Appliqué by hand or machine on a solid color ready-made cloth. Fold the cloth to find the center. Join the appliquéd pieces with Outline or Chain Stitch.

For design B, the green crown can be cut all in one or in four separate designs (one point with an opening and one without). There are eight white pear drops with the stems in Outline or Chain Stitch.

CHILDREN'S HAPPY APPLIQUÉ

Full Size Pattern

Add Seams

CHILDREN'S HAPPY APPLIQUÉ

Use the bold bright designs as shown here or mix and match them for curtains, pillows, bedspreads, clothing and all manner of delightful things for a child to enjoy. The patterns are full size and the lines are simple enough for either machine or hand appliqué.

CHILDREN'S HAPPY APPLIQUÉ

Full Size Pattern

Add Seams

CHILDREN'S HAPPY APPLIQUÉ

Full Size Pattern
Add Seams

CHILDREN'S HAPPY APPLIQUÉ

Full Size Pattern

Add Seams

Index

KNITTING KNOBBY

LACE

LAYOUTS

LININGS

MACRAMÉ

MARKING FABRIC FROM PATTERN

MEASURING

MITERED CORNERS

NAPPED FABRICS